LIVING BY VOW

LIVING BY VOW

A PRACTICAL INTRODUCTION TO EIGHT
ESSENTIAL ZEN CHANTS AND TEXTS

Shohaku Okumura

EDITED BY DAVE ELLISON

Wisdom Publications
199 Elm Street
Somerville MA 02144 USA
www.wisdomexperience.org

Library of Congress Cataloging-in-Publication Data
Okumura, Shohaku, 1948–
 Living by vow : a practical introduction to eight essential Zen chants and texts / Shohaku Okumura ; edited by Dave Ellison.
     pages cm
Includes bibliographical references and index.
ISBN 1-61429-010-5 (p : alk. paper)
1. Zen literature—History and criticism. 2. Zen Buddhism—Rituals. 3. Buddhist chants. I. Title.
BQ9273.O58 2012
294.3'438—dc23

                     2011048873

ISBN 978-1-61429-010-0   ebook ISBN 978-1-61429-021-6

24 23 22 21
7   6   5   4

Cover art by Eiji Imao: www.eonet.ne.jp/~eijin/index.html. Cover design by JBTL. Interior design by Gopa&Ted2. Set in Diacritical Garamond 11.9/11.5.

Please visit fscus.org.

Contents

Editor's Preface

ON THEIR FIRST ENCOUNTER with the sutras many Zen beginners are perplexed. A few words might look familiar from other reading. Perhaps the overall gist seems apparent. But on first reading many sutras are an impenetrable mixture of meaningless foreign phrases and illogical paradoxes. To the experienced student, sutras can present another sort of problem. After years of study and practice, many of us fall into narrow, knee-jerk interpretations of the sutras we've recited so often. This book is aimed directly at both problems. As an experienced practitioner of Zen, Shohaku Okumura speaks clearly and directly of the personal meaning and implications of Zen practice. He uses his own life experiences to illustrate the practical significance of the sutras to the beginning student. As a scholar of Buddhist literature he reveals the subtle, intricate web of culture and history that surrounds the words so familiar to the longtime student. The net effect is of a sympathetic friend who has practiced Zen for decades (and also happens to be a Buddhist scholar) patiently explaining, annotating, and illuminating eight of the most important sutras. Esoteric Sanskrit terms take on vivid, personal meaning. Worn-out, empty phrases gain rich new poetic resonance. Both the neophyte and the experienced practitioner will come away with a richer appreciation of these sutras.

For instance, take the word "vow." Many modern readers, scientists, skeptics, and secular humanists might find this concept distinctly uncomfortable. Some may feel it carries the taint of ancient dogma draped in musty, jewel-encrusted robes. It hints of rigid rules for diet, sexual practices, clothing, and social hierarchies. Okumura Roshi uses the teachings and poetry of the Buddha, Dōgen, Katagiri Roshi, Uchiyama Roshi, and others to elucidate the central role of vow in Zen practice. In the process he gives fresh meaning to the word. Instead of a static pledge, vow is shown to be a dynamic, day-to-day expression of the most fundamental aspect of our true nature. He shows how our sitting practice, our Zen community, and our livelihood can all be animated and illuminated by vow.

Emptiness, or *śūnyatā*, like many concepts in Zen, is slippery and paradoxical. In his chapter on the *Heart Sutra*, Okumura Roshi uses the words of masters selected from the twenty-five-hundred-year tradition of Zen to elucidate this challenging but crucial reality. The result is multilayered, cross-cultural, philosophical, and at the same time personal. His interpretation of the five *skandhas* can be read as a paraphrase of a modern neuroscience text. He quotes Nāgārjuna, who lived nearly two thousand years ago, to demonstrate how awareness of emptiness leads naturally to a more peaceful, stable life in our modern world. Impermanence and interdependence are not merely philosophical abstractions. They are fundamental aspects of our daily existence. Ongoing recognition of this reality leads naturally to generosity, egolessness, and inner calm. The appreciation and application of this concept is a very practical antidote to the pervasive angst of our modern consumer society.

This book offers the thoughtful reader an opportunity to apply the cumulative insights of twenty-five hundred years of disciplined spiritual research to their own everyday existence. It is neither a quick, effortless panacea nor an abstract metaphysical treatise, but rather a series of signposts to guide and inspire the determined seeker.

Dave Ellison

AUTHOR'S PREFACE

THIS BOOK IS based on a series of lectures I gave as the interim head teacher at the Minnesota Zen Meditation Center (MZMC) in Minneapolis from September 1993 to August 1996. The center was founded by Dainin Katagiri Roshi. He originally came to the United States in 1963 to serve at Zenshūji Sōtō Mission, the Sōtō Zen temple for the Japanese-American community in Los Angeles. A few years later, he moved to Sōkōji to assist Shunryū Suzuki Roshi, the resident priest at Sōkōji and the founding teacher of the San Francisco Zen Center. He practiced and taught there as the assistant teacher until Suzuki Roshi's death in 1971. The next year he moved to Minneapolis and founded the MZMC, where he served as abbot until his death in March 1990 at the age of sixty-three.

The MZMC is located on the eastern shore of Lake Calhoun in South Minneapolis near the Uptown neighborhood. The center was named Kōun-zan Ganshōji by Katagiri Roshi. The mountain (*zan*) name Kōun means "cultivating the clouds" and is taken from one of Dōgen's well-known poems.[1] The temple name Gansho means "living by vow" and alludes to one of the definitions of a bodhisattva: "Ordinary people are those who live being pulled by their karma (*gosshō no bonpu*); bodhisattvas are those who live led by their vows (*ganshō no bosatsu*)."

I had the opportunity to practice with Katagiri Roshi for one month at Daijōji monastery in Kanazawa, Japan, in 1988. He was the head teacher of the one-month special training period sponsored by Sōtōshū Shūmuchō for Western Sōtō Zen teachers. I was one of the assistants during the training period. Katagiri Roshi gave lectures on the *Shōbōgenzō* chapter Kūge (Flower of Emptiness) in English to the Western teachers. When I listened to his lectures, I was astonished and very inspired. I already had some experience giving dharma talks in English to Westerners, but until then I did not think I could give lectures on *Shōbōgenzō*. Later I had several opportunities to visit the MZMC to lecture his students while he was sick with cancer. That was why I was invited to be the interim head teacher three years after Katagiri Roshi's death.

When I accepted the invitation from the MZMC I resolved to continue Katagiri Roshi's style of practice and transmit the same essential spirit of bodhisattva practice, or living by vow (*ganshō*), to his students. Therefore, when I started to teach, my first seven talks were on the bodhisattva vows.

Some of the differences and similarities between Katagiri Roshi's style of practice and my own can be understood in terms of the history of our lineages. From Shakyamuni Buddha until the seventy-fifth ancestor, Gangoku Kankei Daioshō (1683–1767), our lineage is exactly the same. Katagiri Roshi was the sixth generation and I am the eighth generation from Gangoku Kankei Daioshō. Soon after he was ordained as a Sōtō Zen priest, Katagiri Roshi practiced for three years with Hashimoto Ekō Roshi, who was the *godō* (instructor for training monks) at Eiheiji monastery. Hashimoto Roshi was a close friend of Sawaki Kōdō Roshi, and my teacher, Uchiyama Kōshō Roshi, was a disciple of Sawaki Roshi. They both emphasized *nyohō-e*, traditional sewing of the *okesa* and the *rakusu* worn by priests and laypeople who receive the Buddha's precepts. Hashimoto Roshi and Sawaki Roshi practiced together under Oka Sōtan Roshi's guidance at Shuzenji monastery. Another student of Oka Roshi was Kishizawa Ian Roshi, with whom Shunryū Suzuki Roshi studied in Japan. The lineages of Kishizawa Roshi, Hashimoto

Roshi, and Sawaki Roshi are thus closely related. In the United States the influence of these three roshis continues through the lineages of Suzuki Roshi, Katagiri Roshi, and Uchiyama Roshi.

Although Hashimoto Roshi and Sawaki Roshi were good friends, their styles of practice were quite different. Hashimoto Roshi emphasized the importance of maintaining the details of Dōgen Zenji's monastic practice. Narasaki Ikkō Roshi and Tsūgen Roshi, the abbots of Zuiōji, retained Hashimoto Roshi's style in Japan. Narasaki Roshi and Katagiri Roshi were very close. Katagiri Roshi also adhered to Hashimoto Roshi's very traditional monastic practice and sent some of his disciples to Zuiōji. Together, Narasaki Roshi and Katagiri Roshi planned to create an international monastery at Shōgoji, in Kumamoto Prefecture in Kyūshū. Katagiri Roshi was going to lead the international summer practice period when the construction of the monks' hall (sodo) was completed. Unfortunately he passed away before that happened.

Sawaki Roshi never had his own temple or monastery. He was a professor at Komazawa University for more than thirty years. He also traveled throughout Japan to teach. Many laypeople started to practice zazen because of his efforts. Sawaki Roshi was called "homeless" Kōdō because he did not have a monastery or temple but instead traveled all over Japan. He called his teaching style a moving monastery. My teacher Kōshō Uchiyama Roshi was ordained by Sawaki Roshi and practiced only with him. After Sawaki Roshi passed away, Uchiyama Roshi became the abbot of Antaiji. He focused on zazen practice with minimal ceremony, ritual, and formality. Uchiyama Roshi started five-day "sesshins without toys," during which we simply sat fourteen fifty-minute periods of zazen. I was ordained by Uchiyama Roshi and practiced at Antaiji until he retired in 1975.

After Uchiyama Roshi's retirement I practiced at Zuiōji, where Narasaki Ikkō Roshi was abbot. There, for a short period of time, I experienced Hashimoto Roshi's style of practice. I learned firsthand that Katagiri Roshi's style of practice and the style taught by Uchiyama Roshi were quite different.

Recently Arthur Braverman, a friend of mine from Antaiji, wrote an article about Uchiyama Roshi in *Buddhadharma* magazine. In it he said:

> While Shunryū Suzuki was igniting a Zen revolution in San Francisco in the late sixties, Kōshō Uchiyama was trying to foster a Zen reformation in Japan. It was perhaps an even more imposing challenge when one considers the power of the traditional Sōtō Zen sect in Japan.
>
> Both masters believed greatly in the power of meditation, and both did a masterful job of transmitting the importance of zazen to their students. While Suzuki Roshi was attempting to get his American students to see the importance of many of the Japanese forms, Uchiyama was trying to teach his Japanese students not to be attached to the forms, but to let the forms grow out of the practice.[2]

This is a very clear explanation of both the difference and the underlying unity of Uchiyama Roshi's style and that of Suzuki Roshi and Katagiri Roshi. Katagiri Roshi also put emphasis on traditional formal Sōtō Zen monastic practice. For me, the decision to follow Katagiri Roshi's style was a big one. For all Dōgen Zenji's descendants, of course, the basic spirit of the bodhisattva practice is the same. I feel that the essence of bodhisattva practice and the common ground of various styles of practice is living by vow.

Katagiri Roshi often spoke about living by vow. In his book *Each Moment Is the Universe*, he says that wholehearted practice of zazen is itself living by vow.

> In zazen many things come up: thoughts, emotions, sometimes anger and hatred. But all you have to do is take care of zazen in eternal possibility. It's completely beyond good or bad, right or wrong, so put aside all kinds of imagination fabricated by your consciousness. Don't attach to thoughts

and emotions, just let them return to emptiness. Just be present there and swim in buddha-nature. This is living the bodhisattva vow to help all beings. Then the great energy of the universe supports you and you take one step toward the future with all beings.[3]

Katagiri Roshi wrote his *yuige* (bequeathed verse) a few weeks before his death:

Living in Vow, silently sitting
Sixty-three years
Plum blossoms begin to bloom
The jeweled mirror reflects truth as it is.[4]

While my practice and understanding were greatly enriched by my study of Katagiri Roshi's style of practice, I also learned from him how to teach Americans. For that I am very grateful. For twenty years I practiced Uchiyama Roshi's style of sesshin with no activities other than zazen. At MZMC I gave lectures and had dokusan (private interviews) during sesshins. It was a challenge, but I learned a great deal.

After lecturing on "living by vow," I spoke on the verses and sutras in the MZMC sutra book. Since these are chanted regularly, they are the Buddhist literature most familiar to Sōtō Zen practitioners, both in Japan and in the West. Many people memorize them. But the meaning of these verses and sutras is rarely explained. That is why I gave lectures on them. I talked about them on Saturday mornings for about three years until 1996, when I finished my term as the interim head teacher at MZMC.

Most of the lectures included in this book were transcribed by José Escobar and Dave Ellison. Some lectures were not recorded and a few tapes were missing. I rewrote these sections to fill the gaps. My talks on the *Heart Sutra* were transcribed and edited by Dave and printed in the MZMC newsletter. Tom Goodell, one of the practitioners at MZMC, was the first person who worked on this project. Since both Tom and

I were very busy, especially after I moved to California to work for Sōtōshū North America Education Center (currently Sōtōshū International Center), the project could not be completed. A few years later, Dave kindly took over the project and patiently continued to work on it for more than ten years. I gave these lectures more than fifteen years ago, right after I moved to Minneapolis from Japan. Even though I had lived in the United States for five years, my English was not fluent. I had a limited vocabulary with which to express my thoughts. I am sure that it was difficult for Dave to understand what I wanted to say. I deeply appreciate his hard work, which "translated" my very Japanese English into readable English.

I would like to express my appreciation to Jōkei Molly Whitehead, a disciple of mine at Sanshinji. While she was busy for preparing for her ordination ceremony, she worked hard on the final stages of this book and gave us many helpful suggestions. I also express my gratitude to Andrea Martin, who allowed me to read a draft of her book *Ceaseless Effort: The Life of Dainin Katagiri* and gave me permission to quote Katagiri Roshi's *yuige*. Finally I am extremely delighted to have Eiji Imao's beautiful painting "Tsukinohikari (Moonlight)" on the cover of this book. I appreciate his generous permission to use a painting of his again, as we did on *Realizing Genjokoan*.

Katagiri Roshi's dharma heirs and their students fulfilled his vow to transmit Dōgen Zenji's teaching and practice to America. The tree of Dharma transplanted by Katagiri Roshi continues to grow as its roots spread and deepen in the soil of American spiritual culture in the Twin Cities and elsewhere. I deeply appreciate their continuous efforts and their friendship.

Gassho,
Shohaku Okumura

Introduction

Aᴌᴌ Bᴜᴅᴅʜɪsᴛ sᴄʜᴏᴏᴌs have rituals, services, and ceremonies. At almost all such formal activities we chant verses, poems, or sutras and dedication of merit (*ekō*). Each Buddhist school has a collection of these writings, often called a sutra book (*kyōhon* in Japanese), used in daily practice. This book presents my lectures on some of the verses and sutras in the sutra book.

In the Sōtō Zen tradition, the official sutra book published by the administrative headquarters (Shūmuchō) is *Sōtōshū Nikka Gongyō Seiten*. This collection was translated into English and published by Shūmuchō in 2002 with the title *Sōtō School Scriptures for Daily Service and Practice*. Before the publication of this sutra book, each Zen center in the United States created its own book, sometimes using different translations. Many centers still use their own versions. The text I used for the lectures in this book is MZMC's sutra book.

As is often said, there is no perfect translation, especially in the case of religious scriptures. A translation optimized for meaning is often difficult to read and chant. But to create a beautiful verse we may have to sacrifice the exact meaning of the original texts. Each teacher and translator has a different interpretation and mode of expression. The translations in the MZMC version, which I use except for the meal chants, are no exception. Sometimes I offer an understanding of certain

words that differs from the meaning expressed in the MZMC translations. My interpretation is based on my study and practice, but it is not
the only correct one. My hope is that this book will help practitioners
understand the meaning of the verses and sutras in the context of their
own practice. Perhaps my commentary will be a foundation for better
translations in the future.

I believe that all verses and scriptures in the Sōtō Zen tradition are
based on the Mahāyāna teaching of the bodhisattva vow. That is why
I titled this book *Living by Vow*. It is meant to be a practical introduction not only to Sōtō Zen practice but also to Mahāyāna teaching in
general.

Sōtō Zen Buddhism is part of the Mahāyāna Buddhist tradition
in which practitioners are called *bodhisattvas*. We receive bodhisattva
precepts and take bodhisattva vows. The historical origin of Mahāyāna
Buddhism is not yet clear. In Japan, until the nineteenth century, all
Mahāyāna sutras were considered the recorded sayings of Shakyamuni
Buddha. When modern historical and critical Buddhist study was established, scholars found that Mahāyāna sutras were created at least several
hundred years after Shakyamuni Buddha's death. When they began to
study the origin of the Mahāyāna Buddhist movement, some scholars
thought Mahāyāna developed from Mahāsāṃghika, one of the early
Buddhist sects. Later, scholars such as Akira Hirakawa (1915–2002)
proposed that Mahāyāna Buddhism grew from lay Buddhist movements in various areas of India, a claim derived from the study of stūpa
worship and biographical literature praising Shakyamuni Buddha's
bodhisattva practice. Examples are texts such as *Mahāvastu*, Aśvaghoṣa's
Buddha-carita, and the Jātaka tales. When I was a university student
this was a new and exciting hypothesis. Many Japanese Buddhist scholars accepted the theory, although opinions differed on details. Scholars hypothesized that there were bodhisattva *gaṇa*s (i.e., sanghas) that
existed independently from monastic sanghas. Today, some Western
scholars criticize this hypothesis and suggest that Mahāyāna began as
a movement of a small number of elite monks who aspired to live and

practice in the forest like Shakyamuni Buddha when he was a bodhisattva in his previous lives.

Either way, one of the fundamental ideas of Mahāyāna Buddhism is to take the bodhisattva vow and practice like Shakyamuni to attain buddhahood. The story that Shakyamuni Buddha took the bodhisattva vow appears not only in biographies of the Buddha but also in accounts of his past lives. I think that Shakyamuni's vow originated when he rose from his seat under the bodhi tree and decided to teach. This story, which probably came into existence several hundred years after the Buddha's death, was the original inspiration for bodhisattva practice. I would like to introduce a story from the Pāli canon. Although it is not a Mahāyāna text, all the essential points of the bodhisattva ideal are already there. One important difference is that in the Pāli tradition the term *bodhisattva* refers only to Shakyamuni himself before he attained buddhahood. Only later did tradition create past buddhas such as Vipaśyin Buddha and the future buddha Maitreya. But Mahāyāna Buddhists believed that any one of us could become a bodhisattva if we aroused *bodhi-citta* (bodhi-mind), took bodhisattva vows, and practiced the six *pāramitās*, or perfections.

This story comes from the Khuddaka Nikāya of the Pāli canon. One part of this Nikāya, the Jātakas, comprises 547 tales of Shakyamuni Buddha's previous lives. One of these stories is of Sumedha (the Buddha in a previous life). When he took a vow to become a buddha the Buddha Dīpaṃkara predicted that Sumedha would successfully attain buddhahood in a future life. This story illustrates the origin of the bodhisattva vow and many of the important points of bodhisattva practice. It is interesting that the archetypal image of the bodhisattva already existed in the Pāli Nikāyas.[5]

This story took place countless eons ago. In a city called Amaravatī lived a Brāhmin named Sumedha, who was an outstanding person from a prestigious family. When Sumedha was still young his parents died. A minister of the state, who was steward of the family's property, showed Sumedha the wealth accumulated for seven generations that he inherited from his parents. The family treasury was filled with gold and silver, gems and pearls, and other valuables.

When he saw the treasure he thought, "After amassing all this wealth, none of my parents and ancestors were able to take even a penny with them when they passed away. Can it be right that I should seek to take my wealth with me when I go?" Then he told the king that he would give all this wealth to the poor and leave home to become a spiritual practitioner.

He saw that a life transmigrating within samsara—the cycle of birth, sickness, aging, and death—was suffering and he wanted to find the path of deliverance into nirvana. Sumedha thought, "Suppose a man, after falling into a heap of filth, hears about a distant pond covered with lotuses of five colors. That man ought to search for that pond. If he does not, that's not the pond's fault. In the same way, there is a lake—the great, deathless nirvana—in which to wash off the defilements of my harmful karma. If I do not seek it that will not be the lake's fault." So he left home and entered a forest in the Himalayas to practice as a hermit. Because he was a person of great capability, he attained superhuman knowledge and supernatural power.

While he was practicing thus, Dīpaṃkara Buddha appeared in the world and started to teach. Dīpaṃkara Buddha visited a city not far from where Sumedha was living. The people of that city invited the Buddha and his assembly of followers for a meal. In preparation they began to fix the road, which was flooded, and decorate it with flowers. Sumedha flew there by means of his supernatural power. He asked why they were working so hard and were so excited. They explained that Dīpaṃkara Buddha was coming. Sumedha was delighted and offered his help. Because people knew that Sumedha had supernatural powers, they asked him to fill the muddy part of the road with soil. But Sumedha, although he could easily have filled the muddy road using his supernatural power, wanted to use his own hands instead. He started to carry soil by hand. Unfortunately, Dīpaṃkara Buddha and his assembly arrived before his work was completed.

Sumedha did not want the Buddha to walk through the mud, so

he loosened his matted hair, lay down on the ground, and asked the Buddha to walk on him—a dramatic expression of his commitment to take refuge in the Buddha, the Dharma, and the Sangha. Even today, some Buddhists make prostrations by laying their bodies full length on the ground. When we make prostrations in the Sōtō Zen tradition, we place five parts of our bodies—both knees, both elbows, and forehead—on the ground. We place our hands palm up at the level of our ears as if to accept the Buddha's feet on our hands. This is the form we use to express our respect and gratitude to the Buddha.

When Sumedha, lying in the mire, looked up at Dīpaṃkara Buddha, he made a vow: "If I want I could now enter the Buddhist sangha and by practicing meditation free myself from deluded human desires and become an arhat. Then at death I would at once attain nirvana and cease to be reborn. But this would be a selfish course to pursue, for thus I should benefit myself only. I want to help all beings as Dīpaṃkara Buddha is doing now. I am determined. I vow to attain what Dīpaṃkara Buddha attained and benefit all beings." Upon seeing Dīpaṃkara Buddha, Sumedha abandoned his earlier intention to escape from samsara. Now he aspired to live like the Buddha, staying in samsara to help all living beings.

Dīpaṃkara Buddha, seeing Sumedha lying in the mud, understood that the young man had vowed to become a buddha. He told his assembly that in the distant future Sumedha would become a buddha named Gautama. Hearing this prediction, Sumedha was delighted and believed his vow would be realized. Having praised Sumedha for his vow, Dīpaṃkara Buddha and his assembly departed. Thus Sumedha became "the Bodhisattva," which in this case means "the Buddha-to-be." This is an early example of the path called bodhisattva practice chosen by Shakyamuni Buddha.

Sumedha then realized that to become a buddha he should practice the ten pāramitās: the perfection of giving (*dāna*), the perfection of moral practice (*śīla*), the perfection of renunciation (*nekkhamma*), the perfection of wisdom (*paññā*, known more commonly by the Sanskrit *prajñā*), the perfection of diligence (*viriya*), the perfection of patience

(*khanti*), the perfection of truthfulness (*sacca*), the perfection of determination (*adhitthāna*), the perfection of loving-kindness (*mettā*), and
the perfection of equanimity (*upekkhā*). This list of ten pāramitās is
found in the Pāli canon. It is interesting to note that five of them (giving, moral practice, patience, diligence, and wisdom) are present in
the Mahāyāna list of six pāramitās. The sixth pāramitā, missing in the
Pāli version, is meditation (*dhyāna*). But in some Mahāyāna sutras,
for instance the *Ten Stages Sutra*, ten pāramitās are mentioned: the six
pāramitās just mentioned and these four: skillful means (*upāya*); vow,
resolution, or determination (*pranidhāna*); spiritual power (*bala*); and
knowledge (*jñāna*).

The image of Shakyamuni as a bodhisattva is broadly similar in early
Buddhism and Mahāyāna. One significant difference is that Mahāyāna
Buddhists have always held that anyone, even ordinary people like us,
can be a bodhisattva if they arouse bodhichitta, take the bodhisattva
vow, and practice the six pāramitās. None of us can expect to receive
a prophecy assuring us of attaining buddhahood, but since all beings
intrinsically have buddha-nature, it is certain that we will complete our
vow and attain buddhahood.

The archetypal image of the bodhisattva in this story suggests that all
Mahāyāna Buddhist practice is based on the bodhisattva vow. The vow
has two aspects: becoming a buddha and helping all beings become
buddhas. These two cannot be separated. We vow to become buddhas
together with all beings. That is, we vow not to become a buddha until
all beings become buddhas. We vow to stay in samsara on purpose
to walk with all beings. This explains why the Zen master Guishan
Lingyou (Isan Reiyū) said he would be reborn as a water buffalo, for the
water buffalo, which walks in muddy water to help farmers grow rice,
symbolizes bodhisattva practice. The bodhisattva vow is an essential
point in Mahāyāna teachings and practice. All the verses and sutras
discussed in this book are based on or relate to this concept.

Repentance, or atonement, is intimately connected to vow. My
teacher Uchiyama Kōshō Roshi always emphasized that vow and
repentance are two sides of one practice. Because our vow is endless,

our practice is never complete. This awareness of incompleteness is repentance. In *The Hungry Tigress* Rafe Martin tells the story of the beginning of Shakyamuni Buddha's search for truth.[6] In this story Shakyamuni was a king named Suprabhasa. One day the king asked his elephant trainer to bring his great white elephant for him to ride. The trainer said that the elephant had escaped to the jungle but it would return because he had trained it well. The king did not believe him, grew angry, lost all self-control, yelled at him, and told him to leave. Next morning, the trainer reported that the elephant had returned. "The training was good," he said. "We have conquered his old, wild ways." When he heard this the king thought, "Though I am a king holding great power over others, I have as yet failed to conquer what is closest—myself. I was unable to control my own anger. This will not do."

Such a reflection and realization of one's own incompleteness is repentance. It is the origin of Shakyamuni Buddha's search for the Way. This same realization gives us the energy to study and practice diligently.

The verse of the Triple Treasure clearly states the connection between refuge and vow. When Sumedha, lying on the muddy road, asked Dīpaṃkara Buddha to walk on him, he took refuge in the Buddha, the Dharma, and the Sangha. Dīpaṃkara noticed Sumedha's gesture and vow and predicted that he would be a buddha. By taking refuge, we make clear the direction we intend to follow. Taking refuge in the Buddha, we vow together with all beings to walk his path of wisdom and compassion; taking refuge in the Dharma, we vow to share the teachings and wisdom as boundless as the ocean; taking refuge in the Sangha, we vow to create harmony without hindrance.

In the Mahāyāna tradition, people become Buddhists when they take the bodhisattva vow, repent their previous way of life, and take refuge in the Triple Treasure. Some of them choose to leave home and practice at monasteries. In the traditional Sōtō Zen monasteries, monks in training live in the monks' hall where they share their entire time and space with other practitioners. Their practice of vow includes not just the study of Dharma teachings and meditation practice but all the activities of daily life, including sleeping, eating, working, washing the face, and shaving the head. In addition to shelter, food and clothing are the most important elements of the monks' lives. The robe chant and the meal chants originate from this way of life dedicated to the bodhisattva vow.

In the robe chant verse, sometimes called the "Verse of the Kesa," we affirm our aim to practice with the same vow that Shakyamuni Buddha and all other bodhisattvas including Dōgen Zenji took—to save all beings. Dōgen Zenji himself took a vow when he first saw Chinese monks venerate the robe (okesa/kesa) by putting it on their heads and chanting. His vow was to introduce the okesa and encourage Japanese people to venerate it as a part of bodhisattva practice.

In *Shōbōgenzō* "Kesakudoku" (Virtue of the Kesa) Dōgen Zenji quotes a Mahāyāna sutra, the *Sutra of Compassion Flower* (*Hige-kyō*), in which Shakyamuni Buddha, when he was a bodhisattva in one of his past lives, took five vows regarding the okesa (or *kaṣāya*). One of his vows was that he would help students put on the okesa with respect and veneration. Then Dōgen Zenji commented on these vows:

> Truly, the kaṣāya is the buddha robe of all the buddhas in the past, present, and future. Although the virtues of the kaṣāya [from any buddha] are boundless, attaining the kaṣāya within the Dharma of Shakyamuni Buddha must be superior to getting it from other buddhas.
>
> This is because when Shakyamuni Buddha was in the causal stage [of practice] as the Great Compassion Bodhisattva, he took five hundred vows in front of the Jewel-Treasury Buddha. He particularly took vows regarding the virtues of the kaṣāya.

Even mundane daily activities like eating are related to vow. In the Zen tradition, monks sleep, meditate, and eat in a building called a *sōdō* (monks' hall). When we have formal meals in this hall, we chant verses to remind ourselves that eating is also a bodhisattva practice. We remember Shakyamuni Buddha's life and give praise. Then we vow to receive the food that comes to us from the network of interdependent origination, share it with all beings, and fulfill the bodhisattva vow to attain buddhahood together with all beings.

The *Heart Sutra* explains the practice necessary to achieve this vow. After Sumedha received Dīpaṃkara Buddha's prediction, he decided to practice the ten pāramitās. In Mahāyāna Buddhism the sixth pāramitā, the pāramitā of meditation (*dhyāna*), should be practiced by all bodhisattvas. The *Heart Sutra*, one of the early Mahāyāna *Prajñāpāramitā Sutras*, emphasizes the pāramitā of *prajñā*, or wisdom, as the most essential of the six. Without prajñā, the other five practices cannot be pāramitās (perfections). Although a relatively recent sutra, the *Heart Sutra* is considered the essence of the large collection of *Prajñāpāramitā Sutras*. It points to the essential role of prajñā in our efforts to fulfill our vows. To follow the bodhisattva path, we study and practice prajñā-pāramitā, the wisdom that sees impermanence, no-self, emptiness, and interdependent origination. When we clearly see this reality; that we and other things exist together without fixed independent entities, our practice is strengthened. We understand that to live by vow is not to accept a particular fixed doctrine but is a natural expression of our life force.

Zen Buddhism originated in China. "Sandōkai," a poem written in the ninth century by the Zen master Shitou Xiqian, is a Chinese expression of Buddhist wisdom that sees emptiness. In the very beginning of "Sandōkai," the author clearly states that the mind of the Buddha has been intimately transmitted through ancestors in the Zen tradition. "Intimately" means from person to person, not through written words and concepts. When the first ancestor of Chinese Zen, Bodhidharma, traveled from India to China, he was practicing his bodhisattva vow: to transmit and share the true Dharma, the mind of the Buddha, with Chinese people. Dōgen Zenji commented on Bodhidharma's practice in *Shōbōgenzō* "Gyōji" (Continuous Practice), "This way of protecting and maintaining practice [*gyōji*] stemmed from his great compassion and his vow to transmit the Dharma and save deluded living beings. He was able to do it because he himself was the dharma-self of transmission and for him the whole universe was the world of transmitting Dharma." In the same way, transmission of Buddha Dharma from Asian Buddhist countries to the West is the result of many Buddhist monks and laypeople who live by vow. Shitou, the eighth-generation ancestor from Bodhidharma expresses prajñā as the merging of the two truths, ultimate (*ri*) and conventional (*ji*). At the end of "Sandōkai" he encourages us to practice wholeheartedly and not waste time.

The "Verse for Opening the Sutra" explicitly points to the importance of vow. When we chant it before a dharma talk (open the sutra), we vow to listen, understand, digest, and apply the teaching to our practice. This is another expression of the third bodhisattva vow. Not only written texts and Dharma lectures but everything we encounter is a sutra that shows us, day by day and moment by moment, the true reality of all beings, continuously deepening our understanding and practice.

In the Sōtō Zen tradition, our practice is based on Dōgen Zenji's teaching of continuous practice and the identity of practice and verification. The bodhisattva Way is not linear. It's not a path that we move along from a starting point to a finish, as in a board game. In *Shōbōgenzō* "Gyōji," Dōgen explained that we practice together with all buddhas, bodhisattvas, and ancestors.

> In the great Way of the buddhas and ancestors, there is always unsurpassable continuous practice which is the Way like a circle without interruption. Between the arousing of awakening-mind, practice, awakening, and nirvana, there is not the slightest break. Continuous practice is the circle of the Way. Therefore, [this continuous practice] is not [activities that we are] forced to do by ourselves or by others [buddhas and ancestors]. It is the continuous practice that has never been defiled [by our three poisonous minds]. The virtue of this continuous practice sustains ourselves and others. The essential point is that, in the entire earth and throughout

throughout heaven in the ten directions, all beings receive the merit of our continuous practice. Although neither others nor ourselves know it, that is the way it is. Therefore, because of the buddhas' and ancestors' continuous practice, our continuous practice is actualized, and our own great Way is penetrated. Because of our own continuous practice, the continuous practice of all buddhas is actualized, and the great Way of buddhas is penetrated. Because of our own continuous practice, there is the virtue of the circle of the Way. Because of this, each and every one of the buddhas and ancestors dwells as a buddha, goes beyond Buddha, upholds Buddha mind, and completes buddhahood without interruption. Because of continuous practice, there are the sun, moon, and stars; because of continuous practice, there is the great earth and empty space. Because of continuous practice, there is the self and its environment, and body and mind; because of continuous practice, there are the four great elements and the five aggregates. Although continuous practice is not something worldly people love, nevertheless it is the true place to return for all people. Because of the continuous practice of all buddhas in the past, present, and future, all buddhas in the past, present, and future are actualized.... Therefore, the continuous practice of one day is nothing other than the seed of all buddhas and [is itself] the continuous practice of all buddhas.

All aspects of our practice—zazen in the monks' hall, chanting of verses and sutras during services, ceremonies in the Dharma hall—and all our other activities in daily life are the practice of the bodhisattva vow actualized moment by moment. We chant these verses and sutras as an expression of this interpenetrating reality with all beings throughout endless time and boundless space.

LIVING BY VOW:
THE FOUR BODHISATTVA VOWS

Sentient beings are numberless; I vow to save them.
Desires are inexhaustible; I vow to put an end to them.
The dharmas are boundless; I vow to master them.
The Buddha's Way is unsurpassable; I vow to attain it.[7]

THIS VERSE, which states the four bodhisattva vows (*shigu-seigan-mon*), is one of the shortest we recite. It is also one of the most important and challenging to understand. It is difficult in part because the meaning of *vow* in this verse departs from the usual English meaning of "solemn promise" or "personal commitment." In Buddhism *vow* has a much larger and more complex meaning. To understand it we need to consider Japanese Buddhist culture.

One of my experiences with the difficulties involved in translating from one cultural tradition to another took place in Kyoto, where I lived for a year in a Catholic convent. Although we were not part of the community, my family and I were given a small house inside the monastery. One day the abbess of the convent, Sister Cleria, visited our house. She was a very elegant old woman, an American. She had been in Japan for more than thirty years as a missionary and spoke fluent Japanese. She asked me to speak on the role of prayer in Buddhism at a gathering of the nuns in the convent. Because they had been so generous to us I couldn't refuse. I began to think about prayer in Buddhism and realized that there is no prayer in Buddhism.[8] That was how I started my talk for the Christian nuns. We don't have prayer in Buddhism, but vow holds the same importance for Buddhists as prayer for Christians. So I talked about the four bodhisattva vows.

Prayer, *inori* in Japanese, is a Christian term that means communion, communication, or oneness with God. Today there are many Catholic priests who practice zazen. Before becoming a Catholic priest, Ichirō Okumura (no relation to me) practiced with the famous Rinzai master Sōen Nakagawa Roshi. Nakagawa Roshi encouraged him to become a Catholic priest, and he has continued to practice zazen. At sixty he was the head of a Carmelite order in Japan. He traveled the world giving meditation instruction to Catholic communities and wrote a book about meditation practice in the Catholic faith. The title of his book is *Inori* (Prayer). An English translation (*Awakening to Prayer*) has been published.[9]

Father Okumura uses an expression from the Old Testament, "to be quiet in front of God," to describe silent sitting practice. This communion with God without language is, he believes, the purest form of prayer. I think this is true in a Christian context, but for me, zazen is not a communication with God or with anything else. I don't think of zazen as a form of prayer. This is a major difference between Buddhism and Christianity. There is no object in our zazen. We just sit.

When I looked in a dictionary of Japanese Buddhist terms, there is no entry for prayer (*inori*). There is a word, *kitō*, which can be translated into English as "prayer" but is actually quite different. Kitō is a Buddhist practice of the Shingon school, a Japanese Vajrayāna school. In India, Vajrayāna Buddhists adopted the practice of kitō under the influence of Hinduism. Hindu gods have an interesting habit. When priests recite special mantras and perform certain rituals, the gods are obliged to grant their requests. In Vajrayāna or Shingonshū there is a similar practice. Believers sit in lotus posture, chant mantras, and enact rituals. The practitioner can then become one with the buddha or bodhisattva enshrined in front of him and his requests will be granted. This is the Shingon practice of kitō. Many Japanese temples practice kitō to insure traffic safety, success in school entrance examinations, easy childbirth, recovery from sickness, or success in business. This is one of the ways Japanese Buddhist temples make money. Sōtō temples are no exception.

Originally, Buddhism had no such practice. From the beginning, however, especially in Mahāyāna Buddhism, vow is essential for all bodhisattvas. In fact, part of the definition of a bodhisattva is a person who lives by vow instead of by karma. Karma means habit, preferences, or a ready-made system of values. As we grow up, we learn a system of values from the culture around us, which we use to evaluate the world and choose actions. This is karma, and living by karma. In contrast, a bodhisattva lives by vow. Vow is like a magnet or compass that shows us the direction toward the Buddha. There are two kinds of vow: general vows, taken by all bodhisattvas, and particular vows for each person. Each bodhisattva makes specific vows unique to his or her personality and capabilities. The four bodhisattva vows are general vows that should be taken by all Mahāyāna Buddhist practitioners. We must live by these vows. That is our direction. Our sitting practice should also be based on these vows.

When I explained the four bodhisattva vows to the Christian nuns, I told them that I see a basic contradiction between the first and second half of each sentence. "Sentient beings are numberless; I vow to save them": but if sentient beings are numberless, we cannot possibly save them all—this is a contradiction. "Desires are inexhaustible; I vow to put an end to them": if they are inexhaustible, how can I put an end to them? That's logically impossible. "The dharmas are boundless; I vow to master them": if they are boundless, then we cannot completely master them. The "contradiction" in the fourth vow is subtler: "The Buddha's Way is unsurpassable; I vow to attain it": if it's so transcendent, can we really expect to realize it? These contradictions are very important and have a profound practical and also religious meaning. But before I discuss them, I will explain each sentence of the verse.

Originally these four vows were connected to the four noble truths. The older version of the verse of four vows is as follows.

> I vow to enable people to be released from the truth of
>   suffering.
> I vow to enable people to understand the truth of the origin
>   of suffering.
> I vow to enable people to peacefully settle down in the truth
>   of the path leading to the cessation of suffering.
> I vow to enable people to enter the cessation of suffering, that
>   is, nirvana.[10]

The four noble truths are the basic teachings of Shakyamuni Buddha. The first is the truth of suffering or dissatisfaction (*duḥkha* in Sanskrit; *dukkha* in Pāli). Human life is full of duḥkha. The second is the truth of the cause of suffering: thirst or delusive desires. The third is the truth of the cessation of suffering: nirvana. The fourth is the truth of the path that leads us to nirvana.

The first bodhisattva vow is related to the first noble truth: "I vow to enable people to be released from the truth of suffering." Perhaps "truth" is unnecessary. "I vow to enable people to be released from suffering." "Suffering" here is the specific kind of suffering mentioned in the four noble truths. The Buddha said that our life is full of suffering, and so his teaching is often interpreted as being pessimistic. The suffering referred to here is not limited to the pain, suffering, unhappiness, or sadness brought about by the circumstances of our lives. The deeper meaning of duḥkha or suffering is related to impermanence or egolessness. Everything is impermanent and always changing. As a result there is nothing substantial that we can grasp. And yet we continue to try. But since everything continues to change, we suffer. This suffering arises because we cannot possess or control anything. As long as we try to do so, we suffer and feel dissatisfaction. The fact that we cannot control the reality of our lives is the root of the suffering described by the Buddha, which is based on our delusions about and attachment to the ego. This is the second of the four noble truths.

The second bodhisattva vow is "I vow to enable people to understand the truth of the origin of suffering." The origin of suffering is our delusive desire, which in this context is called *bonnō*. This Japanese word is a Chinese translation of the Sanskrit *kleśa*, often rendered in English as "delusion," although it actually refers to the hindrances, troubles, defilements, or passions that drive us to unwholesome action. According to the Yogacāra school, there are four fundamental bonnō or delusive ideas that defile our minds and our lives. The first, *gachi*, is ignorance of the Dharma, of the reality of impermanence and egolessness. The second is *gaken*, or egocentric views based on ignorance. We cling to established views of things around us. The third one is *gaman*, or arrogance. When we justify ourselves or try to be righteous we become arrogant. We put ourselves above others. The fourth is *ga-ai*, or self-attachment. *Ai* in Japanese is often used as a translation for "love," with a positive meaning. But in Buddhism *ai* is more often a kind of attachment and carries a negative connotation. *Gachi, gaken, gaman, ga-ai*—ignorance, egocentric view, arrogance, and self-attachment—are the four basic desires (*kleśa*). Perhaps "desire" isn't the best word to characterize these things, but they are the cause of suffering and unwholesome karma. The second vow relates to this truth. Bodhisattvas vow to help people understand the truth of the origin of suffering. This is what the second vow means when it says, "Desires are inexhaustible; I vow to put an end to them."

The third vow in the older verse is "I vow to enable people to peacefully settle down in the truth of the path leading to the cessation of suffering." This is about the fourth noble truth, the truth of *mārga*, the path leading to nirvana. (The order of truths is different in the two versions.) The path referred to is our practice of the eightfold noble path: right view, right thinking, right speech, right action, right livelihood, right effort, right mindfulness, and right meditation. The third vow has to do with the fourth noble truth, to enable people to settle in the way of practice. It begins with "The dharmas are boundless." Here the original word for "dharmas" is *hōmon* (dharma gate), which means teachings about reality and about reality-based practice. "The dharmas are boundless; I vow to master them" means that we vow to study and settle down in the way of practice. That is the fourth noble truth and the third vow.

An older version of the fourth vow, "The Buddha's Way is unsurpassable; I vow to attain it," is "I vow to enable people to attain nirvana." This vow is related to the third noble truth. In this context, "Way" is a translation of *bodhi*, or awakening, not of *mārga*, or path. "The Buddha's Way" refers to the Buddha's awakening or nirvana. So this vow says, "The Buddha's awakening is unsurpassable, but I vow to attain it."

This is the meaning of the four vows. It is important to understand that they are directly connected with the four noble truths, the fundamental teaching of Shakyamuni Buddha.

It is interesting to compare the older version of the four vows with the version we usually recite. Again, the older version is:

> I vow to enable people to be released from the truth of
> suffering.
> I vow to enable people to understand the truth of the origin
> of suffering.
> I vow to enable people to peacefully settle down in the truth
> of the path leading to the cessation of suffering.
> I vow to enable people to attain nirvana.

In this version of the four bodhisattva vows, "I" refers to a bodhisattva who has taken vows, been released from suffering, and understood the truth of the origin of suffering. This is someone who has already settled down in practice, in the four noble truths: someone who is already in nirvana. These vows are for someone who is already enlightened. However, the verse we usually recite is, once again:

> Sentient beings are numberless; I vow to save them.
> Desires are inexhaustible; I vow to put an end to them.
> The dharmas are boundless; I vow to master them.
> The Buddha's Way is unsurpassable; I vow to attain it.

This person still has inexhaustible desires or delusions, and so still has something to study, something to learn. The person has not yet attained the Way. The person him/herself still has inexhaustible delusive desires, and therefore the person vows to eliminate them. This is not a vow to help others to be released from inexhaustible desires. The older version is the vow made by an already enlightened bodhisattva, someone who is above all deluded sentient beings, making a vow to help all people.

In the newer version, the one we now chant, we still suffer but vow to save all beings. We have inexhaustible desires but vow to put an end to them. "The dharmas are boundless...." There are so many things to learn, and yet we vow to master them. We must make an effort to study the dharmas, the teachings, and practice, but we realize that practice is endless and so we resolve to practice endlessly. "The Buddha's Way is unsurpassable." We are not yet enlightened, but we vow to attain it. We are ordinary human beings and yet, if we take these four vows, we are bodhisattvas. In reality, we are ordinary human beings with inexhaustible desires. We have to study the teachings and practice endlessly, day by day, moment by moment, to attain the Buddha's enlightenment. That is our vow. In making these four vows, we are bodhisattvas.

As we said, there is a contradiction inherent in these vows: we vow to do things that are impossible. This means that our practice is endless and that we cannot completely fulfill the four vows. Our practice and study are like trying to empty the ocean with a spoon, one spoonful at a time. It is certainly a stupid way of life, not a clever one. A clever person cannot be a bodhisattva. We are aiming at something eternal, infinite, and absolute. No matter how hard we practice, study, and help other people, there is no end to it all. When we compare our achievement with something infinite, absolute, and eternal, it's like nothing.

We shouldn't compare our practice, our understanding, or our achievements with those of other people. When we do, we become competitive. We think, "I'm better than them" or "I'm practicing harder." Our practice becomes a competition based on egocentricity, something totally meaningless as a practice of the Buddha's Way. We cannot peacefully settle down in such a competitive practice. No matter how hard or long we practice, if our practice is based on ego, we are totally deluded. Such practice leads to a selfish view, arrogance, and self-attachment. Even though we think we are practicing the Dharma, we are against the Dharma completely. When we understand that our goal is eternal, infinite, and absolute, no matter how hard we practice, no matter how many things we master, no matter how deep our understanding of Buddha's teaching, compared to the infinite, we are zero. We cannot afford to be arrogant.

There is another side to this. Even if we cannot practice as hard, sit as long, study as much, or understand as deeply as others, we don't need to feel guilty or inferior. Compared to the eternal, the absolute, or the infinite, we are all equal to zero. There is something deeply meaningful in our comparison with the absolute. Understanding ourselves in this way frees our practice from competition based on selfishness. This is a most important point. We cannot be proud of our practice, and we don't need to be too humble about our lack of practice or understanding. We are just as we are. Our practice is to take one more step toward the infinite, the absolute, moment by moment, one step at a time.

According to Dōgen Zenji this one step, or even a half-step, in our practice is the manifestation of absolute enlightenment. This is what he meant when he spoke of "just sitting," or *shikantaza*. When we sit, we just sit. That doesn't mean we don't need to do anything else. It doesn't mean we are all right only when we are sitting. It means that when we sit, there is no comparison. We are right now, right here, with this body and mind, awakening to reality. This is the complete manifestation of absolute, infinite, eternal enlightenment. Even a short period of sitting is bodhisattva practice. And our practice is not only sitting. All of our day-to-day activities should be based on the four vows and the four noble truths, which are the basic teaching of Shakyamuni Buddha.

When I explained all this to the Christian nuns, they liked it! They felt that the teachings of Catholicism are the same as those of Buddhism. In Christianity the absolute, the infinite, is God. Being in front of God, no one can be proud of their achievement. Therefore, believers have to be still in front of God. The philosophical or doctrinal basis is different, but the attitude toward our everyday lives is the same. When we talk to people of other religions, we don't need to discuss the differences in theory. Of course, it is important to understand the differences, but we don't need to argue about which are true.

The four bodhisattva vows are an essential point, not just in our practice of zazen but also in our day-to-day lives. Each of us has a job or a family and in each situation we try to practice the four noble truths and the four bodhisattva vows. Our practice is the whole of our life, not something special that we do only in the monastery or at a sesshin or retreat. Those are important parts of our practice, but the Buddha taught us to just awaken to the reality of our lives and live on the basis of that reality. We have to live right now, right here, with this body and mind, and in the company of others. The guiding force, the compass that leads us to live out this reality, is the bodhisattva vows.

SHAKYAMUNI BUDDHA'S VOW

According to the Sanskrit literature, Shakyamuni sat alone under the bodhi tree and was enlightened. He saw that beings suffer in samsara—in the six realms of the world: the realms of hell, hungry ghosts, animals, asuras, human beings, and heavenly beings. This is the meaning of suffering as the first noble truth. The Indian folk belief was that we are born into one of these six realms, and when we die we are reborn into another realm according to our deeds in this life. The transmigration continues endlessly until we are free from twisted knots of karma created by the three poisonous minds of grasping, aversion, and ignorance.

I don't know if these realms actually exist after death, but I see that they exist in human society and inside each of us. *Hell* is when people live together and make each other suffer. Everything each one does irritates the others. This sort of thing often happens even within ourselves: two conflicting parts of us argue and fight. We have a constant internal struggle. That's hell.

Hungry ghosts are beings consumed by unsatisfied craving. In this realm we always feel something is lacking. We consume or try to obtain things we desire but are never satisfied.

Animals are happy when they are fed; they feel content and go to sleep. Some animals, like cows or elephants, work from birth to death; they just work, work, work. Many Japanese people live like this. Some of my friends who work in Tokyo leave their homes at seven in the morning and start work at eight thirty or nine. It may take them two hours to get to their jobs. They work until nine in the evening and then return home and go to bed around eleven or twelve. That's their life. When I heard this, I was amazed. Their lives are much harder than intensive sitting practice during sesshin! I can't imagine how a person could live that way. It's living in the realm of animals.

Asuras are fighting spirits. Asura was a mythical Indian god of justice. When we believe we are right, we criticize others based on our own concept of justice. If necessary we fight with others until we win. Exterminating people who oppose us becomes the purpose of our lives. Such people cannot be satisfied without enemies. They can't live without something against which they can struggle. We all have this sort of attitude sometimes. When we have someone to criticize, we feel safe, righteous, and good.

Human beings seek fame and profit. Animals are satisfied when their stomachs are full, but we with our human minds are never full, because we think of our future. I want to make sure I will be fulfilled tomorrow, the day after tomorrow, and for the rest of my life, and that my children will live long, happy lives. Even if we don't have any problems at this moment, we are not satisfied because we worry about the future. Animals don't worry about safety or security in the future. Only human beings save something extra for tomorrow.

Heavenly beings are those whose desires are completely met. They need nothing; they seem happy, and yet they are not. Since they have everything, they don't need to seek anything and are unable to find motivation to do anything. These people become lazy and also worry about losing what they already possess. It can be difficult for them to find truly intimate friends because they think others befriend them only to take something. Even if they live successful lives, they lose everything when they die. When such people face death, they might question the meaning of their hard work and achievements. Even someone who has it all cannot be happy in an absolute way as long as the goal in life is to satisfy ego-centered desires. This is the insight the Buddha attained under the bodhi tree.

The Buddha contemplated the causes of these forms of suffering and tried to find their root cause. Later in Buddhist history people assumed that the Buddha contemplated the twelve links of causation—the way our lives become suffering and how we can be liberated from suffering. He found that the ultimate cause of suffering is ignorance and delusive desires based on that ignorance. This ignorance is *mumyō* in Japanese, *avidyā* in Sanskrit. *Myō* means "brightness" or "wisdom," and *mu* means "no." *Mumyō* means that we cannot see the reality of life. As we try to fulfill our desires, we do things that are good or bad. As a result of our deeds, we transmigrate through the various realms of samsara and we suffer. This is the teaching of causality based on our karmic deeds. Our desires and the actions that arise from them are based on our ignorance. The consequences of our deeds cause suffering. When we clearly see our ignorance it disappears. When we see with the eye of wisdom that ignorance causes our suffering, we are free from both ignorance and suffering. This is called nirvana or enlightenment.

Shakyamuni Buddha remained sitting for several weeks to savor his enlightenment. He was released from all ignorance and suffering and he enjoyed it. He felt that what he now saw, the causes of suffering, was very difficult to understand. He feared that if he tried to teach others what he had discovered, no one would understand. He thought, "The content of my enlightenment, the concept of interdependent origination, is extremely difficult to comprehend. Those who enjoy clinging take pleasure in attachment and are fond of their ties of dependence, and they will never be able to understand it." He expressed this thought in verse:

That enlightenment which I have attained through
    many hardships
Should I now teach to others?
Those who hold fast to greed and hatred

Cannot easily understand this Truth.
Against the common stream,
Subtle, profound, fine, and difficult to perceive,
It cannot be seen by those
Who are lost in desire, cloaked in darkness.[11]

Pondering thus, he was not inclined to teach the Dharma.

Here "the common stream" refers to the cycle of birth and death within samsara. The Buddha initially thought that people would find it too difficult to understand what he had discovered. In the Sanskrit story Brahmā Sahāmpati, a god, divined what the Buddha was thinking. (Perhaps this is not a description of real events but an account of what was happening in the Buddha's mind.) When he saw that the Buddha had decided not to teach, he asked him to reconsider. "In this world there are some people who bear only a small amount of hindrance and whose wisdom is outstanding," he said. "Please preach your Dharma to them." Still the Buddha hesitated. Brahma repeated his request, and again the Buddha did not consent. After the third request he accepted. Then he said, "The gateway of ambrosia (deathlessness) is thrown open for those who have ears to hear."

The Buddha's hesitation to teach is understandable. When I first studied the Buddha's teaching I had difficulty accepting it. It was not so hard to understand it intellectually. It's easy to understand as an abstract theory that the cause of suffering is ignorance and desire, or to see examples in other people. But it's difficult to see when we ourselves suffer and are ignorant. It's also hard to accept that we are deluded. We believe that we are special, important, and valuable. It's really not a matter of intellectual understanding, not a set of abstract hypotheses. If we agree with the Buddha's teaching, we need to practice it and make an effort to transform our lives.

Because of Brahma's request, the Buddha went to Benares and taught a group of ascetic monks who had practiced with him. These monks accepted his teaching. The Buddha's determination to start teaching was the origin of the vow in Buddhism. After that the Buddha traveled all over India by foot and continued teaching for over forty-five years. He lived by his vow from his enlightenment until his death at the age of eighty.

The Buddha's vow was to help people awaken to reality and save them from suffering. This is the vow we take as a bodhisattva: "Beings are numberless, we vow to free them." A bodhisattva is a disciple or a child of the Buddha, a person who aspires to learn the Buddha's teaching and follow his example. Vow is essential for us as Buddhist practitioners. It is a concrete and practical form of wisdom and compassion. This is the important point to understand when we think about vow.

Katagiri Roshi's Poem on Vow

Katagiri Roshi, the founding teacher and abbot of the Minnesota Zen Meditation Center until his death in 1990, named the center Ganshōji, which means "temple born of vow." After I became the head teacher there, I used his office. In it was a cabinet holding his writings. Since I wanted to understand his goals, attitude, and teaching, I read much of his work. I found a poem he wrote in 1988 that is quite wonderful.

Peaceful Life

Being told that it's impossible,
One believes, in despair, "Is that so?"
Being told that it is possible,
One believes, in excitement, "That's right."
But whichever is chosen,
It does not fit one's heart neatly.

Being asked, "What is unfitting?"
I don't know what it is.
But my heart knows somehow.
I feel an irresistible desire to know.
What a mystery "human" is!

As to this mystery:
Clarifying
Knowing how to live
Knowing how to walk with people
Demonstrating and teaching,
This is the Buddha.

From my human eyes
I feel it's really impossible to become a Buddha.
But this "I," regarding what the Buddha does,
Vows to practice
To aspire
To be resolute,
And tells me, "Yes, I will."
Just practice right here, now
And achieve continuity
Endlessly
Forever.
This is living in vow.
Herein is one's peaceful life found.[12]

This is a poem about vow. I also found his original poem in Japanese. When I read it closely, I saw that it is a lucid explanation of the four noble truths. The first stanza expresses the truth of suffering. "One believes in despair … one believes in excitement … whichever is chosen; it does not fit one's heart neatly." This is the reality of our lives. In Japanese this stanza reads, *Hito ga dame da to ieba / gakkarishite so dana to omoi / Hito ga iinda to ieba hashaide so o nanda to omou.* The phrases he used for "possible" and "impossible" are *dame da* and *iinda. Dame da* means both "impossible" and "not good." *Iinda* can be interpreted as "good." We encounter many such judgments in our lives. Sometimes people say you are good, sometimes not good. Each time we are judged we feel despair or excitement. We live based on opinions, not just other people's but also our own. When we are successful, we think, "Yeah, this is great." When we've had a hard time, we feel small. We may even feel that life is not worth living. This up and down is samsara, the reality of our life that is described as transmigration through the six realms.

This is our life as human beings. We always feel somewhat unsatisfied. "Whichever is chosen; it does not fit one's heart neatly." Happy or sad, there is some dissatisfaction. We feel that there is something unsettled in ourselves and in our way of life. We are moved by others' expectations, by the situation, or even by our own self-image. We can't find a peaceful, steady, absolute foundation for our life. As we move in samsara.We always feel somewhat unsafe, somewhat unsettled. Something is lacking even if we are in the heavenly realm and all our desires are fulfilled. Of course, if we are in hell, we really suffer. This is our life. So we start to question: What's wrong? What's the problem? What causes this feeling of emptiness? We want to understand this feeling. In the second stanza Katagiri says, "Being asked what is unfitting; I don't know what it is." Our motivation to question and understand is called bodhi-mind. Katagiri writes, "My heart knows somehow. / I feel an irresistible desire to know." We want to know the real cause of the problem. This is unique to human beings. We alone ask who we are and how we should live. Other animals don't have this problem.

Dōgen Zenji said that "to study the Buddha Way is to study the self." I think a human is a being that has to study the self. Other living things do not have to do this; they have no questions. But for us, this self is a big question. We humans are troublesome, mysterious creatures. We need to understand this mystery. This questioning, this need to understand, is our bodhi-mind—a mind that awakens to the reality of our life.

Katagiri continues, "As to this mystery: / Clarifying / Knowing how to live / Knowing how to walk with people / Demonstrating and teaching, / This is the Buddha." The Buddha understood or clarified this mystery. He saw the answer to the questions: What are human beings? What is the cause of human suffering? He awakened and understood how we can live in a wholesome way with peace.

The reality that the Buddha found in his enlightenment is

interdependent origination. Katagiri's phrase "knowing how to walk with people" refers to this interdependence. It means that we can't live without other people and things. For Buddhists, studying the self means studying how to walk with others. That's why the Buddha emphasized the importance of the sangha, a place where people live and practice together.

Katagiri's comment in the last stanza, "From my human eyes / I feel it's really impossible to become a Buddha," reminds us that even though we study the Buddha's teaching we are still human. The Buddha's achievement is so great that it's almost impossible for us as humans to follow his Way. Even so, one "vows to practice." In the Japanese version, the word for "vow" is *negau*, which means "to wish." We wish to practice and aspire to become buddhas. Katagiri uses the word "aspire" as the translation for *inori*. *Inori*, we've seen, is usually translated as "prayer," but here it means "deeply wish for something that doesn't seem possible." Even though we know that it is impossible to follow the Buddha's Way, we deeply wish to make it possible. Then Katagiri says he vows "to be resolute." Here the Japanese version has *kesshin*, which means "to make up one's mind, to be fixed and determined." Next, he says he tells himself, "Yes, I will." Even though he feels it's impossible, he cannot help but say this. That vow comes from the deepest part of the self. Intellectually it seems impossible. But from our deep life force we can't help but say, "Yes, I will." That is vow. A vow should not be made by our intellect or an emotional impulse. It should come from the deepest part of us.

"Just practice right here, now" means that we start practicing immediately. We can't postpone it because the wish is so deep. Somehow we have to start searching for our own self. There is no time to wait. "And achieve continuity" means to practice continuously. Because it's impossible to achieve what Buddha did, we have to practice forever. There is no end, no goal, and yet we take small steps one by one, moment by moment. We try to walk along the Buddha's Way one step or just half a step in all situations. Sometimes we are happy because we feel we are good practitioners and doing the right thing. Sometimes sitting in this posture every morning is boring or painful, and yet we do it. In any situation we try to adopt the attitude Katagiri describes. "Being told that it's impossible / One believes, in despair, 'Is that so?' / Being told that it is possible, / One believes, in excitement, 'That's right.'" Even in our practice we need to work with this attitude of up and down. Sometimes sitting in our zazen we feel great; we feel that we are enlightened. Sometimes we feel we are in hell. In either situation we just go through it endlessly, forever.

Katagiri Roshi said, "This is living in vow." It means to sit, to try to help others, to live and work with others each day of our lives. When we are living in vow, in our emotion, in our human sentiment, there are good times and hard times. Like all people in samsara, we are still in the six realms. And yet, we can find a peaceful basis, a foundation for our life which is never moved by human sentiment. That is vow. That is the reality of our life.

The last line of his poem is "Herein is one's peaceful life found." When we vow, we feel we have a duty. Usually, taking a vow is like making a promise: if we don't keep it, we feel bad or fear that we might be punished. But vow in Buddhism is not like that. It's not something we do with our intellect or shallow emotion. We vow toward the Buddha, toward something absolute and infinite. As a bodhisattva, we can never say, "I have achieved all vows." We cannot be proud of our achievements, because in comparison with the infinite anything we achieve is insignificant. Each of us has different capabilities, of course. If we cannot do very much, we practice just a little. There is no reason for us to feel small or to say we're sorry. We just try to be right here with this body and mind and move forward one step or just half a step. This is our practice in a concrete sense.

Katagiri Roshi used the expression "living in vow" because it sounds natural in English. I like "living *by* vow," perhaps because D. T. Suzuki has this expression in his book *Living by Zen*.[13] In the Japanese translation of this book he says something like "All living beings are living in Zen but only human beings can live by Zen." Saying that all living beings—dogs, cats, plants, flowers—are living in Zen doesn't mean they abide in meditation or samādhi, but rather that they are living the reality of life as it is, or *tathātā* in Sanskrit. Everything lives in the reality of life, in Zen; but only human beings have to make a conscious effort to do so. We devote ourselves to the study and practice of Zen and consciously live *by* Zen. As Suzuki says, only human beings do this, but that doesn't mean that we are superior to other beings. Because of our doubts and delusions we cannot *simply* live in reality. We have to consciously return to reality and make an effort to live on that basis. That, according to Suzuki, is living by Zen.

A life led by vow is a life animated or inspired by vow, not one that is watched, scolded, or consoled by vow. These verbs create a separation between the person and the vow. The simple phrase "living by vow" emphasizes that the person and the vow are one. Our life is itself a vow.

D. T. Suzuki's Vow

The Japanese translator of *Living by Zen*, Sōhaku Kobori, wrote about a conversation he had with Suzuki when he was young. Kobori asked a question that had popped into his mind: "What is your kenshō?" In Rinzai Zen, *kenshō* means enlightenment. Suzuki replied, "Well, my kenshō is *shujō mu hen sei gan do*."[14] The Japanese expression means "Living beings are numberless; I vow to save them." That was his enlightenment. I was surprised when I first read this conversation, but I now believe Suzuki was a real bodhisattva. His many books in English have introduced Zen around the world. He worked continuously until he died at the age of ninety-six. The basis of his effort was the vow "Sentient beings are numberless; I vow to save them." In this respect there is no distinction between Rinzai and Sōtō. We are all Buddhists or bodhisattvas. Zen in the West began with D. T. Suzuki's bodhisattva vow, just as Buddhism began with the Buddha's vow.

In his writings Suzuki elaborated on the bodhisattva vow:

Let me remark ... that "vow" is not a very appropriate term to express the meaning of the Sanskrit *pranidhāna*. Pranidhāna is a strong wish, aspiration, prayer, or an inflexible determination to carry out one's will even through an infinite series of rebirths. Buddhists have such a supreme belief in the power of will or spirit that, whatever material limitations, the will is sure to triumph over them and gain its final aim. So, every Bodhisattva is considered to have his own share in the work of universal salvation.[15]

Suzuki's kenshō was his strong determination and vow to help liberate all living beings from a delusive way of life. He carried out this vow till death.

UCHIYAMA ROSHI AND VOW

Uchiyama Roshi placed great emphasis on living by vow. Although we didn't chant much at Antaiji, before and after each of his lectures we chanted the four bodhisattva vows verse instead of the "Verse for Opening the Sutra." In fact, the bodhisattva vows verse was the only verse we regularly chanted in our practice life at Antaiji. Uchiyama Roshi felt that the vows were essential to our practice. He writes:

A classic Mahāyāna text says, "The true mind of every sentient being itself teaches and leads each sentient being. This is the vow of Buddha." Vow is not a special speculative approach to something outside us. The true mind of sentient beings— that is, universal self—itself is vow. Thus, when we consider universal self from the vantage point of the personal self, we realize that we cannot live without vow.[16]

As human beings living at the intersection of the universal self and the ego-centered self, we cannot live without being led by vow as the direction of our lives. Uchiyama Roshi took two personal vows based on the four general bodhisattva vows. One was to study the truth of life from not only Zen or Buddhism but also other spiritual traditions, to digest it through his own way of life, and to share it through his writings with Japanese and Westerners alike. His other vow was to produce determined practitioners of zazen who are thoroughly settled in the life of zazen practice.

Uchiyama Roshi often used the expression *ichiza nigyō sanshin*. The first word, *ichiza*, means "one sitting," referring, of course, to our practice of zazen. *Nigyō* means "two practices," vow and repentance. *Sanshin*, "three minds," refers to three mental attitudes described by Dōgen Zenji: joyful mind, parental mind, and magnanimous mind. "One sitting," Uchiyama Roshi says, is the center of our zazen practice. By "one sitting" he doesn't mean one of many. In this context "one" means absolute. In the chapter of *Shōbōgenzō* titled "Zammai ō zammai," Dōgen Zenji writes:

> That which directly goes beyond the whole world is *kekka-fuza* (full-lotus sitting). It is what is most venerable in the house of the buddhas and ancestors. That which kicks away the heads of non-Buddhists and demons and enables us to be inhabitants of the innermost room of the house of the buddhas and ancestors is kekkafuza. Only this practice transcends the pinnacle of the buddhas and ancestors. Therefore, the buddhas and ancestors have been practicing zazen alone, without pursuing anything else.[17]

This is the meaning of "one sitting."

According to Dōgen Zenji, our sitting is not part of our practice, but rather other activities are part of our zazen. This is what is meant by the phrase "our zazen is absolute." This is a very important point. In *Bendōwa*, Dōgen Zenji said, "Even if only one person sits for a short time, because this zazen is one with all existence and completely permeates all time, it performs everlasting Buddha guidance within the inexhaustible dharma world in the past, present, and future."[18] In this sense, sitting is absolute. This means that we become awakened to the reality that we are one with all beings, all times, and all space. This too is the meaning of "one sitting."

According to Uchiyama Roshi zazen has two aspects. One is vow and the other is repentance. In this context "aspect" doesn't mean that there are two parts to our zazen. It means that the whole of sitting is the practice of vow and, at the same time, the practice of repentance. Whether or not we aware of it, we are living out the reality of life. Unfortunately, we lose sight of this reality. Our life is like a hand. When we see it as a hand, there is no distinction between the fingers. But when we see it as a collection of fingers, each finger is independent and has its own name and characteristics. Each has a unique shape and function. They can act independently and are not interchangeable.

In the same way, human beings are individuals. If we cut off a finger, it can't function as a finger anymore. A finger always works with other fingers. This is the reality of human life as well, but we often forget and think of ourselves only as individuals. This is a fundamental delusion for us. We have to wake up to the reality that we can be a finger only in relationship to other fingers working as one hand. The hand can be a family, a sangha, a society, or the whole universe. Yet if we think of this community as an entity in itself, it can become just another, bigger ego. We shouldn't consider either the hand or the finger to be a separate, independent thing. Both are like a bubble. The bubble doesn't exist as a separate thing, but only as a condition of water and air: it is air trapped inside a film of water. But we can't deny that the bubble exists. The bubble is there. "Bubble" is just a name for a condition of air trapped in water. So we can say neither that the bubble doesn't exist nor that the bubble exists independently. Air and water are themselves the same in that they are merely collections of atoms. In the same way, atoms are aggregates of even smaller particles.

Although this is the reality of our life, we are almost always unaware of it. We think of this person which is ourself as most important, as the center of the universe. We need to return to the reality that exists before egocentricity arises, before the separation of this body and mind from the rest of the world. This is what Uchiyama Roshi meant when he said we are living at the intersection of the universal self and the ego-centered self.

To vow to save all beings doesn't mean that we believe that we have the power to help all those who are in trouble. Imagining that were so would truly be quite arrogant. To save all beings means to *be one with* all beings. We cannot become one with others by means of our individual efforts. But we can wake up to the reality that from the beginning we are one with all beings. That is why we study the obstacles that prevent us from seeing this reality. That is how we become free from delusion. To become free from delusion, we have to study the Buddha's teachings. Reality itself is also a teaching. All beings in this universe—trees, leaves, and animals—teach us to awaken to the reality that is impermanent and egoless. We are not sensitive enough to hear this teaching without effort, so we must actively listen and study. In our practice together, we vow to attain the Buddha's Way, the Buddha's enlightenment, and to be one with all beings. As the Buddha said in the *Lotus Sutra*, "But now this threefold world is all my domain, and the living beings in it are all my children."[19] That is the Buddha's attitude, and we vow to attain such an attitude. We know it's almost impossible, but we vow to do so.

Each of the four bodhisattva vows is a kind of a paradox or contradiction. It is impossible to accomplish or completely achieve the vows. Since we are working at something infinite and absolute, it's important to reflect on the fact that we can never accomplish it. We cannot be perfect. This awakening to our own imperfection is repentance.

In Buddhism repentance does not mean saying "I'm sorry" because of some mistake I have made. That kind of repentance is relevant, but as Buddhists repentance means awareness of our imperfections and limitations. Vow and repentance are two kinds of energy that enable us to continue our practice. Zazen is itself the practice of vow. Zazen is itself the practice of repentance.

When we sit, we face the absolute, the infinite, and we let go of thought. This means that we don't judge things by our own yardsticks, but instead we are measured against the absolute. That is our practice of vow and repentance. Facing the infinite or absolute, we are really nothing. No matter how long we practice zazen, we cannot be proud of what we have accomplished. At the same time, we don't need to feel guilty or inadequate because we cannot practice enough, or because we cannot help others so much. No matter how great or small our accomplishments, they are all the same compared to the infinite. The important point is that even if it is only a small thing, we just do it. We don't need a fancy way to attain perfect enlightenment or a means to help all living beings. Just sit a little more, or help others a little more. We should be down to earth. This is our practice.

THE THREE MINDS

As we have seen, our practice of zazen has two aspects. One is vow, to resolve to take one more step ahead. The other is repentance, to be aware of our imperfection. This zazen has to be applied to our day-to-day lives. According to Dōgen Zenji, the attitude we should maintain toward the things we encounter in our everyday lives is "three minds." He discusses this in "Tenzokyōkun" (Instructions to the Cook). In this text, he talks about the attitude the person who is in charge of cooking in the monastery must have. Of course, he is recommending this for all people who are working as a community. Three kinds of mind are mentioned in the final part of "Tenzokyōkun."

Joyful Mind

> On all occasions when the temple administrators, heads of monastic departments, and the tenzo are engaged in their work, they should maintain joyful mind, nurturing mind, and magnanimous mind. What I call joyful mind is the happy heart. You must reflect that if you were born in heaven you would cling to ceaseless bliss and not give rise to Way-seeking mind.[20]

Heaven is the realm in samsara in which people's desires are all ful-filled; only pleasure and happiness remain. There is no suffering. But if we don't encounter some hardship or difficulty, we don't arouse bodhi-mind. We won't seek after the Way when our life is full of happiness and joy. Heaven is not a good place to practice.

> This would not be conducive to practice. What's more, how could you prepare food to offer to the three jewels? Among the ten thousand dharmas, the most honored are the three jewels. Most excellent are the three jewels. Neither the lord of heaven nor a wheel-turning king can compare to them. The Zen'en Shingi says, "Respected by society, though peace-fully apart, the sangha is most pure and unfabricated."[21]

The *Zen'en Shingi* is a collection of regulations for monastic life in the Chinese Zen tradition. It recommends that the community of Buddhist practitioners should be pure and unfabricated. Here "unfab-ricated" is a translation of *mui*, which can mean "nondoing," or "non-action." In this context it means free of artifice. The Buddhist sangha or community is a place where people can escape from artificial ways of thinking and return to reality. This passage means that the sangha should be pure and free from attachment, delusion, and egocentricity.

The great importance of the Buddhist sangha isn't of course restricted to the Zen center as an institution. If we think of "sangha" as referring to a specific group of Buddhists, it becomes a sort of group ego. We should see sangha as more inclusive. The community of people living in this area is a sangha. This country, the community of all countries, and the society of all human beings should also be considered sanghas. Anywhere we go to return to reality or live according to reality is a sangha and is therefore most precious.

Dōgen remarks further, "Now I have the fortune to be born a human being and prepare food to be received by the three jewels. Is this not a great karmic affinity? We must be very happy about this." His expres-sion "great karmic affinity" is a translation of *dai innen*. Here *innen*

means the causes and conditions that enable us to practice and participate in a sangha. The conditions cannot be taken for granted:

> Consider that if you were born in the realms of hell, hungry
> ghosts, animals, fighting gods, or others of the eight diffi-
> cult births, even if you desired refuge within the sangha's
> power, you would never actually be able to prepare pure
> food to offer the Three Treasures. Because of suffering in
> these painful circumstances your body and mind would be
> fettered. However, in the present life you have already done
> this [cooking], so you should enjoy this life and this body
> resulting from incalculable ages of worthy activity. This
> merit can never fade.[22]

The sangha has power because in community we encourage one
another to practice in the Buddha's Way. When we can work as a tenzo
or in any other position to support others' practice we should appreciate this good fortune.

Furthermore, "You should engage in and carry out this work with
the vow to include one thousand or ten thousand lives in one day or
one time." Here he is alluding to the oneness of this moment, this day,
and all eternity. As far as our attitude is concerned, eternity and this
moment are one. This means that what we do this moment is not a step
to the next stage. We cook not to feed people but to cook. When we
cook, cooking itself should be our practice. It should not be preparation
for something else. Cooking is in itself a perfect action if it is cooking
just for the sake of cooking. When the food is ready, just offer it. Offering is not the result of cooking as preparation. Offering is just offering.
Eating is just eating. Each moment is perfect in itself, not a step to the
next one. Each moment is one with eternity. This is the attitude we
should maintain.

The same is true of zazen. When we sit in this posture, we are one
with all beings, all time, and all space. It's all very dynamic, not limited
to one single person or one moment of work. Even though we and our

work are small, they are connected with the whole universe. When we are without a limited attitude or purpose, our work has no limits.

"This will allow you to unite with these virtuous karmic causes for ten million lives," says Dōgen Zenji. "The mind that has fully contemplated such fortune is joyful mind." This positive attitude we can sustain even in hard times. As a tenzo, if we don't have fancy ingredients, we just work with what we have. Dōgen Zenji uses the expression "Pick a single blade of grass and erect a sanctuary for the jewel king; enter a single atom and turn the great wheel of the teaching."[23] We pick up just one small piece of bread and build the loftiest of the Buddha's temples. That's our practice.

Whatever we accomplish, it cannot be just for ourselves. "Truly, even if you become a virtuous wheel-turning king but do not make food to offer the Three Treasures, after all there is no benefit. It would only be like a splash of water, a bubble, or a flickering flame." If we do things for our private gain or personal benefit, then no matter how hard we work, no matter how much we achieve, it will come to an end. Instead we dedicate our work to all beings. That is our attitude toward work and toward other people. That is joyful mind.

Parental Mind

The second aspect of sanshin is nurturing or parental mind. "As for what is called nurturing mind," Dōgen continues, "it is the mind of mothers and fathers. For example, it is considering the Three Treasures in the way that a mother and father think of their only child." We try to care for the Three Treasures, the Buddha, Dharma, and Sangha, as if they were our only child. It is especially important to have this attitude when we practice in a community. The attitude of parents is to take care of others. When we live together, caring and being cared for are the same. The reality of what is happening is the same. The inner attitude of the caregiver, however, is very different from that of the one who expects to be cared for. This difference determines the quality of the community. A place where people want to be taken care of is very different from a place where people care for others. We should understand that this small difference in our inner attitude has very large effects on the world around us.

> Even impoverished, destitute people firmly love and raise an only child. What kind of determination is this? Other people cannot know it until they actually become mothers and fathers. Parents earnestly consider their child's growth without concern for their own wealth or poverty. They do not care if they are cold or hot but give their child covering or shade. In parents' thoughtfulness there is this intensity. People who have aroused this mind comprehended it well. Only people who are familiar with this mind are truly awake to it.[24]

When we are small, we are not capable. We can't survive without being taken care of by our parents or society. We should be grateful for the support and help we receive from our parents and others. When we become mature enough, we should take care of things around us, the way parents take care of their children. When you have this attitude you understand what it is.

For Dōgen this attitude is one of "watching over water and over grain." Here he is talking about the tenzo's work. When the tenzo cooks, he must take care of water, grain, fire, everything that happens in the kitchen. We have to pay careful attention to everything. When we prepare meals, many things are going on at the same time. As we cook the rice, we have to prepare soup and other side dishes. It's even more difficult when you cook with firewood. It's very easy to forget about the fire when you're doing something else. You have to be very careful, attentive to each thing. Even when we are caught up with several different things, we must remember the fire.

This attitude, concentrating on a particular thing while remaining aware of everything else, is the same as in our zazen. We don't concentrate our mind on a certain object in our zazen. Our mind is nowhere and at the same time everywhere. It's the same as when we are driving.

We don't focus our attention on a particular object like the steering wheel but are just awake. Our mind is really nowhere, which means everywhere. When our mind is nowhere and everywhere, we can react very naturally to whatever happens. That is our zazen. Our minds should not be fixed in one place but rather be nowhere and everywhere. That is our awakening. That is parental mind. Dōgen Zenji continues:

> Therefore, watching over water and over grain, shouldn't everyone maintain the affection and kindness of nourishing children? Great Teacher Sakyamuni even gave up twenty years of a buddha's allotted life span to protect us all alike in these later times. What was his intention? It was simply to confer parental mind. Tathāgatas could never wish for rewards or riches.[25]

According to Buddhist scriptures, the Buddha could have lived one hundred years, and yet he died when he was eighty in order to donate twenty years of his life span to all beings. This is how the Buddha manifests parental mind, the attitude of caring for things and other people.

Magnanimous Mind

The third aspect of the attitude advocated by Dōgen Zenji is magnanimous mind. "As for what is called magnanimous mind," he said, "this mind is like the great mountains or like the great ocean; it is not a biased or contentious mind."

We must try to avoid bias or a one-sided perspective and instead strive to see the whole situation. If we say, "This is me and that is them," our community is divided and our minds become one-sided. This leads to internal conflict and struggle and our group cannot be called a community or sangha. A sangha is a peaceful community of people, a mixture of water and milk, not water and oil. The attitude of magnanimous mind is no separation.

"Carrying half a pound, do not take it lightly; lifting forty pounds should not seem heavy." Here again Dōgen is talking about cooking. Sometimes we cook for one or two people. Sometimes we have to cook for one or two hundred people. We should not think that to prepare a meal for one or two people is easy or that to prepare a meal for many people is heavy or difficult. We take the same careful, attentive attitude in either case.

"Although drawn by the voices of spring, do not wander over spring meadows; viewing the fall colors, do not allow your heart to fall." Here spring and fall are used to represent favorable conditions and adversity. In spring we are happy and we wander around and forget reality. During the fall we become sorrowful and forget about reality. Too often we are moved by emotions, by circumstances, by good times and bad. Magnanimous mind, according to Dōgen, means that "the four seasons cooperate in a single scene." Spring, summer, autumn, and winter are one season. We should accept them as one reality of life. That is magnanimous mind.

"Regard light and heavy with a single eye," he goes on to say. "On this single occasion you must write the word 'great.' You must know the word 'great.' You must learn the word 'great.'" The attitude of magnanimous mind is the same as that of our zazen. Let go of thought, resist the pull of discrimination, and accept the situation as one.

These are the three attitudes or three minds with which we want to practice as a community, as a sangha. Our vow functions as the three minds, to nurture the Dharma, to practice with others, to create a situation or place to practice with other people. To do this we have to maintain these three attitudes, especially magnanimous mind. We must not be fettered by circumstance. We try to keep practicing steadily. That is the attitude we learn from our sitting practice. Whatever happens, whatever the situation, we just keep sitting. Sometimes we are busy, sometimes we are tired, sometimes we are involved in things. But we always come back to the zendo and sit down quietly. This is our practice.

VOW AS SANGHA

Sangha, or community, is an important manifestation of the concept of vow. We see this in the life of Guishan Lingyou, a famous Chinese Zen master who established a large and influential sangha in China.[26] How he accomplished this is instructive.

Guishan was instrumental in the establishment of Zen monasteries. Before his time there were no formal Zen Buddhist orders. People simply came together to practice. But then Zen monks started to create their own unique form of monastic practice. It was the beginning of Zen as a distinct school of Chinese Buddhism. This at least is the traditional view of the history of Chinese Zen.

Guishan was tenzo, the chief cook in the monastery where he practiced with his teacher, Baizhang Huihai. One day Guishan was standing near the abbot's room where Baizhang was staying.

Baizhang asked Guishan, "Who is it?" and Guishan replied, "It's me, Lingyou" (Guishan's dharma name). Baizhang said, "Would you dig in the firepot and see if there is fire or not?" It was winter and the firepot was their source of heat. Guishan stirred the firepot and said, "No fire." Then Baizhang got up and came over, dug deep into the ashes, and found a tiny ember. He showed it to Lingyou and said, "What is this? Isn't this fire?" Guishan was enlightened.

The fire in this story refers to the buddha-nature. Buddha-nature is not something solid or immovable, but rather an energy that motivates us to practice—and not just zazen or Buddhist practice. Buddha-nature is the fire of the life force that enables us to aspire to be better persons, to be more helpful to others, to settle into a healthy way of life, and to practice the Way. It's difficult to find the fire of buddha-nature inside ourselves, but we must. It's there. We are alive, so we have this force that drives us to practice and wake up to the reality of life. It may be only an ember, but all of us without exception have it. When we practice with other people, we gather together small fires. If we try to build a fire in a hibachi or firepot with a single piece of charcoal, it soon dies out. But even one tiny ember, if fed with charcoal, becomes a big fire. This is the meaning of sangha. We practice together with other people in a sangha. Each one of us has a small fire, which alone will die out sooner or later. Together we become bigger than ourselves. This was Guishan Lingyou's enlightenment.

Baizhang sent Guishan to Mount Gui, an isolated, precipitous, and awe-inspiring mountain suitable for a great monastery. He practiced there alone for several years. Dōgen Zenji comments on Guishan's practice, which he greatly admired, in a chapter of *Shōbōgenzō* titled "Gyōji." *Gyōji* means continuous or ceaseless practice. Here Dōgen talks about many Chinese Zen masters and their practice, Guishan being one of them. For Dōgen, Guishan's practice offered an important example of how to establish a monastery or sangha. He remarks:

> After the bestowal of the prophecy (Dharma transmission), Zen master Dayuan (Daien) of Mount Gui [i.e., Guishan Lingyou] went directly to the steep Gui Shan. There he made friends with bears and animals, lived at a thatched hermitage, and kept practicing. He didn't avoid hardships with wind and snow. He ate only chestnuts or horse chestnuts. There were neither temple buildings nor temple provisions. However, he ceaselessly devoted himself to continuous practice for more than forty years. Later, his temple became well known throughout the country and many excellent practitioners gathered there.[27]

People came to practice with him, and eventually his sangha grew huge. It is said that he had fifteen hundred students and forty-one dharma successors. Even though in the beginning he practiced alone, his practice was not for himself. He vowed to create a monastery or sangha to practice with others.

Dōgen Zenji discusses the inner attitude we should maintain when we vow to create a sangha or practice place. He continues, "When we make a vow to found a temple (a sangha or a monastery) we should not be motivated by human sentiment, but we should strengthen our aspiration for the continuous practice of Buddha Dharma." Our vow, then, should not be based on the human tendency to undertake things that we see as good, useful, or beneficial for ourselves alone— things we expect to bring us fame, profit, or self-satisfaction. This human sentiment isn't necessarily bad, but when we practice Buddha Dharma with others it is a hindrance. If each person seeks his or her own happiness and holds his or her own views, opinions, values, and ways of thinking, then there will be conflict. If we practice with other people on the basis of human sentiment, it may work for a while, but eventually it will fail. So our practice should be based not on human sentiment but on an aspiration for the continuous practice of Buddha Dharma.

Dōgen Zenji continues, "Even if we don't have lofty temple buildings, if we practice, the place can be called a *dōjō* of ancient buddhas." *Dōjō* means a place for practice. We now use the word *dōjō* for martial arts like karate or aikido, but originally this term referred to the place where the Buddha was enlightened under the bodhi tree. *Dōjō* is both a place for practice and a place of enlightenment because practice and enlightenment are one.

"We hear that ancient people practiced on the ground or under a tree. Such places are sacred forever. A single person's continuous practice creates a dōjō for many buddhas." This is the basic point of Dōgen Zenji's practice. We don't need lofty temple buildings for our practice. We don't need a formal zazen hall. When we vow to establish a dōjō, monastery, or sangha, we should not forget this. The number of buildings or people is not essential. The critical points are practice and aspiration. Dōgen said:

> Foolish people in this degenerate age should not be vainly engaged in construction of temple buildings. The buddhas and ancestors never had desires for buildings. Many people today meaninglessly construct a Buddha hall or other temple buildings although they haven't yet clarified the eye of their own self. Such people build temples, not in order to

offer the buildings to buddhas, but to make them their own homes of fame and profit.

They don't understand Buddha Dharma, but they construct lofty buildings. That's why there are so many temples in Japan now. They are monuments to their founders. Today, Japan is prosperous. Even Buddhist priests have money. They construct gorgeous buildings, huge Buddha halls, and beautiful zendos. I was surprised when I visited a big temple in Japan. They had just built a huge two-story building. The first story had a spacious hall for giving lectures. On the second floor, there was a zendo with a big Mañjuśrī statue. But there were no monks practicing there. They used the building only once a month to have *zazen-kai*, day-long meditation retreats, and retreats for laypeople a few times a year. To me this is a waste of wealth. It has no meaning as Buddha Dharma. Dōgen Zenji made this same criticism. My teacher, Uchiyama Roshi, was also very critical of this kind of activity. Many people, sincere practitioners who would like to practice as Dōgen Zenji did, try to have a formal sōdō and a statue of Mañjuśrī, and everything Dōgen Zenji described. These people build a zendō for the sake of human sentiment. They think that buildings are essential and that they cannot practice without formal monastic buildings. Uchiyama Roshi said that we can practice zazen with only three square feet for each person, a *zafu* (round cushion) and *zabuton* (square mat) to sit on, and our aspiration to practice. That's all we need. This is a very important point.

Dōgen Zenji continues:

> We have to quietly contemplate Guishan's continuous prac-
> tice in ancient times. To contemplate means to think of it
> as if we were living on Mount Gui right now. Listen to the
> sound of rain at midnight. The raindrops have power to
> pierce not only moss but also a rock. On a snowy night in
> winter, even birds and animals don't come to us. Unless we
> devote ourselves to continuous practice, valuing Dharma
> more than our own lives, we cannot stand such a life.

Guishan practiced alone, but I think this is not just a description of his solitary lifestyle. This is a description of our zazen. When we sit in zazen, even if we are with other people in a busy city, we are totally alone. The sound of raindrops and the sounds of the birds and animals are the sounds of our life. The snow is the scenery of our life. We just see it. We don't need to worry about what we should do today or tomorrow. Of course, we have a schedules, goals, and projects. But we just sit, right now, right here. We try to see that this is the only reality and everything else is the scenery of our life. We don't consider this practice as a step to something else. This practice right now, right here, brings about the next step. We don't need to worry about the next step. We should be fully right here, right now, in this situation, and awake to the reality of this self. That is an essential point.

> So Guishan didn't hurry to cut the grass to prepare the land, or engage in constructing temple buildings. He only continued to practice and put his whole energy into cultivating the Way. We cannot help but have sympathy for the authentic ancestor who transmitted the true Dharma and who had to undergo such hardships in a secluded steep mountain. I heard that on Mount Gui there was a pond and a brook which might be covered with layers of ice and mist. Although it was too solitary for a human being to tolerate, practice of the Buddha Way and the innermost truth vigorously came together there through his continuous practice.

This is the most important point in this chapter. Practice of the Buddha's Way is not something abstract but rather our concrete practice of the innermost truth of Buddha Dharma. This is the Buddha's teaching of the reality of our life. Even though our practice is very small, it merges with the innermost truth—Buddha's teaching of the reality of this universal life. This is an important aspect of our practice. Dōgen Zenji frequently talks about our concrete practice with our body and mind and that our personal practice actualizes the boundless, universal truth. Without our small, individual practice with this body and mind, the Buddha's teaching, or universal reality, is just an abstraction, something written in scriptures that we read and try to imagine. The universal truth or life force can only be manifested through our practice. If no one practices, Buddhist texts remain only words. If no one lives the teaching, it's just another part of our library; it's not alive. Even if our bodhi-mind or aspiration is weak, our practice is the manifestation of the universal truth taught by the Buddha.

Without the practice of this limited body and mind, temple buildings and zendos are meaningless. According to Dōgen Zenji, the meaning of our practice is practice at this moment, right now, right here, actualizing the Buddha's teaching. Without our practice there is no Buddha's teaching.

KATAGIRI ROSHI'S VOW

In 1988 Katagiri Roshi gave a lecture titled "Twenty-five Years of Dharma Transmission in North America" in which he spoke about his experiences in the United States and his vow and vision of his activities.[28] One of his experiences in his early time at the San Francisco Zen Center made him question the attitude of some American practitioners in the 1960s. At that time there were many young hippies living in the San Francisco area. Katagiri Roshi invited them to participate in practice at the center. One of them came to all the activities there. Katagiri Roshi said to him, "You come so often. What do you do? What's your job?" He answered, "I get unemployment." After he worked for six months or so, he could collect unemployment and meanwhile participate in activities at the center. After his unemployment payments expired, he would find another job. Katagiri Roshi was surprised by this reply. He had thought that this person was a good Zen student, but in fact the young man was engaging in an irresponsible way of life—irresponsible to his work, his society, and himself. According to Katagiri Roshi, taking advantage of the social welfare system to fulfill one's desire, even a desire to study Dharma, didn't have anything to do with the Dharma and was inconsistent with the bodhisattva practice of vow. Katagiri Roshi felt that a vow entails responsibility to one's own life, to other people, and to the whole of society. The most important point was always to walk together with all living beings.

In the lecture Katagiri Roshi also talked about his plans for the Zen community of MZMC. He mentioned four projects. I was surprised that he was so ambitious. First, he wanted to establish a monastery at Hokyōji,[29] where people could practice together as a sangha in an intimate setting. For Katagiri Roshi, Dharma means living beyond our egocentricity, individuality, and distinctions based on nationality and culture. It means living together as practitioners. This is the essence of Buddhism. Second, to educate and train his priest-disciples, he planned to establish a place where people could practice with experienced teachers. Finally, within Hokyōji's compound Katagiri Roshi wanted to build a separate facility as a retreat center, not just for monks but for anyone who wanted to experience a quiet life in nature. Fourth was Ganshōji, the Zen center in Minneapolis. This center is meant to have a function in the larger community, not just for the members of this sangha. Katagiri Roshi established a Buddhist study program that would appeal to a broad group of laypeople.

THE POWER OF RAINDROPS

In his comments about Guishan Lingyou's practice, Dōgen Zenji talks about raindrops. He asks us to contemplate Guishan's practice in the mountains. We should try to feel as if we were in Guishan's place. "Listen to the sound of raindrops at midnight. The raindrops have the power to pierce not only moss but also rock." Guishan sat by himself in the deep mountain. Our practice of zazen, like his, resembles a raindrop. We are small and can sit for only a short time. Each drop alone has little power, but still we continue to practice. As raindrops eventually pierce not only moss but also rock, continuous practice of zazen has the power to make a hole in even a rock. This is an essential point. Our practice doesn't have a mystical, mysterious, or magical power to clear away all delusions. But like the raindrops, we sit moment by moment, day after day, year after year, and this sitting generates the power to erode a rock. When we think of our plans to establish a monastery, it's the same. Our effort is like raindrops; it doesn't create change in one day, or a few days, or a few years. But if we just keep doing it, when conditions are ripe, it happens.

We should remember Guishan Lingyou's example. Our actual practice is most important. We need time to work toward our goals, but to accomplish any project the appropriate cause and conditions are essential. The cause may be compared to the seed of a plant, and the conditions to temperature, humidity, and sunshine. If we put a seed on a desk, it won't sprout. It needs the right conditions. But even when conditions are perfect, if the seed isn't healthy it won't sprout. So we must be careful to keep our practice healthy and deeply rooted. We should keep the root of our practice wholesome.

The changing of the seasons is similar. When I came to Minneapolis in August, all the trees had green leaves. It was very beautiful. After a few weeks, the trees turned many different colors, and this too was beautiful. If we tried to paint each leaf by hand, it would take forever. But when autumn comes, all the leaves change color suddenly, almost at once, because there is a cause inside of the tree. That's how things happen. If we don't have the right conditions, not even a single leaf will change color. This is important to consider in the context of vow. Vow is kind of a long-range project or plan. We don't need to be in a hurry. Just practice and recharge our energy in the sangha. Practice, sit, keep the seed alive, and when conditions ripen, it will grow.

Katagiri Roshi's vow was huge. This is the same as practice. Buddha Dharma is something universal, infinite, and absolute. As individual human beings, we are small and limited. But when we sit in this posture and let go of individuality, we are one with everything. We are infinite, absolute, part of the universe. When we give up our limited attitudes, there is no separation between this small individual self and the boundless universe. The smallness of individuals and universality of reality is a main point in Dōgen Zenji's teaching. It can also be described as the merging of difference and unity. Difference is individuality; each person is different. Unity means that everything is one; there is no separation. This is our reality. We are independent, small, and limited. Yet when we sit in this posture and let go of thought and of our limited desires, we are moved by a vow that comes from the very core of our being, and there is no separation between us and the whole universe.

Dōgen Zenji often referred to this merging of individuality and universality. For example, in *Eihei Kōroku* he quotes Hongzhi Zhengjue (Wanshi Shōkaku), a famous Chinese Zen master and the Dharma brother of Changlu Qingliao (Chōro Seiryō). Hongzhi was asked, "What is the self before discrimination?" He answered, "A toad in a well swallows the moon."[30] A tiny being in a small well swallowed the moon, a symbol of universality, the reality of our life.

In *Eihei Kōroku* Dōgen Zenji changed the expression to "A toad in the bottom of the ocean eats gruel." This is a strange image, since there are no toads in the ocean. Here's how we can understand it. The toad in the bottom of the ocean symbolizes a practitioner in a monastery; the gruel is what practitioners eat almost every day for breakfast, and the ocean represents the sangha. So we are all toads in the ocean. A well refers to narrow egocentricity, or individuality. When we practice in a sangha, we are still toads, although we no longer live in a well but in the ocean.

Dōgen continues, "A jewel rabbit in the sky washes the bowl."[31] As a child in Japan, I was taught that there was a rabbit in the moon, because the pattern of the moon's craters resembles a rabbit, at least for the Japanese. So "jewel rabbit" refers to the moon. What does Dōgen mean when he says that a toad in the ocean eats gruel and a jewel rabbit washes the bowl? I think he means that we are very limited beings, but when we practice with the sangha and eat gruel for breakfast, the rabbit, meaning the moon, comes to this person and washes the bowl. So this practitioner is not a toad anymore, but the jewel rabbit in the moon. There is a transformation here. Hongzhi's expression is poetic, not about day-to-day activity. But Dōgen Zenji expresses very well the reality of our practice. We are small living beings like toads, and yet, when we practice with the sangha, we are not just individuals but part of the ocean of beings, of all existence. Eating gruel for breakfast is a very concrete activity. Even a small act by a small person manifests the universal reality, which is the reality of our life. Any effort, however small, is enough. We do what we can in this moment, and then in the next moment, and then tomorrow; one moment at a time. It is the same as our practice of zazen, and our practice in our daily activities.

MEANINGS OF LIVING BY VOW

Vow is one of the most important aspects of practice as a bodhisattva. It can be understood from three different perspectives. First, a vow is a direction for an individual. We live the reality of life whether we are deluded or enlightened. This reality is called as-it-is-ness, or *tathātā*. It is also true that we frequently deviate from this reality of life because we are deceived by our egocentricity. The reality of our life is not so simple for us human beings. Enlightened or deluded, we are living out our as-it-is-ness, and yet we are always blind to it. This is our life as human beings. First we have to realize that we are deluded. Then we have to go back to the reality of life through the practice of this reality. As-it-is-ness for human beings is dynamic. We live in the reality of life, yet always lose sight of it, so we must return to it. These three points are the movement, the actual reality of our lives. To go back to the reality of life in the midst of this reality is our practice. This practice is based on vow. This vow is not a special promise we make to the Buddha but rather a manifestation of the foundation of our being. This is the most fundamental meaning of taking a vow. We go back to the reality of life within that reality.

The second aspect of living by vow is to live within a sangha and practice with other people, that is, to walk together with all living beings. We do this with the three minds—joyful mind, parental mind, and magnanimous mind. Our vow is manifest in our day-to-day lives as these three minds. Finally, we practice as a sangha, not simply as an individual but as one whole body. The sangha itself needs to have a direction to grow. That is the meaning of living by vow as a sangha. By working on the vow as a sangha little by little, one thing at a time, like raindrops, we meet the challenges and create a new stage in the history of Buddhism in the West.

All the karma ever created by me since of old
Through greed, anger, and self-delusion
Which has no beginning, born of my body, speech, and thought
I now make full repentance of it[32]

TRADITIONALLY in Chinese and Japanese Buddhism, there are two kinds of repentance. One is formal and concrete repentance, called *ji-sange*, in which we repent concrete offenses by means of rituals conducted with the help of a particular buddha, teacher, or sangha member. Another kind of repentance is called *ri-sange*. *Ji* and *ri* are important concepts in Chinese Buddhism. *Ji* refers to the relative, conventional, phenomenal, and formal level, whereas *ri* refers to the absolute, supreme, total, and formless level. A verse different from the one quoted above is used for ri-sange.

Sitting in zazen and letting go of thoughts is formless repentance. This kind of repentance has been emphasized in the Sōtō tradition since the Edo period (seventeenth–ninteenth centuries). But in Dōgen Zenji's writings, as far as I know, only the verse of ji-sange is recorded. I think both are important. Formal repentance is for our misdeeds that break the bodhisattva precepts we receive when we become the

Buddha's students. Formless repentance is to awaken to the total inter-penetrating reality beyond separation of subject and object, self and others. This is zazen.

The original Buddhist repentance was ji-sange, or formal repentance. In the original Buddhist sangha in India, when someone made a mistake the Buddha admonished the person not to repeat the deed. These admonitions were memorized and compiled in a category of Buddhist scripture called Vinaya by one of the ten great disciples, Upāli, at the first council after the Buddha's death. Since then, people receiving ordination as monks and nuns took these precepts as guidelines and vowed to uphold them. Sangha members held meetings for repentance called *uposatha* (Jap., *fusatsu*) twice a month on new and full moon days. A leader of the sangha recited the precepts text, called the Prātimokṣa, and people who had transgressed against the precepts made confession and repentance. They incurred penalties depending upon the severity of their violations. Lay Buddhists received five precepts and could participate in uposatha gatherings.

So the original meaning of repentance is to reflect on one's misdeeds and confess them to the sangha. This is a concrete, formal repentance. In order to make repentance, we first have to receive the precepts. The precepts are guidelines for our day-to-day lives. When we become aware of our deviation from these guidelines, we repent and go back to the precepts. This is the meaning of receiving the precepts as standards for our lives and making repentance.

Since Mahāyāna Buddhism was initially a lay movement, practitioners didn't have their own Vinaya. They received only the bodhisattva precepts. Later Mahāyāna monks lived in monasteries and practiced based on the Vinaya.[33] In China, Mahāyāna Buddhist monks received both the Vinaya and Mahāyāna precepts: the ten major precepts and the forty-eight minor precepts. However, in almost all schools of Japanese Buddhism except the Ritsu (Vinaya) school, both monks and laypeople receive only the bodhisattva precepts. This tradition originated with the founder of the Japanese Tendai school, Saichō (767–822). In the Sōtō Zen tradition founded by Dōgen, both priests and laypeople receive only sixteen bodhisattva precepts: the three refuges, the three-fold pure precepts, and the ten major precepts.

In our *jukai* (precepts-receiving) ceremony, we recite this verse of repentance before accepting the precepts. Repentance is like washing a cloth before dying it a certain color. By repenting the way we have been living, we cleanse our body and mind. This is a decisive turning point in our lives. We change our direction from the pursuit of wealth, fame, and success to the bodhisattva Way of living at one with all beings.

Many recite this verse not just once in a lifetime at the jukai ceremony but also at bimonthly repentance ceremonies called *ryaku-fusatsu*. Katagiri Roshi's practice at MZMC was to recite it at the beginning of the morning service together with the verses of the three refuges and the four bodhisattva vows. Even though we have received the precepts, we often forget them and lose our direction as bodhisattvas. So we remember that the precepts are the guidelines of our lives and renew our aspiration and commitment. This is the meaning of the recitation of repentance in our daily practice.

There is another, deeper meaning of repentance. We live in the reality of our life whether or not we observe the precepts. No one can escape from this reality. Even when we are deluded, we live in reality as deluded human beings. Ultimately there is no separation between reality and delusion. In other words, reality includes delusions. Even though we live in the reality that is beyond discrimination, we have to discriminate in our day-to-day lives. We have to decide what is good or bad. Without discrimination we can do nothing. Even as we practice the Buddha's teachings, we have to make choices. This is the unavoidable reality of our concrete lives.

Zazen is the only exception. When we sit in this posture and open the hand of thought, we are truly free from discrimination. Whenever thoughts come up, we just let them go. In our daily activities, however, we have to make choices based on discrimination even though we practice the reality that is beyond discrimination. For instance, right now I am thinking, "How can I express the Buddha's teachings in the most understandable way in English?" This is my intention. Even when we try to manifest the reality beyond discrimination, we have to discriminate and make choices about the best way to do so. Repentance means that although I think this is the best thing to do in this situation, I recognize that it might be a mistake. It might even be harmful to others and to me—I don't know.

When I was at Pioneer Valley Zendo in Massachusetts, I had to cut many trees to clear the land and plant a garden. I killed many small animals, insects, and worms. Once, for example, after I dug a well the hole filled with rainwater and a skunk drowned. My intention was to work for the Buddha Dharma and to create a place for practice. To do so, I harmed other creatures. Even when we try to work for the benefit of all beings, we may harm others. We cannot predict the consequences of our actions. All of us have to eat to live. Even if we don't eat meat, we have to eat vegetables. This means we have to kill vegetables. To live as a human being is to be supported by others' lives and deaths. Even if we are not conscious of it, we may create evil karma that can injure ourselves and others. As bodhisattvas we cannot live without repentance.

"All the karma ever created by me since of old": This translation does not specify bad karma, but the original does. *Shoakugō* means "bad karma." Some other translations use words such as "unwholesome," "twisted," or "harmful" to avoid the duality between good and bad. We practice repentance on the basis of total interpenetrating reality. We live only with the support of all beings but recognize that we may harm some. Even when we live as well as we possibly can, we still need to repent because from our limited viewpoint we can't know which acts might result in harm.

"Through greed, anger, and self-delusion": In Buddhism these are the three poisons. Self-delusion or ignorance is the cause of the other two. In this case it refers to ignorance of the reality of impermanence and ego.[34] The *Heart Sutra* tells us that all five skandhas are empty. The five skandhas make up our body and mind. This means that we are empty, and yet we don't often see the emptiness of our body and mind. It feels as if we have a body and mind. We assume there is something called an "ego" that owns and operates our body in the same way a person owns and drives a car. In reality there is no driver but only this body and mind. There is no driver, but somehow the car runs. This is really an "auto-mobile."

When we are unaware of impermanence and egolessness, the ego appears to be the center of the world. Anger and greed arise because the ego tries to protect itself. Greed prompts us to accumulate more and more to satisfy egocentric desires. Anger is caused by the ego's need to stay secure and powerful. These three poisons are the basic causes of our bad karma.

Body, speech, and thought create our good and bad karma. "No beginning" means we cannot see the origin of our karma. Our body and mind are influenced even by things that have happened before we were born. Everything that has happened in the whole universe since the Big Bang influences our ways of thinking and behaving. It is all really without beginning.

"I now make full repentance of it": The original word was *sange*, which as we've seen means "repentance." Repentance includes confession but is not necessarily limited to confession. As the Buddha's students, we receive the precepts and vow to live by them. This is why we have to repent deeds against our vow. In the first line the Japanese word *issai* ("all") means all the misdeeds or mistakes we have made, even if we are not conscious of them. Vow and repentance are inseparable. When we closely look at our past deeds, we cannot help but repent. When we awaken to the total interpenetrating reality of our being and look to the future, we cannot refrain from making the vow to live with all beings and to practice according to the Buddha's teachings. Vow and repentance are two sides of the single practice of zazen.

Another important verse of repentance is from the *Samantabhadra Sutra*. It addresses formless repentance (*ri-sange*) and repentance of true reality (*jissō-sange*).

> The ocean of all karmic hindrances
> arises solely from delusive thoughts.

If you wish to make repentance,
sit in upright posture and be mindful of the true reality.
All misdemeanors, like frost and dew,
are melted away in the sun of wisdom.[35]

In this repentance we do not actually say something like, "I'm sorry because of this or that specific mistake." Rather, our zazen is itself repentance.

"The ocean of all karmic hindrances / arises solely from delusive thoughts": Here "karma" means all of our activities—not just our mistakes or misconduct. Even when we do good things we may create karmic hindrance. Almost all of our actions, good or bad, are based on self-centeredness. Therefore they are not in accord with the reality of oneness, impermanence, and interdependent origination. Any actions (karma) caused by our ignorance of the reality of life are a hindrance because they prevent us from awakening to reality and liberating ourselves from self-clinging. Any activity we do solely for ourselves, for our family, community, or nation—including Buddhist practices—can be a hindrance to actualizing total interpenetrating reality.

Even our charitable acts often have egocentric motivations. We seek satisfaction by trying to be better or more important. To gain respect from others, we try to be seen as compassionate. When there is the slightest deviation between our actions and our true mind, we create karmic hindrances. When we do something evil or make a mistake, we find it easy to repent. We have no difficulty in seeing it's our own fault, and if we don't recognize our misdeeds, others will help us by showing their anger. But when we are doing good things, it is really difficult to notice our karmic hindrances because people praise us and we feel good. Our good deeds that generate karmic hindrance make us arrogant and careless. We become blind to the fact that we are still limited, ordinary, self-centered human beings.

"If you wish to make repentance, / sit in upright posture and be mindful of the true reality": To be bodhisattvas, we have to be free from the hindrance of even our good deeds. To do that, we just sit and try to be mindful of the reality of our life. To be mindful of true reality does not mean *thinking* about reality. When we sit in the zazen posture, we keep our body straight and breathe quietly through our nose, smoothly and deeply, feeling the air as it fills our chest. We let go of thoughts. Whatever comes up in our mind, we just let it go. We don't hide anything, even negative feelings or stupid thoughts, even thoughts about the Buddha's teaching. We just let them come up and go away. Repeatedly we return to zazen, to our posture and breathing.

In this practice we are mindful of true reality that exists independent of our thoughts. To be mindful means to settle down right now, right here, without seeking after or escaping from anything. We refrain from either affirming or negating anything. We accept everything as it is, as the reality of our own life. In this sitting and letting go, true reality manifests itself. We can become intimate with ourselves as a whole. In this way we can be free from the egocentricity that makes us do "good" things. In other words, we do not become attached to what we think is good, meaningful, or important according to our own system of values.

"All misdemeanors, like frost and dew, / are melted away in the sun of wisdom": This is true formless repentance, in which we liberate ourselves even from Buddhist teachings. This is what Linji (Rinzai) meant when he said that if you meet the Buddha you should kill the Buddha. Dōgen Zenji said that sitting Buddha is killing Buddha. We see the reality of things with ever-fresh eyes, unclouded by even our good will. We are not caught in one particular place. We don't rely on anything inside or outside ourselves.

If we did something good yesterday, we should forget it and face what confronts us today. What we did yesterday is no longer real. We cannot be proud of what we did in the past or think we are a great person because we did such and such. Nor should we be caught up in our mistakes. We let go of them and start again. We start right from this posture in silence, from the ever-fresh life force that is free from any defilement. Moment by moment, we start again and again. This is not where our human evaluation and discrimination works. This is true repentance.

A Japanese Sōtō Zen master, Banjin Dōtan (1698–1775), comments on this verse in his *Zenkai-shō* (Comments on Zen Precepts):

> The essence of repentance is that delusion and enlighten-ment, or living beings and buddhas, are one. Because of this, a person who practices repentance is endowed with all vir-tue. We usually think that delusive thoughts and true real-ity are separate and distinct, as an owner and that which is owned. When we are completely liberated, we see that there is no person who possesses delusions nor are there delusions that are possessed. This is the true path of Buddha Dharma. We should not understand this verse to mean that we have to get rid of delusive thoughts by sitting upright and being mindful of the true reality. Repentance is another name for the Three Treasures. To repent is to take refuge in the Three Treasures. When the dharma of repentance is carried out, it completely includes the three refuges and the threefold pure precepts. Repentance, the three refuges, and the threefold pure precepts are not apart from falsehood caused by delu-sions. We are, however, able to attain liberation within delu-sions. We could say that before delusions leave, true reality has arrived. This is what is meant by the expression "Before the donkey leaves, the horse has arrived." We should learn that repentance is nothing other than the Dharma, the prac-tice of the Buddha's awakening.[36]

Banjin Dōtan says that to awaken to the reality that exists prior to the separation between delusion and enlightenment, between living beings and buddhas, is the essence of repentance. Because of awakening, a per-son who practices the repentance of sitting in upright posture in zazen is endowed with all virtues of the Buddha, the reality of life.

We usually think that delusive thoughts or desires are incompat-ible with the enlightenment of true reality. We believe that in order to attain enlightenment, we have to eliminate delusions. Banjin Dōtan, however, says that when we are completely liberated, we see that there is no one who possesses delusions, nor are there any delusions that are possessed. When we are sitting in zazen and letting go of thoughts, we are completely liberated. We see that both persons and delusions are without substance. This is the emptiness of reality, the true path of Buddha Dharma.

Our practice is not a means to get rid of delusive thoughts. Being mindful of true reality is not a method to eliminate delusions. In fact, when we sit in zazen, we sit squarely within the reality before the separation of delusion and enlightenment. We usually think of ourselves as deluded human beings and of buddhas as enlightened beings. We imagine that our practice is a method to transform a deluded being into an enlightened one by removing delusion. This idea is itself dualistic and contrary to the reality before separation.

So should we give up practice and pursue our delusions? No, what we must do is sit in zazen and let go of all dualistic ideas. In doing so, true reality manifests itself. Delusion and enlightenment are both here. Neither is negated or affirmed; neither is grasped. We sit on the ground of letting go. This is the meaning of Dōgen Zenji's expression "Practice and enlightenment are one." There is no state to be attained other than our practice of letting go. We practice within delusions and manifest enlightenment through sitting practice and day-to-day activities based on zazen. These practices enable us to settle our whole existence on that ground.

Banjin Dōtan also said that repentance is itself the Three Treasures. When we really repent in zazen and let go of thoughts, we take refuge in the Buddha, Dharma, and Sangha. Repentance in Buddhism is not something negative. It is a very positive activity through which we become true Buddhists. Our practice doesn't make us perfect or holy people. In a sense, practice means giving up trying to become perfect; it means realizing our imperfect nature. We accept even our delusions and take care of them as if they were as precious as our children. If we ignore our delusions (or our children), they can do great harm. When we take good care of them, they can be quieted. We can be liberated within delusions only if we face and care for them. If we don't, they become an impregnable barrier. There is a path of liberation within delusions and suffering. When we see reality clearly, we can see delusions as just delusion.

"We could say that before delusions leave, true reality has arrived. This is what is meant by the expression 'Before the donkey leaves, the horse has arrived,'" writes Banjin Dōtan. Donkeys do not run fast, and we usually consider them lazy and foolish. We think a horse is better than a donkey. But this expression says that before the donkey (a deluded human being) leaves, the horse (true reality) has arrived. This means that right within this moment, our life force, this body and mind, both donkey and horse, are present, and we don't need to hit the donkey to force it to go. We should not, however, mistake the donkey for the horse. Taking good care of the donkey is our practice. Within this practice is the horse. We can find egocentricity deep inside our good deeds. But this doesn't mean we should carry out good deeds until we have completely eliminated our egocentricity. We strive to practice good and keep awakening to delusions, even those in our benevolent deeds. If we practice in this way we cannot avoid repentance. This formless, true repentance is in fact our zazen.

I think this repentance is essential for modern human beings because we have such powerful technologies. We can kill all the living beings on the earth. Most of the major problems we face today are a result of human activities. They are not caused by bad, foolish, or cruel people. Wars, ecological destruction, and so on have been caused by sincere, brilliant people under the banners of justice, liberty, human welfare, and national prosperity. These people are often respected as great leaders. Many religions cause problems by encouraging us to cling to doctrines and beliefs. We have to become aware of our self-delusion and clinging even while we try to accomplish good. Only in this way can we become free from the defilements caused by performing good deeds with imperfect motives. This is the true meaning of repentance.

FINAL SHELTER: 3
THE VERSE OF THE THREE REFUGES

THE ENGLISH TRANSLATION of the verse of the Triple Treasure in the MZMC sutra book is:

> I take refuge in the Buddha, vowing with all sentient beings, acquiring the Great Way, awakening the unsurpassable mind.

> I take refuge in the Dharma, vowing with all sentient beings, deeply entering the teaching, wisdom like the sea.

> I take refuge in the Sangha, vowing with all sentient beings, bringing harmony to all, completely, without hindrance.[37]

When we become Buddhists, we first make repentance and take refuge in the Three Treasures of Buddhism: the Buddha, Dharma, and Sangha. These refuges are the first three of the sixteen precepts we receive in the Japanese Sōtō Zen tradition established by Dōgen Zenji. Without these three there is no Buddhism. Shakyamuni Buddha, born in India about twenty-five hundred years ago, is our original teacher. He awakened to the reality of our life. Both his teachings about this reality and the reality itself are called Dharma. Sangha is the community of people who study the Buddha's teaching and follow his way of life. His first students were the five monks who had practiced with him before his enlightenment. They understood, became his disciples, and established the first sangha. That was the birth of Buddhism. From the very beginning, the Buddha as teacher, the Dharma as teaching, and the Sangha as community have been the essential elements of Buddhism.

TAKING REFUGE IN THE BUDDHA

When we become Buddhists, we vow to take refuge in the Buddha, the Dharma, and the Sangha. When we accept the Buddha's teaching as a student of the Buddha, we make this vow with all sentient beings. It would be better to translate this as "all living beings." The original word in Japanese is *shujō*. *Shu* means "many" or "various"; *jō* means "life" or "living beings." The next phrase, *taige taidō*, or "acquiring the Great Way," is an interesting expression. *Tai* means "body" and *ge* means "to understand," so this can be translated as "understanding with the body." We have to understand the Great Way with our bodies. The Buddha's teaching is not something we can understand merely with our intellects; we have to practice it in our day-to-day lives. To understand and agree with his teaching is not enough. If we agree with his teaching, we have to carry it out, to live it. *Taige* means to embody, study, learn, or incorporate into our everyday lives. *Taidō*, or "Great Way," means "awakening." Here the "Way" is a translation of the Sanskrit word *bodhi*. This phrase means we have to embody the Great Awakening of the Buddha in our daily lives.

The first refuge includes the phrase "awakening the unsurpassable mind." Unsurpassable mind (*mujō-shin*) is the same as bodhi-mind (*bodai-shin*). Both are abbreviations of the Sanskrit *anuttarā-samyaksambodhi-citta*. *Anuttarā* means "unsurpassable," "supreme," or "highest." *Bodhi* means "awakening." *Mujō* is the translation of *anuttarā* and *bodai* is the transliteration of *bodhi*. When we embody the Great Awakening, we awaken to the awakening mind. It's a strange expression, but that is the reality. We awaken the awakening mind in order to wake up. We usually think we are awake except when we are asleep at night or napping, but actually we are usually asleep and dreaming. We imagine this world, our lives, and ourselves. We create dream-worlds and then believe that they are reality. And yet, they are only constructs of our mind. We create a story in which we are the hero or heroine. We think we are the center of the world, and all other people and things are resources to make a happy ending for our story. This is how we live in a dream. To awaken means to drop off body and mind, become free from dreaming and encounter reality. We try to act based on the reality that exists before we process the world through the intellect. Our intellection is based on our education and all our experiences since birth. But these experiences are a limited way of viewing the world, so we must wake up to reality.

Another aspect of "unsurpassable mind" is compassion for all beings. When we awake to the reality that has not yet been processed by our ego-centered mind, we cannot help having compassion for all beings. We realize that we live together with all beings, supported by networks of interconnection. We share air, water, and life by offering ourselves to each other. We live supported by all beings. In turn, we must support all other beings. This is compassion. We have to awaken to the reality that we live together as knots within Indra's net. We do not and cannot live independently, as limited and conditioned individuals. This is the meaning of taking refuge in the Buddha.

TAKING REFUGE IN DHARMA

The next section begins, "I take refuge in the Dharma." The Sanskrit word *dharma* has many meanings, but two are important here—the Buddha's teaching and the reality of all beings. It continues, "Vowing with all sentient beings, deeply entering the teaching." The original word for "the teaching" is *kyō zō. Kyō* means "sutra," and *zō* means "warehouse," "storehouse," or "treasury." Buildings in Buddhist temples where sutras or texts are stored called *kyō zō. Jin nyū kyō zō* means "deeply entering into the storehouse of sutras." Another possible interpretation of this word *kyō zō* is "sutra *piṭaka*," that is, one of the three "baskets" (*piṭaka*) of Buddhist scriptures: sutras, commentaries on the sutras (*Abhidharma*), and precepts (*Vinaya*). Either way, we vow to study the sutras thoroughly. In a chapter of *Shōbōgenzō* titled "Sansuikyō" (Mountains and Waters Sutra), Dōgen Zenji wrote, "These mountains and waters of the present are the manifestation of the Way of the ancient buddhas." This implies that the reality of all beings is itself a sutra. Not only the mountains and waters but also the birds singing, the sun shining, and everything happening around us are sutras teaching us the reality of being. They teach impermanence and interdependence. Nothing lasts forever, everything is always changing, and there is no fixed ego or substance. All beings in the universe teach this reality, but we don't listen; we don't really see it. We think, "I want to do this" or "I wish to do that," and we are blind to the reality of impermanence and interdependence. The phrase "deeply entering the teaching" doesn't require that we read all the Buddhist texts. Although reading is an important part of entering the teaching, the deeper meaning is really to awaken to the reality before our eyes, the reality that we actually live.

The phrase "wisdom like the sea" refers to an unlimited and boundless perspective. We are like a frog in a well that can see only a small patch of sky. Our view is limited, yet we think we are the center of the world and know everything. We base our actions on our conditioned understanding, perceptions, and opinions. The beginning of wisdom is to see that our view is limited. The view we have at sea is wider than in a well. There is no limitation to something so vast and boundless. By studying the Buddha's teaching we become free from our limited views and open ourselves to boundless reality. The meaning of taking refuge in the Dharma is that we value Dharma more than our own limited opinions and views based on our personal karma.

TAKING REFUGE IN SANGHA

The third vow begins, "I take refuge in the Sangha." *Sangha* is a Sanskrit word meaning an association or union of people. In India at the time of the Buddha, cities were forming, and some people were freed from the daily labor of agriculture. Classes of merchants, craftsmen, warriors, and nobles arose. People established unions or associations called sanghas (or *gaṇas*). A sangha is a democratic community of members who share the same interests and status. The vow continues with "vowing with all sentient beings, bringing harmony to all." The phrase "bringing harmony" is a translation of the Japanese word *tori*, which means "unify." Buddhist sangha members are unified by the Dharma. To have a community instead of a collection of individuals, to have harmony, we need something that unifies. To make soup we chop the ingredients and put them in a pot, then add seasoning and cook it until the individual flavors blend to make one taste. Similarly, we need to cook ourselves and make these individuals into one community with one taste—the taste of Dharma. Harmony unifies a collection of individuals into a community in which we can take refuge.

The next phrase is "completely, without hindrance." With harmony and unity, there is no hindrance. When individuals think "me first," endless problems and obstacles arise. But when we wake up to impermanence and egolessness, and share the life of this moment, there is no hindrance. Of course, there are still difficulties to overcome, but with harmony we can work on them. If we have discord, we cannot. This is the meaning of sangha and of taking refuge in the Three Treasures.

THE REASON FOR TAKING REFUGE

Shōbōgenzō is a collection of about ninety-five of Dōgen Zenji's independent writings. One of the chapters is called "Taking Refuge in Buddha, Dharma, and Sangha" (Kie-buppōsōbō). Here he quotes a section from *Kusharon* (*Abhidharmakośa bhāṣya*), chapter 14, about why we take refuge in the Three Treasures. This text was originally written in India and translated into Chinese. The Indian text says, "Many people out of fear take refuge in the deities of mountains, forests, trees, gardens, shrines, and so on."[38] We take refuge in gods because of fear. We need shelter—in this case spiritual shelter—because we are weak and afraid. Human beings are not necessarily the strongest animals. We are not as big as elephants, as fast as cheetahs, or as strong as gorillas. All phenomenal elements, such as too much or too little rain, cause suffering in our lives. Full of fear and uncertainty, primitive people needed something to worship, to rely on. Even in civilized society it's dangerous to rely on things outside of ourselves. Everything outside of us is uncertain, always changing and unreliable. We worship, pray to, or rely on this thing that we believe to be eternal and unchanging. This is one of the reasons we need religion. Buddhism, of course, is one of the religions. But the Buddha didn't teach us to take refuge in a deity beyond this phenomenal world. He taught us to find refuge within this world, within ourselves. This is the basic teaching of the Buddha and a difference between Buddhism and other religions.

The Indian text continues, "Taking refuge in such deities, however, is not excellent and worthwhile. It is not possible to be released from various pains or sufferings by means of taking refuge in such kinds of deities." So we cannot find security through worship of things in nature or beyond nature. "If people take refuge in the Buddha and take refuge in the Dharma and the Sangha, they will, in keeping with the four noble truths, constantly contemplate with wisdom: they know suffering, they know the cause of suffering, they know eternally going beyond suffering, and they know the eightfold noble path." Shakyamuni Buddha taught that people who take refuge in the Buddha, Dharma, and Sangha are able to see with the wisdom expressed in the four noble truths. Wisdom is important in Buddhism, together with compassion and faith. In other religions, we can't understand, so we believe. But in Buddhism we have faith because we have the wisdom to see. This is an important point. By taking refuge in the Buddha, the Dharma, and the Sangha, we learn to find stability, peace, and liberation from fear by examining what's happening. We see that the cause of fear is inside us.

With the four noble truths, the Buddha taught the reality of suffering or duḥkha. In Buddhism it said that there are four kinds of suffering: birth, aging, sickness, and death. All of us are born crying with pain. Life is filled with suffering, as is death. Another four kinds of suffering are often mentioned: separating from beloved people, meeting with people we don't like, not being able to gain what we want, and not being able to control the five *skandhas*. The first three are the painful experiences all of us often experience in our social lives. Sometimes we have to separate from people we love, and at other times we have to associate with people we don't like. That is the reality of our life. Often we cannot acquire something we really want, and so we suffer. The most fundamental form of suffering is the last one, which is inherent in human nature. We are collections of five skandhas or aggregates: form, sensation, perception, mental formations, and consciousness. These elements, of which we and all other beings are formed, are impermanent and always changing. They cannot be controlled because there is nothing to control them. We cannot control our lives. This body and mind is not a possession that can be mastered. Therefore, human existence itself is always unsatisfactory and we feel suffering. This is the meaning of suffering in Buddhist teachings.

The second of the four noble truths is the cause of suffering. The Buddha taught that delusive desires and attachments based on fundamental ignorance are the cause of all suffering. We are always thirsty and hungry and chase after things to fill our empty stomachs, and when we can't find anything we suffer. When we are successful, we want more, or we fear losing what we have.

Third is the truth of the cessation of suffering, or nirvana. When we first hear that Buddhism teaches that life is full of suffering, we think it must be very pessimistic or nihilistic. But the Buddha taught that it's possible to be in nirvana, to become free from suffering. This is because suffering has causes and conditions. If we work on changing those causes and conditions, we can release ourselves from suffering. Shakyamuni Buddha's teaching is not at all pessimistic.

The fourth noble truth, the way to eradicate the causes of suffering, is the eightfold noble path. To follow this path we must view things correctly, base our thinking on reality instead of egocentricity, speak truthfully, act in accord with the right view, engage in a wholesome livelihood, make diligent efforts, and practice right mindfulness and meditation. The Buddha gave us these eight guidelines for our practice.

He taught that we can find the real foundation for a peaceful life within ourselves, within this phenomenal world, without relying on a deity. This teaching and practice of the Middle Way to which the Buddha awakened are the shelter and foundation of our life.

The *Abhidharmakośa* text continues, "Therefore, taking refuge in the Three Treasures is supreme and most venerable." We take refuge in various things in this world. In a financial context, taking refuge might mean trusting money or insurance. We rely on insurance to provide security when we are unable to work. We do this to be free from fear, but when life insurance is actually paid you are no longer there. So it's really no benefit to you at all. We rely on many different things, but nothing is really certain; nothing has a truly stable foundation. The only stable foundation for our life, according to the Buddha, is the Dharma and the self. In the *Dhammapada* the Buddha said:

> Your own self is
> your own mainstay,
> for who else could your mainstay be?
> With you yourself well-trained
> you obtain the mainstay
> hard to obtain.[39]

In another old scripture, the *Suttanipāta*, the Buddha said:

> The independent man does not tremble or get confused. But
> a man who is dependent on something is clutching, grasping
> at existence in one form or another, and he cannot escape
> from existences.[40]

The Buddha's advice to us is not to count on others but depend on the Dharma and rely on our own self. Neither the Dharma nor the self is eternal, and everything is changing. We can't really rely on anything, yet this reality of egolessness (no-self) and impermanence is itself the foundation of our life. We can find peace and liberation by seeing deeply the impermanence and egolessness of life itself. This is the only possible stable, peaceful foundation of us because it is the only reality that is here and now. Nothing in the past, nothing in the future, nothing beyond this reality is reliable. Reality is ever changing and therefore ever fresh and new. My teacher, Uchiyama Roshi, urged us to open the hand of thought and awaken to the reality that is always changing. This is the most reliable foundation of our life. This refuge is supreme and most venerable.

In *Abhidharmakośa* the final reason to take refuge in the Triple Treasure is that "By taking refuge, people are surely released from various sufferings." This is why the Buddha and other masters encourage us to take refuge in the Buddha, the Dharma, and the Sangha. I think that of these three, the sangha is most significant to us today. Of course, the Buddha and the Dharma are the basis of Sangha. However, without Sangha, a living community of people, the Buddha is someone who lived in the past, and his teaching is something printed in a textbook. Because there is a community of practitioners who follow his teaching and manifest reality in their daily activities, the Buddha and the Dharma come alive right now, right here. I have been a monk-priest for about twenty-five years. I don't think that I could have lived the Buddha's teaching and practiced by myself for so long. With the help of my teacher, my dharma brothers, and the people who practice with me, I can practice. A sangha of practitioners is most important. We really have to take refuge there. This vow brings Sangha vividly alive.

THREE MEANINGS OF THE TRIPLE TREASURE

The basic original meaning of the Buddha, the Dharma, and the Sangha is straightforward. "Buddha" refers to Shakyamuni Buddha, who was born in India about twenty-five hundred years ago. "Dharma" is both the reality to which he awakened and his teachings about that reality. "Sangha" is the community of the Buddha's students. As Buddhism evolved, the understanding of the Three Treasures became more complex. The death of Shakyamuni Buddha was a great loss for his students.

He was not only their teacher, he was the only teacher. None of his disciples could become a second Buddha and assume his position in the sangha. They were sad and also confused as to who could be their teacher. Then they remembered that Shakyamuni said that people who see the Dharma see the Buddha. For them, Shakyamuni Buddha was not just a person who had a physical body and had died. The Buddha was still there as the teaching and as the reality. They called this the dharma-body (*dharmakāya*) of the Buddha, as opposed to the material body (*rūpakāya*) that perished with Shakyamuni's passing away. They believed that the Dharma, the Buddha's teaching, was the Buddha himself.

The Buddha said, "Monks should not take care of the Buddha's dead body." Monks were supposed to concentrate on practice not the past. Consequently, Shakyamuni Buddha's funeral was left to lay students. They performed the funeral, separating his ashes or relics into eight sections, which were enshrined at eight different sites in India. Lay followers built stūpas and made pilgrimages to them to pay homage to the Buddha. The Buddha's statue or relics enshrined in a stūpa symbolized Shakyamuni Buddha. So there are three meanings of Buddha: the historical Buddha, the Buddha as dharma-body, and the Buddha as a statue, image, or relic.

People also started to think that there were three kinds of Triple Treasure. Historically "Dharma" meant the Buddha's teachings, but in "dharma-body" it refers to reality itself. This reality was there before Shakyamuni awakened to it. He said, "I didn't invent the truth, teaching, or reality. I was like a person who finds an old castle hidden in a forest." This reality is the original meaning of *dharma*. All beings and all things in this universe are the manifestation of this original reality. Since all beings manifest this reality, they are always awakened because they are reality itself. All beings in the universe can be called members of the universal sangha. Ultimately speaking, the dharma-body is the Buddha Treasure; the Dharma, the true way of things as they are, is the Dharma Treasure; and all beings as an expression of Dharma are called the Sangha Treasure. This very idealistic interpretation of the Three

Treasures is known as Ittai Sanbō. *Sanbō* means "three treasures"; *ittai* means "one body." In this context *one* means "absolute." So the Three Treasures are one body, one reality. The Buddha, the Dharma, and the Sangha are just one reality. Ittai Sanbō is referred to as the Absolute Three Treasures or the Unified Three Treasures.

The historical Three Treasures—Shakyamuni Buddha, his teaching, and his community of students—are called Genzen Sanbō (Manifesting Three Treasures) because they are historical, real-world manifestations of the Absolute Three Treasures. After the Buddha's death, his followers continued to practice his teaching. For several centuries the sutras were transmitted as an oral tradition. Eventually they were written down in Sanskrit or Pāli. In India the sutras were written on the leaves of *tala* trees. The Buddha's teaching was recorded as a kind of a scripture and called the Dharma Treasure. The Buddha's images or relics were considered symbols of the Buddha, or the Buddha Treasure, and the sangha was called the Sangha Treasure. These were called *Jūji Sanbō. Jūji* means "maintaining." In order to maintain the Buddha's teaching after he died, the Buddha's image, sutras, and the communities of practitioners were considered to be Three Treasures. When we become Buddhists, we take refuge in the Buddha, the Dharma, and the Sangha. There are three kinds of Three Treasures and we take refuge in all of them. There are sanghas, or communities of the Buddha's students, throughout the world. The Buddha's teachings have been translated into many different languages, and each translation is a dharma treasure and should be respected.

THE TRIPLE TREASURE AS TEACHER, MEDICINE, AND FRIENDS

In the chapter of *Shōbōgenzō* entitled "Taking Refuge in Buddha, Dharma, and Sangha," Dōgen Zenji mentions the reason why we take refuge in those three. He says, "We take refuge in the Buddha because the Buddha is our great teacher, we take refuge in the Dharma because the Dharma is good medicine for us, and we take refuge in the Sangha because the people in the Sangha are excellent friends for us."

Dōgen's word for "excellent friends" is *shōyū*. *Shō* means "excellent," "superior," or "good." We have three kinds of good friends in Buddhism: teachers, fellow practitioners, and people who support our practice. According to Dōgen Zenji, the Buddha is a great teacher, the Dharma is good medicine, and the Sangha is a community of good friends. Another text says that the Buddha is like a doctor, the Dharma is good medicine, and the people of the Sangha are our nurses. The doctor makes a diagnosis and gives a prescription. To study the Dharma and practice according to the teaching is taking the medicine. Sangha is the community of co-practitioners—people who like nurses take care of the practice with each other. In modern society nurses are professional people, but in ancient times there were no nurses. Family or friends took care of the sick. So here "nurse" doesn't mean a professional but rather a member of the sangha. The people of the sangha should care for one another.

To say that the Buddha is a doctor, the Dharma is medicine, and Sangha members are nurses implies that we are sick. According to the Buddha's teaching, all people are indeed sick. We may be sick physically and are usually sick spiritually. What kind of sickness do we have? Before Shakyamuni Buddha left home and started to seek the Way, he was a prince. He was healthy and wealthy, certainly not sick in the common sense. But he needed something, and so started to practice. He came to see all sentient beings as sick and practiced to find a way to release them from sickness. Eventually he realized that the cause of our sickness is ignorant egocentricity and the desires that arise from it.

Many religions originate in our weaknesses and fears. Before civilization conditions of life were very severe. There were many dangers and people needed something to pray to. In many primal religions people worshiped natural phenomena: the ocean, mountains, thunder, or ancient trees. They worshiped things larger, more powerful, and longer lasting than themselves. Gradually civilization developed and human beings became better at survival. We then became each other's enemies. We started to fight, and at the time of Shakyamuni, about the fifth century BCE, people had enough wealth to fight over territory. They fought each other to establish countries and kingdoms. Stronger nations conquered weaker ones. We needed some principle to live together in harmony. This is the second reason for religion: to teach us to live together with other people. I think this is the point of all religions and philosophies in the history of humanity. We live in civilizations that have developed over twenty centuries in America, Japan, and Europe, and yet we are still spiritually sick. We still don't know how to live in peace with people from different national, racial, religious, or cultural backgrounds. The Buddha's teaching is a prescription for curing this sickness.

FINAL PLACE TO RETURN

Dōgen Zenji quotes another phrase from an old Buddhist scripture titled *Daijō-gi-shō* about why we take refuge in the Three Treasures. It says, "We take refuge in these Three Treasures because they are the final place to return."[41]

Dōgen's word for "final place to return" is *hikkyō-kisho*. *Sho* means "place," *ki* means "to go back or return," and *hikkyō* means "finally," "final place," and "to go back." Our life is a journey. Childhood is like our home, where we are born. We don't need to go anywhere. We are happy simply to be there. When we grow up, we become travelers. We search here and there for treasure—something valuable or meaningful. We yearn for something better. We seek happiness and satisfaction. Sometimes we are happy, sometimes sad. Finally, at the end of our lives we face death. Regardless of our success or failure, each of us has to face it. When we do, we are afraid. Wealth, fame, and social position don't help us then. We face death alone.

Where, then, is the final place to which we return? This is, I think, the fundamental question we have to keep in mind. In modern society it's easy to forget. In the past people were born, lived, got sick, and died, all at home. Life and death were right there in front of everyone. But in our modern society people are born at the hospital. When they are sick, they go to the hospital, and when they die, it's usually in the hospital. Life and death are hidden from us. While we are young and healthy, we can forget about life and death. Suddenly we are aging or sick; the matter of life and death is in front of our eyes, and we are afraid. This is the reality of our life. Before we have to face death, we should try to think about life and death, to awaken from the dream of success even while dreaming it. We must wake up to the reality of the impermanence of our lives. Because of impermanence, our death is inevitable. We must find the best and most peaceful way of life. Success, wealth, and fame are not significant in the final stage of our lives. The important point is to return to the matter of life and death, to wake up to the reality of this body and mind, and on that basis create a way of life. This, I think, is the meaning of taking refuge in the Buddha, the Dharma, and the Sangha.

You don't have to become a Buddhist and take refuge. Buddhism is only one of many paths, one way to wake to the reality of our life. When we become a Buddhist due to various causes and conditions, we follow the path of the Buddha. We seek to manifest the universal life force which we have been given. We live on this earth with everything we need as a gift from nature. It seems that our society doesn't live in accordance with nature. It acts like a cancer, independently, in its own way. When a cancer becomes too strong, the body dies. When the body dies, the cancer also must die. Cancer is paradoxical. Modern civilization is similar. We have no direction. We just try to live in an ever more convenient way. We chase after prosperity. We live separate from nature and build an artificial world around us. As we get stronger and stronger, we destroy more of the environment. When nature dies, we die.

How can we go back to nature, to the vital life force? This is the essential koan for us, the question we have to work on. In a sense this whole universe is like a hospital. We are all sick. How can we recover from this human sickness? The Buddha's teaching and the Buddhist Way can be one of the paths to recovery. The Buddha is the doctor who guides the healing process; dharma practice is the medicine he prescribes; the sangha, and all living beings in this universe, are nurses to aid our recovery. This is what the text means by "These three treasures are the final place to return." They release us from the suffering of a life based on egocentricity and return us to the original, wholesome way of life.

CULTIVATING THE VIRTUOUS FIELD: THE ROBE CHANT

VERSE ON THE KESA

Great robe of liberation.
Virtuous field far beyond form and emptiness.
Wearing the Tathāgata's teaching
I vow to save all beings.[42]

Dai sai gedappuku
Musō fukuden e
Hibu nyorai kyō
Kōdo shoshu jō

WHEN DŌGEN ZENJI went to China and began to practice at Tiangtong monastery in 1223, he found that in the sōdō (monks' hall), the monks rested their folded okesas (the formal term for the *kesa*, or monk's robe) atop their heads with veneration and chanted this verse after early morning zazen each day. He had read of this practice in the *Āgama Sutra* but had never seen it. When he experienced the traditional chanting of this verse and saw the monks put on their okesas, he was deeply impressed. Dōgen Zenji wrote about this experience in the chapter *Shōbōgenzō* "Kesakudoku" (Virtue of the Kesa): "At that time, I felt that I had never before seen such a gracious thing. My body was filled with delight, and tears of joy silently fell and moistened the lapel of my robe."[43] The young Dōgen vowed to transmit this practice to Japan. As a result, for the last eight hundred years in Dōgen Zenji's lineage we have chanted this verse every morning after zazen when we put on our okesas or rakusus.

The Buddha himself decided the kesa's design. A king who was a lay student of Shakyamuni Buddha went to visit the Buddha one day. On the way he saw a religious practitioner walking across the road. He thought this person was a disciple of the Buddha and got off his cart to greet him. When he found that he was not a Buddhist monk he felt a little embarrassed. He asked Shakyamuni Buddha to make a special robe for his disciples so they could easily be recognized as Buddhist monks.

One day the Buddha, walking in the countryside with his attendant Ānanda, noticed the beautiful patterns of rice paddies newly planted with green seedlings and surrounded by footpaths. They are especially beautiful in the rainy season when the rice is new. The Buddha remarked to Ānanda, "These are so beautiful. Could you make a robe like this?" Ānanda agreed. The Buddha conceived the pattern and Ānanda created the design. Since then, Buddhists have worn the okesa in all traditions and in all countries.[44]

In Japanese the first words of the verse of the kesa is *dai sai*. *Dai* means "to be great" or "magnificent." *Sai* has no meaning by itself but functions as an exclamation mark: "How great!" The next part of the verse gives three different names for the okesa. In the chapter "Virtue of the Kesa" Dōgen Zenji introduced many names for the okesa. He said, "We should understand that the kesa is what all buddhas have respected and taken refuge in. The kesa is the Buddha's body and the Buddha's mind. The kesa is called the robe of liberation, the robe of the field of virtue, and the robe of formlessness. It is also called the robe of supremacy, the robe of patience, the robe of the Tathāgata, the robe of great compassion, the robe of the victory banner (against delusion), and the robe of unsurpassable enlightenment. Truly, we should receive and maintain it gratefully and respectfully."[45] These are all different names for the okesa used in various Buddhist scriptures. In this verse, the first three names are mentioned: the robe of liberation, the robe of formlessness, and the robe of the field of virtue.

The first name for the okesa is the robe of liberation. The Sanskrit word *kaṣāya* refers to a muted or broken color (*ejiki*). To make okesas, Indian monks collected abandoned rags from graveyards and refuse heaps, so that they would have no attachment to the material. They cut the rags into pieces and washed, dyed, and sewed them together. They didn't dye them pure colors—blue, yellow, red, black, or white—but instead mixed different colors together to darken the cloth, rendering it valueless by ordinary standards. The okesa was made out of materials that had no value and were not attractive to people. Even today if we have new material from which to make an okesa, we cut it into pieces so that the material loses its value. No one would want to steal it. This is why the okesa is free from attachment. In Buddhism, things free from attachment are immaculate. When we become Buddhists, we receive the okesa as a symbol of our faith in the Buddha's teachings. This means we also become free from ego attachment.

The construction of the okesa symbolizes the emptiness of the five skandhas. The pieces come from all over, are sewed together, and stay for a while in the shape of a robe. The okesa is an example of emptiness or egolessness (*anātman*), impermanence, and interdependent origination. So the robe is much more than a uniform; it embodies the basic teachings of the Buddha.

When I first studied "Kesakudoku" (Virtue of the Kesa), I was confused because Dōgen discussed the virtue of the okesa in various ways. He wrote that the okesa had been transmitted from Vipaśyin Buddha, the first of the seven buddhas. It is said that each buddha's life span was shorter than the last. Their bodies also became smaller and smaller. And yet the okesa transmitted from the previous buddha perfectly fit all of the following buddhas. I wondered how Dōgen could say such a thing, since he knew that the okesa was designed by Shakyamuni Buddha and his disciple Ānanda. How could all the buddhas before Shakyamuni have worn and transmitted it?

Dōgen also discusses the fact that Shakyamuni's okesa was transmitted to Mahākāśyapa, and then from Mahākāśyapa to the next ancestor. It was then transmitted through each subsequent ancestor to Bodhidharma. Bodhidharma brought it from India to China, and then the okesa was transmitted through six generations to the sixth ancestor, Huineng. The okesa was used as the symbol of the Dharma and also of the authenticity of the Dharma's transmission.

Dōgen Zenji encourages us to sew our own okesa and venerate it as the symbol of the Buddha's vow to save all living beings, the symbol of the Dharma itself, and the symbol of the authenticity of transmission in his lineage.

Later I realized that this corresponds to the Three Treasures he mentions in *Kyōjukaimon* (Comments on Teaching and Conferring the Precepts). Here he comments on the precepts of taking refuge in the Buddha, the Dharma, and the Sangha and on the Absolute Three Treasures, the Manifesting Three Treasures, and the Maintaining Three Treasures.[46]

The okesa used by all buddhas in the past, present, and future—and which perfectly fits all of them despite their differences in size—corresponds to the Absolute Three Treasures. The okesa designed by Shakyamuni and Ānanda corresponds to the Manifesting Three Treasures. And the okesa used as a symbol of transmission and the okesa Dōgen encourages us to sew, wear, and venerate correspond to the Maintaining Three Treasures. When Dōgen discusses the virtue of the okesa, he freely switches among these three meanings of the word. This is why I was confused. The okesa is the symbol of the Dharma itself in its various facets.

The second name of the okesa is the robe of formlessness (*musō*). In our sutra book, *musō* is translated as "far beyond form and emptiness." This is a questionable translation. It seems to me that "far beyond form and emptiness" refers to a line in the *Heart Sutra*: "That which is form is emptiness and that which is emptiness, form." In this case "form" is a translation of the Sanskrit word *rūpa*, one of the five aggregates, which means materials that have physical form and color. The Chinese translation of rūpa is *se*, and the Japanese pronunciation is *shiki*. The *Heart Sutra* says that material beings are emptiness and emptiness is material beings. But here the word used is not *shiki* but *sō*, a translation of the Sanskrit *nimitta*, which means "appearance," as opposed to *shō*, "nature" or "essence." Other possible translations of *nimitta* are "mark" or "attribution." *Musō* is *animitta* in Sanskrit. This use of "form" does not imply material beings. Instead, it means temporal form or appearance. The reality of emptiness has no fixed form. The robe of formlessness (*musō-e*) means that this robe has no form (*animitta*), not that it is beyond form and emptiness.

In this English translation, the phrase "far beyond form and emptiness" modifies "virtuous field" (*fukuden*). This is not a correct interpretation of the line because *musō-e* and *fukuden-e* are the two different names of the okesa.

The *Diamond Sutra* says, "To see all forms as no-form is to see the true form." What is beyond form and emptiness? Form is emptiness and emptiness is form. There is nothing beyond form and emptiness. And in this verse there is no word that refers to emptiness. Here "formless" means that the okesa has a form and yet the form itself is formless or empty. Emptiness means moving and changing moment by moment. In this moment, this robe exists in the form of the okesa but has no fixed, permanent form. *Musō* also means free from attachment. Because it is formless, we cannot attach ourselves; we cannot grasp it. If we grasp this as the Buddha's teaching, as something important and hold on to it, we miss the point of the Buddha's teaching. Instead we open our hands. This is the meaning of formlessness.

It is the same with our lives. Our body and mind are collections of many different elements that exist in this moment. Because they are always changing, we cannot grasp them as "my" body, "my" mind, or "my" property. And yet we attach ourselves to the present, transient form. But since nothing is substantial, we cannot actually grasp it. When we try to control it, we diminish our life force. Instead, we open our hands. This is what we practice in our zazen. The okesa and our body and mind are the same. This subtle difference in attitude can change our lives completely. When we grasp something, we lose it. When we open our hands, we see that everything we need is an offering from nature. If we have something extra, we offer it to others. This is the life attitude of a bodhisattva. Just open our hands. The okesa is a symbol of this attitude.

As noted just now, the third name of the okesa in this verse is the robe of the field of virtues (*fukuden-e*). *Fuku* means "happiness," "blessing," "fortune," or "virtue," while *den* means "rice paddy." In Asian countries people consider rice paddies the foundation of everything good. Rice is the most important product and the basis of the whole economy. When rice grows we are blessed by nature. The Buddha's teachings, the Buddha-mind, and the practice of Dharma are often compared to a rice paddy.

The *Suttanipāta* is one of the oldest collections of short suttas in Pāli. In it we find the *Kasībhāradvāja Sutta* (The Farmer Bharadvaja), which records the Buddha's conversation with an Indian farmer. When the Buddha was staying in a farming village, he woke up one morning, put on the okesa, and went out to the village for *takuhatsu* (begging for food). The Buddha came across a rich farmer's house. The farmer was giving food to his workers. The Buddha was standing in front of the farmer to receive food.

The farmer said, "I eat after cultivating fields and planting seeds. I eat after working. Why don't you work? Why do you beg for food?" The Buddha replied, "I am a farmer, too. I also work." The farmer asked further, "You say you are also a farmer. But I never saw you farming. I ask you, what do you mean when you say you are a farmer? Tell me so that I can understand." Then the Buddha answered, "Faith is a seed. Practice is rain. Wisdom is my yoke and plow. Repentance (having a sense of shame) is my plow bar. Aspiration is a rope to tie a yoke to an ox. Mindfulness is a plow-blade and digging bar. I behave prudently. I am discreet in speech. I eat moderately. Truth is my sickle to mow grass. Gentleness is untying the yoke from an ox when finished working.

Diligence is my ox which takes me to peacefulness (nirvana). I go forth without backsliding. Once I reach peacefulness, I have no anxiety. My farming is done in this way. Its result is sweet dew. If you engage in this farming, you will be released from all kinds of suffering."[47]

The farmer left home and became the Buddha's disciple. In the Buddha's simile, farming is a practice aimed at freedom from ego-attachment and a peaceful life. When we wear the okesa, we are also farming. This is the meaning of "robe of virtuous field" (*fukuden-e*). This body and mind is the field we work. It is not a field of fortune from which we can expect to receive blessings without practice. We have to cultivate our life.

The third line of the verse is "Wearing the Tathāgata's teaching" (*hibu nyorai kyō*). *Hi* means "to open," "unfold," or "uncover," so I translate this line as "I unfold and wear the Tathāgata's teaching." First we have to unfold the Buddha's teaching and cover ourselves with it. *Bu* means "humble," "thankful," or "respectful." Then what is meant by "the Tathāgata's teaching" (*nyorai-kyō*)? The Buddha taught the interdependent origination of all beings. Since no beings have self-nature, we should not attach ourselves to anything. We should be free from ego-attachment, transform our way of life, and choose a path to peacefulness. We unfold this teaching through practice. We receive the teaching of the Tathāgata, unfold it, wear it, and are covered by it. This is the meaning of wearing the okesa and practicing zazen.

Formlessness means the same as emptiness, egolessness, and interdependent origination. Since we are not substantial, we cannot live alone without being supported by other beings. We have to live together with others. This is another essential point of the Buddha's teaching. We cannot be completely peaceful unless all living beings are in peace. We cannot be completely happy if we are aware of someone who is unhappy. When we awaken to this reality, the bodhisattva vows arise naturally. The vow to save all beings is not a duty or a promise to the Buddha. The vow does not mean that we are great people and we have to save all others, like millionaires who give money to the poor. When we open our eyes to the reality of our lives, we simply cannot help but share happiness and sadness, pleasure and pain with all beings. To be peaceful, we have to do something for other beings. We live within the Buddha's vow to save all beings.

Zen Master Dongshan Liangjie (Tōzan Ryōkai, 802–869) was the founder of the Chinese Caodon (Sōtō) school. Dongshan asked a monk, "What is most painful?" The monk replied, "To be in hell is most painful." Dongshan said, "No, it isn't." Then the monk asked, "What do you think, then, is most painful?" Dongshan replied, "Wearing the okesa yet not having clarified the great matter is most painful." Hell is the worst part of samsara and is considered the most agonizing. But Dongshan said that there is a more painful condition. When we wear the okesa, we are in nirvana. We are apart from samsara, and yet when we chase after something, even enlightenment, our practice becomes an activity within samsara. When we look for something better through zazen, that striving is more painful than hell. If you suffer in samsara because you don't know the Buddha's teachings, you can be saved by studying the Buddha Dharma and practicing zazen. But if you already know the Buddha Dharma, receive the precepts, wear the okesa, practice zazen, and *still* chase after something, there is no way to be saved. One of the most famous sayings of Kōdō Sawaki Roshi is, "Wear the okesa and sit in zazen: that's all." That's it. There is nothing else to search for. There's nowhere to go. Still, we look for something more valuable. Even when we sit in the zendo we are often hungry ghosts in samsara.

Whenever we deviate from where we are now, we immediately return to what's right here, right now, by letting go. This is our zazen. This is the meaning of wearing the okesa after reciting this verse.

CONTINUOUS CIRCLE OF OFFERING: THE MEAL CHANTS

DŌGEN'S COMMENTS ON THE SIGNIFICANCE OF TAKING FOOD

MEAL CHANTS are the verses we recite during formal *ōryōki* meals at Sōtō Zen monasteries and Zen centers during sesshin. Dōgen Zenji's comments at the beginning of "Fushukuhanpō" (The Dharma for Taking Meals) are a good introduction to these verses. He describes how to eat, use the bowls, and comport ourselves during an ōryōki meal. "The Dharma for Taking Meals" is a section of *Eihei Shingi*. The word *shingi* means regulations or standards, and Eiheiji is the monastery founded by Dōgen Zenji. "The Dharma for Taking Meals" is one of the six sections of *Eihei Shingi*; another is "Tenzokyōkun" (Instructions for the Cook). Dōgen Zenji teaches that cooking and receiving food are both important parts of our practice. Eating is an essential part of our practice because it's a necessary part of our life. We eat three times every day of our lives but rarely think about the significance of eating. Both "Tenzokyōkun" and "Fushukuhanpō" show us how activities in our daily lives can become spiritual practice.

In "Tenzokyōkun," Dōgen Zenji describes the attitude we should maintain toward foods, fire, water, and utensils when we cook. "When steaming rice, regard the pot as your own head; when washing rice, know that the water is your own life."[48] Everything is part of our life. As tenzo we should think about the people who eat, who receive the food, and who practice. According to Dōgen Zenji, practice itself is enlightenment, so people who practice are enlightened, and therefore as tenzo we prepare meals to offer to the Buddha. Through work with food in the kitchen, the tenzo's energy becomes part of the Buddha, so the tenzo should be sincere and careful. This is an important point. Since the tenzo doesn't sit in the zendō all the time, the kitchen is the tenzo's place of practice. When the tenzo cooks, the food is the Buddha and the cooking is the tenzo's zazen. We should receive the food gratefully and with the same attitude with which it was cooked. That's the meaning of this ritual.

It's difficult when we begin to study the rituals of ōryōki and memorize the chants because many of us don't like formality. I myself don't like it much, but I try to follow it because it's our practice. If we think of the meaning or significance of this practice, we can appreciate this formality on a deeper level. That is the point of this section of "Fushukuhanpō" (The Dharma of Taking Meals):

> A sutra says, "If you can remain the same with food, all dharmas also remain the same; if all dharmas are the same, then also with food you will remain the same." Just let dharma be the same as food, and let food be the same as dharma. For this reason, if dharmas are the dharma-nature, then food also is the dharma-nature. If the dharma is suchness, food also is suchness. If the dharma is the single mind, food also is the single mind. If the dharma is bodhi, food also is bodhi. They are named the same and their significance is the same, so it is said that they are the same. A sutra says, "Named the same and significance the same, each and every one is the same, consistent with nothing extra." Mazu said, "If the dharma realm is established, everything is entirely dharma realm. If suchness is established, everything is entirely suchness. If the principle is established, everything is entirely

the principle. If phenomena are established, all dharmas are entirely phenomena." Therefore this "same" is not the sameness of parity or equality, but the sameness of awakening to the true sameness [*anuttarā-samyaksambodhi*]. Awakening to the true sameness is the ultimate identity [of all the suchnesses] from beginning to end. The suchness of the ultimate identity from beginning to end is the genuine form of all dharmas, which only a buddha together with a buddha can exhaustively penetrate. Therefore, food is the dharma of all dharmas, which only a buddha together with a buddha can exhaustively penetrate. Just at such a time, there are the genuine marks, nature, substance, power, functions, causes, and conditions. For this reason, dharma is itself food; food is itself dharma. This dharma is what is received and used by all buddhas in the past and future. This food is the fulfillment that is the joy of dharma and the delight of meditation.[49]

The quote at the beginning, "If you can remain the same with food, all dharmas also remain the same; if all dharmas are the same, then also with food you will remain the same," comes from the *Vimalakīrti Sutra*.[50] Dōgen Zenji comments on this passage, "Just let dharma be the same as food, and let food be the same as dharma." This sutra says that as practitioners of Mahāyāna Buddhism we should maintain the same attitude toward everything we encounter. We should not discriminate between things as valuable or worthless on the basis of conventions. We should not discriminate between good times and hard times, delusion and enlightenment, samsara and nirvana, or deluded human beings and buddhas. This is the basis of the Mahāyāna teaching of śūnyatā. We must go beyond discrimination and keep the same attitude toward all things because everything we encounter is the Buddha's life. The *Vimalakīrti Sutra* says that as a practitioner of Mahāyāna Buddhism, we should have the same attitude toward all food and not discriminate between something expensive or delicious and something cheap or not so tasty on the basis of preferences or worldly values.

Subhūti, one of the ten greatest disciples of Shakyamuni Buddha, was doing takuhatsu, begging for food. Vimalakīrti offered him some delicious food, saying he could eat it if he didn't discriminate between delicacies and the food of the poor. In his comment Dōgen Zenji twisted the meaning slightly. He said: "Just let dharma be the same as food, and let food be the same as dharma." Dōgen Zenji says that dharma and food are the same. He doesn't discriminate between good and bad food. He simply says that dharma and food are the same.

We have to be careful here about the meaning of the word *dharma*. It can be used to mean the Buddha's teaching. A second meaning is the truth about which the Buddha taught, the reality of our life. A third meaning of *dharma* is all beings or things. The phrase often used to express this, "myriad dharmas," means all beings, everything. In this usage, Dōgen is saying that food, as one of the "myriad dharmas," reveals the reality of all beings, and therefore the food itself is the teaching (Dharma) of the Buddha. The Buddha awakened to and taught this reality, so his teaching is called Dharma. His teaching became a kind of law, principle, or basic standard of morality. In "The Dharma for Taking Meals," "dharma" means an etiquette or standard of behavior that we should follow when we eat meals. In his commentary Dōgen is playing with words. He uses "dharma" not to designate a kind of ritual but as reality itself as well as the teachings about that reality. He says that our practice and the food we eat is dharma, reality, or truth itself. We should receive our food as we receive the Buddha's teaching and reality itself.

He continues, "For this reason, if dharmas are the dharma-nature, then food also is the dharma-nature." Dharma-nature is almost synonymous with buddha-nature. For human beings the term "buddha-nature" is used. For other beings or inanimate objects, all of reality, the phrase "dharma-nature" is used. Our food is dharma-nature. Dharma-nature and food are really one, so "if the dharma is suchness [reality or truth], food also is suchness." Suchness means the way all beings, all dharmas, are. So food is nothing but suchness itself. In the same way, "If the dharma is the single mind," another name for Buddha mind, "food also is the single mind," the One Mind, or Buddha mind. So we should receive food with the same attitude we receive the Buddha and his teachings. Dōgen says, "If the dharma is bodhi, food also is bodhi." Bodhi means enlightenment or awakening to the reality of all beings. So dharma is awakening. We usually think of awakening as something subjective that happens inside a person, and dharma as the object of awakening. In the teachings of Mahāyāna Buddhism, there is no separation between subject and object, between the person who sees reality and the reality that is seen. When we separate the two, wisdom becomes delusion. Awakening, beings, and reality are one. The dharma is bodhi, awakening itself. Awakening is not some special psychological state or stage of development. When we are one with all beings we are awake. When we are mindful, right now, right here, our body and mind completely present in this moment and engaged with what we are doing, we are awake and enlightened. The dharma is bodhi, and food is also bodhi. Food and dharma are both dharma-nature, buddha-nature, and suchness.

Dōgen continues, "They [dharma and food] are named the same and their significance is the same, so it is said that they are the same. A sutra says, 'Named the same and significance the same, each and every one is the same, consistent with nothing extra.'" This means that when we receive this body and mind and the things we encounter in our daily lives as self, we are connected with all beings in the whole universe. This whole universe is one reality. We should receive the rituals of meals and universe with the same attitude. Dōgen quotes Mazu (Baso), "If the dharma realm is established, everything is entirely dharma realm." "Dharma realm" is a translation of *dharmadhātu*, this dharma universe. This whole universe is dharma universe; there is nothing extra. Everything is entirely the dharma world; nothing is outside it. He continues, "If suchness is established, everything is entirely suchness." If we see this whole reality as suchness, everything is entirely suchness. There is nothing that is not suchness. Within delusion there is suchness as delusion. The fact that we are deluded is reality. When we see delusion as delusion, delusion is part of reality and there is nothing to be eliminated, nothing to be negated. We should accept everything as the

Buddha's life. Mazu continues, "If the principle is established, everything is entirely the principle," and "If phenomena are established, all dharmas are entirely phenomena." These two concepts, principle and phenomena, or *ri* and *ji*, are important in the "Merging of Difference and Unity," the title of a text by Shitou discussed below. *Ri* means reality as a whole regardless of differences among individuals. A hand has five fingers. If we see it as one hand it is actually one thing. We cannot separate it into parts. But we can also see it as five fingers, each with a different shape, function, and name. So *ri* refers to the entire totality of a being, and so does *ji*. There is nothing that is half-and-half. *Ri* means all of this one hand, and so does *ji*, the five fingers. When we see this as one hand, there are no separate fingers. When we see it as five fingers, there is no single hand. This is the way we see reality. We call principles "absolute" and phenomena "relative." The absolute and relative ways of seeing things are reality at work.

Dōgen Zenji continues, "Therefore, this 'same' is not the sameness of parity or equality, but the sameness of awakening to the true sameness." "Awakening to the true sameness" is a translation of the phrase *anuttarā-samyaksambodhi*. A common Chinese translation of this phrase is *shōtōgaku*. *Shō* means "true," "correct," or "absolute"; *tō* means "sameness" or "equality"; and *gaku* is "awakening." This "sameness" is a difficult concept. We cannot use the word "equality" here because Dōgen Zenji said, "Therefore this 'same' is not the sameness of parity or equality." This is not a matter of comparing two things and finding them to be the same or equal, as in one hand and five fingers. This is one thing with two names. Food and dharma really are the same thing. This sameness, Dōgen says, is sameness within *anuttarā-samyaksambodhi*. *Samyak* means "sameness," "equality," or "identity." This sameness is not a matter of comparison: good versus bad food, or like versus dislike. This sameness means that we should encounter each thing as an absolute reality, as a whole, as the Buddha. When I drink water, water is the Buddha. This means that this water is connected with all beings. Someone brings a glass of water for me. The water came from a river or lake, and before that from the sky. The water in the sky came from the ocean. Everything really is connected. This interpenetrating, connected reality is the Buddha, and we are part of it. There is no separation between myself and the water. The water becomes part of me when I drink it. This glass, this body and mind, and the water are all Buddha. When we see them as Buddha we are part of the whole universe. When we see them as separate entities, each of them and each of us is a small, individual thing or ego.

Dōgen Zenji goes on to say, "Awakening to the true sameness is the ultimate identity [of all the suchnesses] from beginning to end." Awakening to the true sameness means accepting all beings as our own life, as the Buddha's life. A quote from the *Lotus Sutra* helps explain the meaning of the following: "The suchness of the ultimate identity from beginning to end is the genuine form of all dharmas [the reality of all beings], which only a buddha together with a buddha can exhaustively penetrate." In the second chapter of the *Lotus Sutra* the Buddha said, "Concerning the prime, rare, hard-to-understand dharmas, which the Buddha has perfected, only a Buddha and a Buddha can exhaust their reality, namely, the suchness of the dharmas."[51] "The suchness of the dharmas" in the *Lotus Sutra* and "the genuine form of all dharmas" in "Fushukuhanpō" are the same word. The reality of all beings can be understood or seen only by buddhas.

The sutra continues by listing the ten suchnesses: "The suchness of their marks (form), the suchness of their nature, the suchness of their substance (body), the suchness of their powers (energy), the suchness of their functions, the suchness of their causes, the suchness of their conditions, the suchness of their effects, the suchness of their retributions, and the absolute identity of their beginning and end."[52] "Ultimate identity from beginning to end" is another translation for the ending of this quote. In Japanese the phrase is *nyoze honmatsu kukyō tō*. *Hon* (beginning) and *matsu* (end) refer to the nine points of reality: form, nature, body, energy, function, cause, condition (secondary cause), effect, and retribution. Each being has its own unique form, nature, body, energy, and function. For example, this glass has a form, round and transparent. This being has a nature as a glass and as a body that is different from other glasses. The Japanese word translated here as "body" is some-times translated as "substance" or "embodiment," but "body" is better. Each being has its own power and energy. Even this glass has chemical, potential, kinetic, and nuclear energy. Essentially there is no difference between energy and being. "Being" is nothing other than various forms of energy in certain conditions. The function of this glass is to contain liquid. Each being has a different combination of these five character-istics: a different form, nature, body, energy, and function. Each being has a cause and a secondary cause as its conditions. "Secondary cause" refers to the way this glass was made. Someone works with materials to form glass into this shape. That person is a secondary cause. In addi-tion to the person who makes the glass there is electricity, water, and raw materials. The person who makes the glass eats food, which is also a secondary cause of this glass. Everything is connected with every-thing else. Each being has causes, secondary causes, and effects. This being has effects because of its function. Because this glass functions to contain water, I can drink the water. That is an effect of this being we call a glass. The last of the nine points is "retribution." This could also be translated as "secondary effect." Because this glass can contain the water, it allows me to drink the water, and the water can become part of my body, which enables me to continue to talk. That's a second-ary effect. The first five suchnesses describe the unique characteristics of each being, each dharma; and the next four are the interconnec-tions between beings throughout time and space. A secondary cause is the relationship between this being and its function and other beings within space at the present moment. Secondary effect is the connection with other beings in the future within time.

Each thing also has its own unique characteristics. In this sense, it is independent. This glass is different from all other glasses. All beings, including this body and mind, have unique characteristics, and yet we are interconnected. We live together with each other. All beings have two aspects: independence and connectedness. This is the same con-cept as seeing one hand or five fingers. The tenth suchness, "absolute identity of their beginning and end," means that the other nine—from the first, form, up to the ninth, retribution—are one. Within this one being, all are included. The universal interconnection within Indra's net is manifested in this one being, in each and every being. It's really hard to comprehend this reality of our life, the way we live with both individuality (independence) and connection (interdependence) at the same time. I have to take responsibility for whatever I do because I am I, not you or another person. And yet my personal action influences the entire world.

Without this being, there are no other beings. This is called wondrous dharma or true dharma. We cannot grasp it with our concepts, and yet, as a reality, it's right in front of us. It means: This is one, this is Shohaku Okumura; and yet, at the same time: This is not Shohaku Okumura, this is not an individual. When we use the principles of logic we avoid contradiction, and so we cannot see reality as a whole. We see only one side of reality, either the individuality of all beings or their identity. When we think about ourselves and the reality of our lives, we cannot see both aspects at once. Sometimes we see five fingers: I am not you, and you are not me. But at the same time, this is one hand and there is no separation. If we think logically, it's contradictory. If we can set our logic aside, we can see reality as it is, five fingers and one hand at the same time. That's the reality of the network of interdependent origination. And so, getting back to Dōgen's text, we should accept food as a part of this reality. There is no separation between the person eating and the food eaten. Both are part of this wondrous dharma.

Dōgen Zenji continues, "Therefore, food is the dharma of all dharmas, which only a buddha together with a buddha can exhaustively penetrate." The phrase "only a buddha together with a buddha" means that no human being can penetrate this dharma. By human beings Dōgen means individuals. When we see this total reality, we are Buddha. The words "I see" are not really adequate because they imply a separation between the person who sees and the reality which is seen. Because we are born, live, and die within the network, we can only see the network from inside. We cannot be an objective observer from the outside. "Accept" is a better word than "see." We should accept this reality and make it manifest through our practice. When we accept food and dharma in this way, Dōgen Zenji says, "Just at such a time, there are the genuine marks, nature, substance, power, functions, causes, and conditions." He lists seven of the ten suchnesses described in the *Lotus Sutra*. I think the other three—effects, retributions, and absolute identity—should be included. All of them are manifested within the one action of eating.

He concludes, "For this reason, dharma is itself food; food is itself dharma. This dharma is what is received and used by all buddhas in the past and future." In this context "dharma" means reality itself. This reality is accepted and used by all buddhas in the past and future. He said, "This food is the fulfillment that is the joy of dharma and the delight of meditation." This joy of dharma and delight of meditation is part of the verse we chant before informal meals. We say, "As we take food and drink, we vow with all beings to rejoice in zazen, being filled with delight in the dharma (*Nyaku onjiki ji tōgan shujō, zennetsu ijiki, hōki jūman*)." When we eat, we should be happy. This happiness is the enjoyment of dharma. We consider the taste of food to be the taste of dharma. When we receive or eat a meal, we shouldn't grasp the taste. Usually when we eat, we encounter our food with our desires. These desires are the cause of delusion or samsara. The Buddha and Dōgen Zenji teach us to become free from the desires caused by objects. This is Dōgen's teaching of *shinjin datsuraku* (dropping off body and mind). Our joy when we receive food is not the fulfillment of our desire. It is the joy of dharma and zazen. I think this is the most essential teaching about food and eating. When we can see this reality that Dōgen Zenji describes in "Fushukuhanpō," not only eating but everything we do becomes our spiritual practice.

Ludwig Feuerbach, a nineteenth-century German philosopher, once said, "We are what we eat." In fact, we are not only what we eat, but what we see, hear, think, and do. When we accept everything that we encounter as it is, and accept all things and beings as ourselves, that is *jijuyū zammai*—samādhi that is self-receiving and self-employing. The most important thing taught by Dōgen Zenji is to accept this body and mind and everything we encounter as our life. Then the self and the entire dharma world become one seamless reality. We should accept and use everything we encounter as samādhi, not as a kind of business. Our life as a whole is samādhi. This means that each and every thing we do in our daily lives becomes a manifestation of our zazen.

FORMAL MEAL VERSES

Verse upon Hearing the Meal Signal

> Buddha was born in Kapilavastu,
> enlightened in Magadha,
> taught in Vārāṇasī,
> entered nirvana in Kuśinagara.

At the beginning of each ōryōki meal we chant this verse and remember the most important events in the life of the Buddha Shakyamuni.[53] The Buddha was born at Lumbinī Park, not far from the palace of his father, King Śuddhodana, at Kapilavastu. The Buddha attained supreme awakening under a bodhi tree at Uruvelā, later called Bodhgayā, in the kingdom of Magadha. The Buddha taught the Dharma for the first time to the five monks at Deer Park (Mṛgadāva) in Sārnāth near Vārāṇasī (Benares). After that, he continued to teach for more than forty years, until he was about eighty years old, when he entered the great nirvana under twin *sāla* trees in Kuśinagara. These places have been considered the four most sacred sites in Buddhism. Following the Buddha's death, Buddhists built stūpas at these places to enshrine his relics, and pilgrimaging there became a common Buddhist practice. People from all over the world still visit these four places even today.

In the *Mahāparinibbāna Sutta*, the Buddha's attendant Ānanda says, "Lord, formerly monks who had spent the rains in various places used to come to see the Tathāgata, and we used to welcome them so that such well-trained monks might see you and pay their respects. But with the Lord's passing, we shall no longer have a chance to do this." The Buddha answered, "Ānanda, there are four places the sight of which should arouse emotion in the faithful. Which are they? 'Here the Tathāgata was born' is the first. 'Here the Tathāgata attained supreme enlightenment' is the second. 'Here the Tathāgata set in motion the Wheel of Dharma' is the third. 'Here the Tathāgata attained the nibbāna-element without remainder' is the fourth. And Ānanda, the faithful monks and nuns, [and] male and female lay-followers will visit those places. And any who die while making the pilgrimage to these shrines with a devout heart will, at the breaking-up of the body after death, be reborn in a heavenly world."[54]

It is difficult for me to imagine that the Buddha called himself Tathāgata, encouraged people to worship his relics, and promised that if they made pilgrimages they would be born in heaven. But it seems certain that such a belief and practice was there when the Nikāyas were written down using the Pāli language several hundred years after the Buddha's death.

One of the four bodhisattva vows is "The Buddha's Way is unsurpassable; we vow to realize it." Even though we are in a very immature stage of the bodhisattva path, because a bodhisattva is a child of the Buddha, the direction of our practice is to live like the Buddha. When we receive food, we are reminded why we are here and why we eat. It is not to satisfy our desire for food but to continue to practice and walk the path taught by the Buddha. In our minds, we make a pilgrimage to those four sacred places.

Verse for Setting Out Bowls

To begin the meal we unwrap our bowls and arrange them on the table before us. As we open the ōryōki bowls we recite this verse:

> Now we set out Buddha's bowls;
> may we, with all living beings,
> realize the emptiness of the three wheels:
> giver, receiver, and gift.

The initial ō in ōryōki means "in proportion to," ryō means "amount" or "quantity," and ki means "container." Ōryōki thus means a container with which we receive a food offering depending on our need to maintain our life for practice. We receive only the amount of food we need. So we have to eat everything we receive without wasting even one grain of rice. To do so, we need to know how much is enough.

In Zen Buddhist tradition, around the eighth century, after the story in which the sixth ancestor, Huineng, received the robe and ōryōki bowl as evidence of his dharma transmission from the fifth ancestor, the bowl was considered the symbol of continuity of Dharma from teacher to disciple. We receive a set of ōryōki bowls from our teacher when we participate in the *shukke tokudo* ceremony to become a monk/priest. Our ōryōki is the Buddha's bowl.

The verse says, "May we ... realize the emptiness of the three wheels." The emptiness of the three wheels is a crucial teaching from the *Prajñāpāramitā Sutra*. The three wheels are the giver, receiver, and gift; these wheels turn the dāna-pāramitā, the perfection of generosity. To practice dāna-pāramitā, there should be no attachment to any wheel.

The *Diamond Sutra*, one of the earliest Mahāyāna sutras, says, "When bodhisattvas give a gift, they should not be attached to ... anything at all. They should not be attached to a sight when they give a gift. Nor should they be attached to a sound, a smell, a taste, a touch, or a dharma when they give a gift."[55]

The famous story of the Bodhidharma's meeting with Emperor Wu makes the same point. The emperor had put on the robes of a monk and gave lectures on one of the group of *Prajñāpāramitā Sutras*. It is said that when he lectured, people saw heavenly flowers falling and the earth turning to gold. He studied extensively and supported Buddhism generously. He issued orders throughout his country to build temples and ordain monks. People called him the Buddha Heart Emperor. When Bodhidharma first met him, the emperor asked, "I have built many temples and allowed many monks to be ordained; what merit is there in this?"

Bodhidharma answered, "There is no merit."[56] "Merit" is a positive effect of certain actions. Even when doing good actions, if we expect to receive merit for ourselves, it is off the mark from the ultimate point of view because it is defiled by our selfish desire.

Ten Buddha Names

After we open the bowls, the *inō* (director of the zendō) recites:

> In the midst of the Three Treasures
> which verify our understanding,
> entrusting ourselves to the sangha,
> we recall: ...

Then everyone recites the ten names of the Buddha. This is an invitation for all buddhas and bodhisattvas to share this offering with us. And this is also an expression of our awareness that we are practicing together with all buddhas and bodhisattvas in the past, present, and future in the ten directions.

> ... Vairocana Buddha, pure dharmakāya;
> Locana Buddha, complete sambhogakāya;
> Shakyamuni Buddha, myriad nirmāṇakāya;
> Maitreya Buddha, of future birth;
> All buddhas throughout space and time;
> Lotus of the Wondrous Dharma, Mahāyāna sutra.
> Mañjuśrī Bodhisattva, great wisdom;
> Samantabhadra Bodhisattva, great activity;
> Avalokiteśvara Bodhisattva, great compassion;
> All honored ones, bodhisattvas, mahāsattvas;
> Wisdom beyond wisdom, mahā prajñā-pāramitā.

These are called the ten Buddha names, but actually there are eleven. Dōgen Zenji added "Lotus of the Wondrous Dharma, Mahāyāna sutra."

The first three names refer to the three bodies of Buddha. Different masters use Vairocana to refer to either dharmakāya or sambhogakāya depending upon the context. Here, Vairocana means the dharmakāya, the Buddha's body, identical with the entirety of Dharma and everything existing. Vairocana as the dharmakāya appears as the main buddha in the *Mahāvairocana Sutra* (Sutra of the Great Radiant One; *Dainichikyō* in Japanese). This is one of the most important sutras in Vajrayāna (Shingon) Buddhism. Vairocana literally means the universal illumination of the radiant light and refers to the light of the sun which illuminates entire world.

Vairocana also appears as the main buddha in the *Avataṃsaka Sutra* (Flower Ornament Sutra) and the *Brahma Net Sutra* (*Bonmōkyō*). Here it is sometimes considered to be the sambhogakāya, the retribution body that is produced upon entering buddhahood as a result of the vows and practice undertaken while the buddha was a bodhisattva. The Chinese transliteration of Vairocana is Pilushena. Locana is another spelling for the shortened form Lushena. In the *Brahma Net Sutra*, the shortened form Locana Buddha is used.

In his commentary on the *Lotus Sutra*, Tientai Zhiyi said that Vairocana is dharmakāya, Locana (Lushena) is sambhogakāya, and Shakyamuni is nirmāṇakāya.[57] "Myriad nirmāṇakāya" refers to the Buddha Shakyamuni, the manifestation of the dharmakāya with a human body in a particular time and space. This expression also comes from the *Brahma Net Sutra*:

> "I have cultivated this Mind-Ground Dharma Gate for hundred of eons. My name is Locana. I request all buddhas to transmit my words to all sentient beings, so as to open this path of cultivation to all." At that time, from Lion's Throne in the Lotus Treasury World, Locana Buddha emitted rays of light. A voice among the rays is heard telling the buddhas seated on thousands of lotus petals, "You should practice and uphold the Mind-Ground Dharma Gate and transmit it to the innumerable Shakyamuni Buddhas, one after another, as well as to all sentient beings. Everyone should

uphold, read, recite, and single-mindedly put its teachings into practice."[58]

Modern Buddhist scholars think the *Brahma Net Sutra* was not translated from an Indian text but composed in Chinese. In the original Chinese text, the *Vai* in *Vairocana* is dropped and *Vairocana* is written as *Locana*. It is said that there are innumerable Shakyamuni Buddhas sitting on the lotus flowers. It seems these ten Buddha names are created within the tradition based on the teachings of the *Avataṃsaka Sutra* (Flower Ornament Sutra) and *Brahma Net Sutra*.

Maitreya Buddha is considered to be the future Buddha. He is now abiding in the Tuṣita heaven, as did Shakyamuni Buddha before he was born in this world. It is believed that Maitreya Buddha will be born 5.6 billion years after Shakyamuni's death.

Dōgen Zenji added the *Lotus Sutra* to the list of ten Buddha names because he thought this sutra was very important. In *Shōbōgenzō* "Kie-buppōsōbō" (Taking Refuge in Buddha, Dharma, and Sangha), he wrote, "The *Dharma Flower Sutra* is the causes and conditions of the one great matter of the Buddha Tathāgata. Of all the sutras expounded by the great teacher Shakyamuni, the *Dharma Flower Sutra* is the great king and is the great teacher. Other sutras and other teachings are all the retainers and people or the family dependents of the *Dharma Flower Sutra*."[59]

The next three names are the most well-known bodhisattvas. Mañjuśrī is the symbol of the Buddha's wisdom to see the reality of all beings. Samantabhadra is the symbol of the Buddha's vow and practice of skillful means to help all beings. Avalokiteśvara is the symbol of the Buddha's boundless compassion toward all beings. In addition to these three great bodhisattvas, all living beings throughout time and space who have aroused bodhicitta (Way-seeking mind) are also bodhisattvas. We are connected with all of them and we practice together with all of them.

The final name is *mahā prajñā-pāramitā*, the Buddha's wisdom that sees the emptiness of all beings. Prajñā-pāramitā is called the mother of all buddhas.

Food Offering Verses

After the ten names of the Buddha are chanted, the head monk (*shuso*) chants the following verses to praise the virtue of the meal offering.

> (*at breakfast*)
> This morning meal of ten benefits
> nourishes us in our practice.
> Its rewards are boundless,
> filling us with ease and joy.

The ten benefits of rice gruel, the traditional morning meal in Zen Buddhist monasteries, are mentioned in the Vinaya of Mahāsāṃghika. They are: making one's complexion healthy and lively, maintaining one's strength, prolonging one's longevity, allowing one to feel ease, keeping one's tongue clean, not upsetting one's stomach, preventing one from catching cold, satisfying one's hunger, keeping one's mouth from thirst, and keeping one's bowels regular.

> (*at lunch*)
> The three virtues and six tastes of this meal
> are offered to the Buddha and the sangha.
> May all sentient beings in the universe
> be equally nourished.

The three virtues of the meal are softness, cleanness, and accordance with dharma (proper preparation). The six tastes are sweetness, spiciness, saltiness, bitterness, sourness, and simplicity. The previous verse is about benefiting the self who eats the food. This verse is about benefiting others: buddhas, sangha members, and all living beings.

Verse of Five Contemplations

When the preceding verses have been chanted, the food is served. Prior to eating, the following verses of five contemplations are chanted.

> We reflect on the effort that brought us this food and con-
> sider how it comes to us.
> We reflect on our virtue and practice, and whether we are
> worthy of this offering.
> We regard greed as the obstacle to freedom of mind.
> We regard this meal as medicine to sustain our life.
> For the sake of enlightenment we now receive this food.[60]

We chant this verse to remind ourselves that eating is a spiritual practice, not just a way to fill our stomachs and satisfy our desires. We acknowledge that we eat "to support our life," but also affirm the important spiritual meaning of the meal. We eat to keep this body in good shape and also to renew our bodhi-mind, our aspiration to practice according to Buddha's teaching.

"We reflect on the effort that brought us this food and consider how it comes to us." The first of the five contemplations is to appreciate the immeasurable work of those who produce the food and prepare the meal. Basically the meal chant is about the practice of dāna-pāramitā. In India, Buddhist monks neither produced food nor prepared meals. Every day after morning meditation practice they went to town to beg for food. Farming was prohibited for monks because farmers have to kill living beings while cultivating the land. Monks simply received the food offered by laypeople.

In China it is said that Zen monks began to cultivate grains and vegetables to support their practice. There are many koan stories in the Zen tradition about masters and monks working in the fields. One of these is the story of Guishan Lingyou (Isan Reiyū, 771–853) and his disciple Yangshan Huiji (Gyōsan Ejaku, 807–883), the founders of the Guiyang (Igyō) school. One day Yangshan was digging on a hillside to make a rice paddy. Yangshan said, "This place is so low, that place is so high." Guishan said, "Water makes things equal. Why don't you level it with water?" Yangshan said, "Water is not reliable, teacher. A high place is high level. A low place is low level." Guishan agreed.

Guishan's teacher Baizhang Huihai (Hyakujō Ekai, 749–814) was also famous for his diligent practice of community work. His saying "A day without work is a day without eating" has been one of the most popular Zen mottos. In the traditional Zen monastery, the monks who grew grains and vegetables and prepared the meals were givers, and the rest of the monks received their offerings. Of course, none of these monks sustained themselves completely by their own labor. Zen monasteries became large institutions supported by the emperor, the government, and the aristocracy, and laypeople donated food. Many monasteries also owned manors cultivated by lay farmers.

Today at American Zen centers, practitioners pay to participate in sesshins and retreats. Food provided during the retreat is purchased with this money, so participants may not consider the food they eat as a gift or think of themselves as recipients. Rather, they may think they are purchasing a service. And yet, if we think carefully about this matter, we realize that we cannot buy food if farmers do not work. And if the weather does not support growing plants, farmers cannot produce crops. Plants need water, air, fertilizer, earthworms, and microorganisms, etc. All the elements in the network of interdependent origination support the farmers' work. All food we receive is a gift from nature.

After the food is grown, we need people to transport it to the marketplace and then to factories to be processed and the various places where consumers shop. On highways we see countless trucks carrying commercial products. Without all these people's work, we could not eat even a single grain of rice.

There are also factors beyond those we can see on the earth. Because of the distance between the sun and the earth, we receive just the right amount of heat. If we had more or less, we could not live the way we live now. This distance is a result of the balance among the planets in the solar system working together.

When we consider these interconnections, we see that our existence itself is a gift from the network of all beings. The totality of this network that enables everything to exist is called the dharma body of the Buddha, the Buddha's life, or the Buddha's compassion. When we awaken to this reality of interconnection, we cannot help but express our appreciation and gratitude.

"We reflect on our virtue and practice, and whether we are worthy of this offering." When we realize that we are supported by this network of interdependent origination, we need to reflect on whether we are worthy of this gift. Since our lives are supported by all beings, we need to appreciate and support them instead of harming them. The first of the four bodhisattva vows, "Beings are numberless, we vow to save them," arises from this awakening to interconnection.

"We regard greed as the obstacle to freedom of mind." In Japanese this line of the original Chinese verse reads as *"Shin wo fusegi, toga wo hanaruru koto wa, ton tō wo shū tosu." Shin wo fusegu* means "to protect our mind." *Toga wo hanaru* means "to keep away from misdeeds." *Ton tō* means "greed," but here it also means the three poisonous minds—not only greed but anger/hatred and ignorance as well. *Shū tosu* means "it is essential." So this line says: to protect our mind, avoid unwholesome deeds, and keep ourselves in healthy shape, it is essential to be free from the three poisonous minds.

Shakyamuni Buddha taught that our six sense organs (eye, ear, nose, tongue, body, and mind), the six corresponding sense objects (forms, sounds, smells, tastes, tactile objects, and objects of mind), and the six kinds of consciousness caused by the contact between these sense organs and their objects (eye consciousness, ear consciousness, nose consciousness, tongue consciousness, body consciousness, and mind consciousness) are the elements of our lives. He taught that these eighteen elements of our lives all burn with the flames of greed, anger/hatred, and ignorance.

The Buddha taught us to extinguish the flames of the three poisonous minds with the fire of wisdom. It is said in the teaching of the four noble truths that the three poisonous minds are the cause of suffering in samsara. Buddhist practice is the path that leads to the cessation of suffering. Our practice protects us from the flames of greed, anger/hatred, and ignorance and so nurtures our virtue.

Because we receive food as part of our Buddhist practice, we need to free ourselves from the three poisonous minds. And yet, food can easily be the object of our greed and anger or hatred.

When I practiced at Antaiji, most of the monks and lay practitioners were young people in their twenties. We were always hungry. Especially during sesshin, because there is no entertainment at all except for the three meals a day, I often ate a lot even though the food was not particularly fancy.

When we have fancy food, we often eat more than we need and suffer later. When the taste of the food is not what we expect, we often dislike it, and we may get angry with the person who prepared it. During a single meal it is possible for us to transmigrate through all six realms of samsara. When I have to eat something I dislike, I feel like a hell dweller. When I am hungry, I feel like a hungry ghost. Sometimes when I eat and become sleepy, I am like an animal. Sometimes, I am as angry as an asura (fighting spirit) with the person who cooked the food. Sometimes when I eat fine food I feel like a heavenly being. These likes and dislikes and transmigration within my mind are caused by ignorance. The taste of food exists only while the food is in my mouth. After I swallow it, whether I love or hate it, it's all the same. It all becomes nutrition that sustains our body and mind in practice.

Receiving food in the zendō during ōryōki meals is a very powerful practice. We cannot complain about the taste, and we receive only the amount of food we can use. There is no way for us to be pulled by the three poisonous minds. We simply receive what is offered to us. This attitude should be maintained throughout our lives.

In the last discourse of Shakyamuni Buddha, recorded in *Butsu-yuikyōgyō*, the Buddha taught the eight awakenings of the great being (Jap., *hachidainingaku*). These are the eight important points of our practice. The first two are to have modest desires (*shōyoku*) and to know how much is enough (*chisoku*). Dōgen Zenji writes:

> The first is having few desires. (Not pursuing too intensively the things we have not yet gained among the objects of the five senses is called "having few desires.") The Buddha said,

"Monks, you should know that people who have many desires avariciously seek after fame and wealth; therefore they experience great suffering and anguish. Those who have few desires, because they have nothing to pursue and desire, are free from such troubles. Having few desires is itself worth learning and practicing. All the more so, as it gives birth to various virtues. Those who have few desires do not flatter to gain others' favor. Also, they are not pulled by their desire for gain. The mind of those who practice having few desires is peaceful, without any worries or fears. They are always affluent with whatever they have and never have a sense of insufficiency. Those who have few desires experience nirvana. This is called 'few desires.'"

The second is to know satisfaction. Even among things which have already been given, you set a limit for taking them. This is called "knowing satisfaction." The Buddha said, "Monks, if you want to be free from suffering and anguish, you should contemplate knowing how much is enough. The dharma of knowing satisfaction is the place of richness, joy, peace, and calm. Those who know satisfaction, even when they lie down on the bare ground, still consider it comfortable and joyful. Those who don't know satisfaction are discontented even when they live in a heavenly palace. Those who do not know satisfaction are poor even if they have much wealth. Those who know satisfaction are rich even if they are poor. Those who don't know satisfaction are constantly pulled by the five sense desires and pitied by those who know satisfaction. This is called 'knowing satisfaction.'"[61]

A meal is an opportunity to practice the Buddha's teachings about having few desires and knowing how much is enough.

"We regard this meal as medicine to sustain our life." Buddhism is not an ascetic practice. Before he attained final awakening the Buddha

practiced austerities for six years, engaging in extremely harsh practices such as holding his breath until almost he died or eating only one grain of sesame or rice a day. It is said that having nearly died, he realized that this kind of practice is not wholesome or meaningful for the purpose of awakening. He received some milk porridge from a young woman named Sujātā, and he bathed in the river. He gave up ascetic practice and sat down under the bodhi tree. When he taught the five monks at Deer Park, the very first thing he said was that he had found the Middle Way.

The Buddha said, "One who has gone forth from worldly life should not indulge in these two extremes. What are the two? There is indulgence in desirable sense objects, which is low, vulgar, worldly, ignoble, unworthy, and unprofitable, and there is devotion to self-mortification, which is painful, unworthy, and unprofitable. Avoiding both these extremes, the Tathāgata has realized the middle path. It produces vision, it produces knowledge, it leads to calm, to higher knowledge, to enlightenment, to nirvana."[62]

An ōryōki meal is a practice of the Middle Way. We become free from the three poisonous minds that lead to indulgence in sensual pleasures. And yet we receive food to keep our body and mind healthy and functional.

"For the sake of enlightenment we now receive this food." The final contemplation is to confirm our determination to receive and eat the food in order to attain the Way. This is the same determination the Buddha made when he received the milk porridge from Sujātā.

Verse of Food for Spirits

O spirits, we now give you an offering;
This food is for all of you in the ten directions.

After we recite the five contemplations at the lunch meal, we offer a small piece of food on the *setsu*, the wooden scraper we use for cleaning ōryōki bowls. This practice is called *saba* in Japanese. We leave this small amount of food for all living beings. When we take food, we are receivers. Before the tenzo obtains the food he will cook, many people work to produce it. The tenzo collects the ingredients, cooks them, and makes them into a meal. To a practitioner who receives, who eats in the zendō, food is an offering from the tenzo and the many other people and living things involved in its production. The idea of saba is that we are donors as well as receivers. We give a small piece of what we have received. This is temporarily our food, but from this food we take a small piece and offer it to all beings.

The original Japanese expression for "O spirits" is *jiten ki jin shū*. This means "many demons and gods." *Ji* is "you," *ten* makes *ji* (you) into plural, and *ki jin* is Japanese or Chinese for unseen beings such as demons and gods. A *ki* is a demon and a *jin* is a god. This phrase refers to two kinds of unseen beings, some harmful and some beneficial. *Shū* means "group" or "assembly."

These unseen beings have vanished from our modern society. Perhaps they live only for a day on Halloween, or in comic books or horror movies. I grew up in a small town named Ibaraki between Kyoto and Osaka. I was surprised to learn that Ibaraki is a sister city of Minneapolis. I lived there from 1952 to 1968. I went to elementary school, middle school, and high school there. When I was a kid, it was a small town of maybe thirty thousand people. Today it has grown tenfold to more than three hundred thousand and has become a part of the metropolis of Osaka. When I lived in Ibaraki there were many Shintō shrines. Each block had its own small shrine that felt like a sacred place, separate from the outside world. When we played in the precincts of the shrines we felt different from the way we did outside. We felt something sacred. We felt that we were protected. In 1970, shortly after I left, they had a World Expo near Ibaraki. In preparation for it, the town was completely changed. We call it development, but in a sense it is a destruction of the living environment. The Shintō shrines were surrounded by houses, shops, and big apartment buildings instead of woods. I've gone back to Ibaraki several times to visit the shrines, but I didn't feel any spirits there or anything spiritually alive. There are just buildings. Today belief in spirits is called animism and is considered to be left over from primitive religion. We don't appreciate it anymore. But we still have a psychological need for this belief. Natural phenomena still influence our mentality or spirituality. Without demons, gods, and natural forces our lives become materialistic, and something is lost. The Buddha's teaching doesn't rely on animistic beliefs; it is rational. The Buddha taught that our life is full of suffering caused by our desires and greed. The essence of Buddhism doesn't rely on demons or gods. And yet Buddhism never opposed folk religions. In fact, in many countries Buddhism accepted and assimilated them. In Japan, for example, Buddhism and Shintoism have coexisted for centuries. Shintō is an animistic folk religion that worships nature, yet nature has been nearly eliminated from modern society. This makes me sad. I don't worship Shintō's demons and gods, and I don't even believe in them as beings. But I think that as symbols of nature—symbols of forces that can become very fearsome or harmful—these spirits can be a kind of blessing. Nature can be frightening and dangerous, certainly, but it also gives us everything we need: food, water, and air. Everything we have is given to us by nature, and yet nature can kill us. Many people believe that beings more powerful than humans control these natural phenomena. They pray to these gods or demons to protect them; they make offerings to insure a good harvest and avoid disasters. Not originally part of Buddhism, these gods and demons became part of people's everyday lives.

Early Buddhist scripture abounds with stories, legends, and myths that mention food offerings to unseen beings. Three are especially well known. The first is about a demon king's wife named Hārītī (Kishimojin in Japanese, which means "mother of demons"). According to the scripture she had ten thousand offspring, whom she fed with human children. The Buddha saw what Hārītī was doing, so he hid her youngest child in the ōryōki. Hārītī was very upset, and she searched all over the world but couldn't find the baby. Finally she came to the Buddha and asked where the child was. He told her, "You have ten thousand children and still, when you lose just one of them, you are sad and you suffer. You are in pain. Human beings have only one child or two. You

should consider the parents' sadness when they lose their children."
After being taught in this way, Hārītī accepted Buddha's teaching and
received the precepts. She said that she would not kill human children
anymore, but then she asked how she could feed her own children.
The Buddha said, "From now on I will tell my disciples to offer a small
amount of food for you at each meal so that your children will never
starve." This is the origin of the offering we make to unseen beings. After
this, Hārītī became the guardian of children and mothers.

The second story, which appears in the Mahāyāna *Parinirvana Sutra*,
involves a demon who ate one person a day. The Buddha taught the
demon and instructed him in the precept of not killing. The demon
asked the same question as Hārītī and the Buddha gave almost the
same answer.

The third story, in the Vinaya, may be more realistic. When the Buddha was still alive monks went to town to do takuhatsu—this is, to beg
for food—and returned before noon to have their meal. Dogs came
hoping to find some food to eat, but some disciples didn't give them
anything. The Buddha taught them that monks should always offer
some of the alms food they received to animals.

These stories convey the original spirit of food offerings made to
birds, animals, and unseen beings. When we receive an offering from
all beings, we should not be the end of this cycle of offering. We cannot live without the offerings we receive, but we should not keep them
all for ourselves. We should offer a small amount to other beings. This
practice makes the offering a circle. We take from nature and we also
give back.

There is a story about the Chinese Zen master Tianhuang Daowu
(Ten'nō Dōgo, 748–807) and his dharma heir, Longtan Chongxin
(Ryūtan Sōshin, ninth century). Before he became a monk, Chongxin
was a cake seller. Every day he offered ten cakes to the master. Each
time, the master returned one cake to him saying, "I offer this to you.
This is for the sake of your descendants." One day Chongxin asked the
master, "I brought these cakes to offer to you. Why do you return one
cake to me? Does it have any special meaning?" The master said, "You

bring the cakes, so what harm is there in returning one to you?" At these words, Chongxin grasped the deeper meaning. Because of this, he left home and became a monk.

Bowl-Raising Verse

After chanting the Verse of Five Contemplations and the Verse of Food for Spirits, we put our spoon in the ōryōki bowl and chopsticks across the second bowl. We return to gasshō and chant the following verse.

> First, this is for the Three Treasures;
> next, for the four benefactors;
> finally, for the beings in the six realms.
> May all be equally nourished.

Then we pick up the ōryōki, hold it with both hands at eye level, and chant the following:

> The first portion is to end all evil;
> the second is to cultivate every good;
> the third is to free all beings.
> May everyone realize the Buddha's Way.

The Japanese reading of the first Chinese verse is *"Jōbun sanbō / Chubun shi on / Gekyū roku dō / Kai dō kuyō."* *Jōbun sanbō* means that the upper portion is for the Three Treasures. *Chūbun shion* means that the middle portion is for the four benefactors. *Gekyū roku dō* means the lower portion is for all living beings in the six realms. *Kai dō kuyō* means to offer this food to support all of them equally.

The expressions *jō* (upper), *chū* (middle), and *ge* (lower) are a reflection of the vertical social structure in ancient China and other East Asian countries influenced by Chinese culture. A correspondence is implied between the upper portion of food and the Three Treasures, the middle portion of food and the four benefactors, and the lower portion of food and living beings in the six realms. Because this vertical idea is not suitable in the modern society, all English translations of this verse avoid using "upper," "middle," and "lower." One translation uses "first," "next," and "finally." Another one has "first," "second," and "third." There is also a translation which avoids even specifying an order: "This food is for the Three Treasures, / For our parents, teachers, leaders, and homeland / And for all beings in the six worlds."

I think there is no problem with using the phrase "to offer the food to the Three Treasures and all living beings in the six realms." But the use of the phrase "to offer" for *kuyō* in relation to the four benefactors needs some explanation.

"Four benefactors" is a translation of *shi on* (Chi., *si en*). *Shi* means four. As for *on* (*en*), this is a difficult word to translate. In a Chinese-English dictionary it is translated as kindness, favor, grace. Another dictionary has: kindness, goodness, favor, mercy, blessing, benefit. In Chinese and Japanese morality, this word also connotes a "debt of kindness." If we receive a kindness from someone when we are in need, we have a debt of kindness to that person. It is very important to repay the debt of kindness with our appreciation and gratitude. We are indebted toward people who did us favors, and we have an obligation to return the debt. This is called *hōon* or *ongaeshi* (repaying the debt of kindness). If we fail to repay this debt we are called *onshirazu* (ungrateful, thankless), that is, someone who doesn't know the importance of repaying the debt of kindness.

According to a Buddhist dictionary, the concept of *on* as a debt of kindness is not emphasized in Indian Buddhism. But in Chinese Buddhism this notion became very important. In Buddhist teachings all of us have four benefactors to whom we have a debt of kindness. There are several different sets of four. According to a sutra titled *Daijōhonshō shinchi kankyō* (Mahāyāna Original-Life Mind-Ground Contemplation Sutra), "four benefactors" refers to one's parents, all sentient beings, rulers of the country, and the Three Treasures. According to another sutra, *Shōbō Nenjo kyō* (True Dharma Mindfulness Foundation Sutra), the four benefactors are one's mother, one's father, the Tathāgata, and one's dharma teacher. The first set is more general, applying to any human being in any society, while the second is limited to the context of Buddhism.

In both cases parents are included. All living beings have parents. We have a unique, intimate connection with them. Parents give birth to us and take care of us until we become independent. In ancient times parents taught their children all the skills necessary to live. Farmers learned how to grow grains and vegetables from their parents. So we all owe much to our parents. We should appreciate their love and kindness. In East Asian countries a very important responsibility of children is to take over the family's work, maintain the family's wealth, and care for their aging parents.

As human beings we are supported not only by our parents but by many other people in society—teachers, friends, and colleagues. We are also supported by many other things—air, water, food, clothes, and houses. We have a debt of kindness toward all beings. This is the second benefactor in the first set of four.

The third benefactor is rulers, kings, or emperors. In these modern times we don't think that presidents or prime ministers have helped us much, so we have no debt of kindness to them. In ancient times, however, people thought that a king or emperor owned the whole country. The king governed people, protected the country from enemies, and kept it peaceful.

The third line of the Bowl-Raising Verse is *gekyū roku dō*, "for all beings in the six realms." This refers to all living beings transmigrating in the six realms of samsara: the realms of hell, hungry ghosts, animals, asuras or fighting spirits, human beings, and heavenly beings.

We express our gratitude to the Three Treasures and to all beings that support our life. This eating of food is not an individual action but rather something we do together with all beings. We can live because we eat food. When eaten, food becomes our energy and part of our body. This body and mind is supported by all beings. We in turn should nurture all beings. That is the idea of *on*, repaying the debt of kindness.

The word *kuyō* is important in Buddhist practice. Unfortunately, in this translation of the meal chant the final line is rendered as "May all be equally nourished." *Kuyō* has disappeared. This word is usually translated as "to make an offering." *Ku* means "offering" and *yō* means "nourish" ot "sustain." The offering here is not limited to offering monks something material such as food, drink, medicine, clothing, shelter, and so forth. The second chapter of the *Lotus Sutra* presents a wide range of offerings:

If anyone goes to stūpas or mausoleums,
To jeweled or painted images,
With flowers, incense, flags, or canopies
And reverently makes offerings;

Or if they have others perform music,
By beating drums or blowing horns or conch shells,
Or playing pipes, flutes, lutes, harps,
Mandolins, cymbals, or gongs,
Producing fine sounds and presenting them as offerings;

Or if they joyfully praise
The Buddha's virtues in song,
Even with just a tiny sound,
They have fulfilled the Buddha way.

If anyone, even while distracted,
With even a single flower,
Makes an offering to a painted image,
They will progressively see countless buddhas.

There are those who worship by prostrating themselves,
Some merely by putting palms together,
Others only by raising a hand,
And others by a slight nod of the head.

All of these,
Honoring images in various ways,
Will progressively see countless buddhas,
Fulfill the unexcelled way themselves.

Save countless beings everywhere,
And enter into nirvana without residue,
As a fire dies out
When the firewood is all consumed.

If anyone, even while distracted,
Enters a stūpa or mausoleum
And even once exclaims, "Hail to the Buddha,"
They have fulfilled the Buddha way.[63]

In *Shōbōgenzō* "Kuyō-Shobutsu" (Making Offering to Buddhas),
Dōgen Zenji introduced ten kinds of offerings and said:

> Such service of offerings we should perform unfailingly
> with sincere mind. It has been performed without fail by
> the buddhas. Stories about it are evident throughout the
> sutras and Vinaya. At the same time, the Buddhist ances-
> tors themselves have personally handed down its authentic
> transmission. Days and months of waiting in attendance and
> doing work are just times of serving offerings.[64]

There are many ways to make offerings. Our practice of zazen is one
offering. Acting for the sake of the Three Treasures instead of fulfill-
ing one's desires is an offering. Because we exist within a network of
support, we need to support others. This is what "repaying the debt of
kindness" and "making offering and sustaining" (*kuyō*) mean. How do
we practice this? How can we pay our debt to all beings? The next verse,
quoted earlier, explains:

The first portion is to end all evil;
the second is to cultivate every good;
the third is to free all beings.
May everyone realize the Buddha's Way.

At the end of this verse, we bow with our ōryōki bowls and begin to eat.

The Japanese interpretation of the Chinese original is "*Ikku i dan issai aku / Niku i shu issai zen / San ku i do sho shu jō / Kaigu jō butsudō.*" *Ikku*, *niku*, and *sanku* mean first, second, and third bites. The first bite is to end all evil, to stop unwholesome deeds. The second bite is for the practice of all good things, and the third is for *do sho shu jō*. This is usually translated as "to save all sentient beings," but the literal meaning of *do* is "to go across." So it means to help all beings to cross the river from this shore to the other. This shore is samsara, in which all beings transmigrate through the six realms. The Buddha taught that we should cross the river to the other shore, nirvana. "To help people" means, in this case, to help all beings cross over to nirvana. This is the first of the four bodhisattva vows. These three points are the same as the threefold pure precepts, one category of the sixteen precepts we receive at the *jukai* (precepts-receiving) ceremony. The first is the precept of embracing moral codes, the second is embracing all good actions, and the third is embracing all living beings. We receive the threefold pure precepts to become Buddha's children or bodhisattvas. These precepts become our vow. We vow to live with this guidance, to refrain from unwholesome deeds by embracing moral codes, to practice only wholesome deeds, and to live together with all living things, doing no harm to any.

A question we should ask now is, What is good or wholesome, and what is bad or unwholesome? The definition of good and bad in Buddhism is clear. Any action we take (or karma we make) that causes suffering to self or others is bad (unwholesome). Actions that reduce suffering or bring joy or happiness to self and others are good (wholesome). The original Sanskrit word for pain or suffering is *duḥkha*, while joy or happiness is *sukha*. So the definition of good and bad in Buddhism has to do with the relation between cause and effect. It is difficult to tell whether one action is good or bad by observing it in isolation. We need to look at the consequences of many related actions. Depending on its results, an action can be good or bad. We can never be entirely certain whether an action is good or bad. An action with good intentions may cause either a beneficial or harmful result. The best we can do is try to do good. This aim to do good is our vow. If our action based on good intentions causes an unwholesome effect, we have to make repentance and try to avoid repeating the mistake. This is our practice of vow and repentance. Vow and repentance together with the precepts are very important aspects of bodhisattva practice. The precepts we receive are the guidelines for our life as the Buddha's children.

The final line is "May everyone realize the Buddha's Way," or in Japanese "Kai gu jō butsu dō." *Kai gu* means "together with all beings." We should not accomplish or complete Buddha's Way alone but with all beings. It's not possible for one person alone to attain buddhahood. When we recite or chant these verses during meals, we renew our vows and reflect on our deeds, our incompleteness, and try to be better. Our practice is to see reality as prajñā, the wisdom that sees the impermanence and egolessness of all beings. In Mahāyāna Buddhism this is called emptiness. We may practice zazen to pacify or calm ourselves, but that is not enough. We have to engage in the activity of our day-to-day lives. Precepts supply guidance for these activities outside of the meditation hall. Precepts, meditation, and wisdom are called the three basic studies of Buddhism. All our activities, all the parts of our lives, should become our practice to accomplish the Buddha's Way with all beings.

Verse of the Rinse Water

When the preceding verses have been chanted, we begin eating. When finished, we wash our bowls. After washing, we offer water and chant the following verse.

> The water with which we wash our bowls
> Tastes like ambrosia.

We offer it to the many spirits;
May they be satisfied.
On ma ku ra sai so wa ka.

After we eat food, we clean the ōryōki bowl and other small bowls with a *setsu*, or scraper. To avoid wasting any food, we clean the bowls with water that we then offer to the various spirits. The meaning of this verse is almost the same as the verse of offering the food before eating, discussed above: "O spirits, we now give you an offering; / This food is for all of you in the ten directions." Here the verse says, "The water with which we wash our bowls / Tastes like ambrosia." I don't know what ambrosia tastes like. The original word, however, is *kanro*, which literally means "sweet dew." Often this word is used as a symbol of Buddha's teachings, the Dharma. Food is Dharma, and Dharma is food. When we offer food, we offer Dharma; and this water tasting like sweet dew is Dharma too.

"We offer it to the many spirits; / May they be satisfied." The original word for spirits is *ki jin*, the same word we saw in the Verse of Offering Food. Although Buddhist philosophy claims there is no soul, Buddhism never negates unseen beings or "spirits." The Buddha never denied reincarnation or transmigration, according to which there is something that never dies and transmigrates when this body dies. Philosophically, reincarnation and the Buddha's teaching of no soul, no ego, or anātman appear contradictory. This contradiction has been an important issue in many philosophical arguments within Buddhism and between Buddhism and other philosophies in India as well as in China.

But since a majority of common people believed in ghosts, spirits, demons, and gods, Buddhism didn't try to eliminate these beliefs but rather accepted them as part of the Buddha's teaching. Many Indian gods, like Indra, were accepted within Buddhism as guardians or protectors of the Dharma. If you think logically, this may strike you as strange. However, when traditional peoples accept the existence of souls and gods, this is not a philosophical concept for them, but rather a feeling, which we share, that we live together with all beings in nature.

We feel an intimacy with nature and we can communicate with it. If we negate these beings, all nature becomes merely a collection of matter, and there is no way to communicate or live together with immaterial things. And if we think of material things as nothing more than objects of our desire, we will use and misuse them in any way to satisfy ourselves.

The next line is a mantra. In Japanese we pronounce this as *On, makurasai, sowaka*. In Sanskrit it goes *Om mahorase svāhā*. We don't know much about this mantra. *Om* and *svāhā* appear in almost all mantras. *Om* is a word that begins the mantra. It is a holy word in India. Vajrayāna Buddhism, in particular, accepted many practices of this kind from Hinduism. According to a commentary on *Chanyuan Qinggui* (*Zen'en Shingi*), *mahorase* is a compound of *mahā* (big) and *urase* (abdomen). Probably this refers to hungry ghosts.

Verse of Purity While Abiding in the World

> Abiding in this ephemeral world
> Like a lotus in muddy water,
> the mind is pure and goes beyond.
> Thus we bow to Buddha.

In "The Dharma for Taking Meals" (Fushukuhanpō) Dōgen Zenji wrote that, in Eiheiji, "hearing the tsui chin, the ino chants the 'Existing in the world' verse. This is the traditional ritual of Sōjō (Bishop) Yōjō [Eisai], so we are following it for now."[65] Dōgen Zenji basically followed the procedure of formal ōryōki meals described in *Chanyuan Qinggui* (*Zen'en Shingi*), but he added this verse, chanted at the end of the meal, from the tradition of Eisai, who was the first Japanese master to introduce Zen to Japan. Eisai was a Rinzai Zen master. Dōgen Zenji first practiced Zen in Japan with Eisai's disciple Myōzen at Keninji, which was founded by Eisai. However, the verse itself is much older than Eisai. It appears in the precepts-receiving ceremony in fascicle 9 of *Chanyuan Qinggui*.

The meaning of this verse is important for us as the Buddha's children. The English translation is a bit different from the original. This is a verse praising the Buddha's virtue. My literal translation of this verse is "Dwelling in this world like empty space, and like a lotus flower without being stained by muddy water. Purity of the mind goes beyond. Therefore we make prostration to the most venerable one." In the English translation, *kokū* (empty space) is an adjective modifying "world," yielding the meaning "this ephemeral world." In the original, however, empty space modifies "abiding." The way the Buddha abides in the world is like empty space and also like a lotus flower.

Like empty space, the Buddha dwells in this world. Empty space or kokū is a symbol of perfect interpenetration. In Buddhism it has three meanings. In a cup, there is a certain amount of water, and above the water there is empty space as a conditioned phenomenal thing. This is a very common meaning of empty space—the space where nothing exists. And yet this space is not really empty. It is filled with air. Empty space in the common sense is not really empty.

Another meaning of empty space in Buddhism is the space that does not disappear even when it is occupied by something. This is considered unconditioned; it never arises or perishes. If a glass is here, the space the glass is occupying doesn't actually disappear. This space allows all beings to exist, and it doesn't disappear even when beings disappear. This space never changes, never appears, and never disappears. It's always there. And this empty space is never defiled or pure. If the space is occupied by dirty things, it is not defiled.

The third meaning of the word *kokū* is empty space as a metaphor for prajñā or wisdom, the emptiness of all beings. Emptiness means the way the Buddha sees all beings—without self-nature or substance, impermanent, and always changing. This way of being is different from the empty space in the cup, which is a lack of being. It is also different from the space that allows all things to exist. This third kind of emptiness is the way all beings exist without self-nature. Since everything is connected with everything else, the reality of all beings, which is emptiness, pervades and penetrates the whole universe. There is no discrimination, no attachment, and nothing to grasp. This meaning of *kokū* is used as a metaphor for the emptiness that is the reality of our life. In this verse, *kokū* means the emptiness of all beings. The Buddha dwells in this world of the five skandhas as emptiness.

Kokū appears in the Verse of the Wind Bell, composed by Dōgen Zenji's teacher, Tiantong Rujing.

> The whole body is like a mouth hanging in empty space.
> Not questioning the winds from east, west, south, or north,
> Equally with all of them, speaking of prajñā:
> Ding-dong-a-ling ding-dong.

Dōgen's teacher wrote this poem about a wind bell hanging under the temple roof. In the *Hōkyōki*, Dōgen recorded his conversation with Rujing about this poem.

> Dōgen made one hundred prostrations and said, "In your poem about the wind bell, I read in the first line, 'The whole body [of the wind bell] is like a mouth hanging in empty space' and in the third line, 'Together expressing prajñā equally to all beings.' Is the empty space referred to one of the form [*rūpa*] elements? Skeptical people may think empty space is one of the form elements. Students today don't understand Buddha Dharma clearly and consider the blue sky as the empty space. I am sorry for them."
>
> Rujing replied with compassion, "This empty space is prajñā. It is not one of the form elements. The empty space neither obstructs nor not-obstructs. Therefore this is neither simple emptiness nor truth relative to falsehood. Various masters haven't understood even what the form is, much less emptiness. This is due to the decline of Buddha Dharma in this country." Dōgen remarked, "This poem is the utmost in excellence. Even if they practice forever, the masters in all corners of the world would not be able to match it. Every

one of the monks appreciates it. Having come from a far-off land and being inexperienced, as I unroll the sayings of other masters in various texts, I have not yet come across anything like this poem. How fortunate I am to be able to learn it! As I read it, I am filled with joy, and tears moisten my robe, and I am moved to prostration because this poem is direct and also lyrical."

When my teacher was about to ride on a sedan-chair, he said with a smile, "What you say is profound and has the mark of greatness. I composed this poem while I was at Chingliang monastery. Although people praised it, no one has ever penetrated it as you do. I grant that you have the Eye. You must compose poems in this way."[66]

Rujing said that this kokū is not the empty space that disappears when it is occupied by something, which is one of the rūpa elements. Neither is it the second meaning. He clearly says this is prajñā itself. Therefore, I am sure that Dōgen Zenji interprets this kokū in the meal chant as meaning prajñā.

The Buddha dwells in this world with prajñā, which sees the true emptiness of all things as neither having form nor being without form. This line echoes the line in the verse for setting out the bowls:

> Now we set out Buddha's bowls;
> may we, with all living beings,
> realize the emptiness of the three wheels:
> giver, receiver, and gift.

The Buddha dwells in this world like a lotus flower. The lotus flower emerges from muddy water. It is a beautiful flower which mud does not defile. It symbolizes the Buddha's virtue, compassion, and wisdom. It is a sacred flower and an important symbol in Buddhism and Hinduism.

According to a Hindu creation myth, when the god Vishnu was

asleep in water a lotus flower grew from his navel. Another god, Brahma, was sleeping on this lotus. Brahma created this world while Vishnu was asleep. The yogic cross-legged posture is called the lotus position because of this myth.

In Buddhism many Buddha statues are sitting or standing on lotus petals. This is for a reason. Right after the Buddha attained awakening, he hesitated to teach because he thought the truth he found was too deep and subtle for anyone to understand. Then Brahma asked the Buddha to teach. Then the Buddha, out of compassion for living beings, surveyed the world. He saw that there are many different kinds of people.

> Just as in a pond of blue or red or white lotuses, some lotuses might be born in the water, grow up in the water, and thrive while submerged in the water, without rising up from the water; some lotuses might be born in the water, grow up in the water, and stand at even level with the water; some lotuses might be born in the water and grow up in the water, but would rise up from the water and stand without being soiled by the water—so too, surveying the world with the eye of a Buddha, the Blessed One saw beings with little dust in their eyes and with much dust in their eyes, with keen faculties and with dull faculties, with good qualities and with bad qualities, easy to teach and hard to teach, and a few who dwelt seeing blame and fear in the other world.[67]

After this survey, the Buddha made up his mind to teach the five monks at Deer Park. In this example, the lotus flower signifies the different capacities of living beings. In another sutra, however, it also represents the Buddha himself. In this sutra the Buddha elucidates the nature of dharma teachings. He said, "I do not dispute with the world; rather, it is the world that disputes with me. A proponent of the Dharma does not dispute with anyone in the world. Of that which the wise in the world agree upon as not existing, I too say that it does not exist. And of that which the wise in the world agree upon as existing, I too say that it exists."

The Buddha did not teach some fabricated dogmatic theory with which wise people did not agree. He taught the truth everyone can see if their eyes are open. In the same sutra, the Buddha said:

> And what is it, bhikkhus, that the wise in the world agree upon as not existing, of which I too say that it does not exist? Form that is permanent, stable, eternal, and not subject to change: this the wise in the world agree upon as not existing, and I too say that it does not exist. Feeling—Perception—Volitional formation—Consciousness that is permanent, stable, eternal, and not subject to change: this the wise in the world agree upon as not existing, and I too say that it does not exist.
>
> And what is it, bhikkhus, that the wise in the world agree upon as existing, of which I too say that it exists? Form that is impermanent, suffering, and subject to change; this the wise in the world agree upon as existing, and I too say that it exists. Feeling, perception, volitional formations, consciousness—that is impermanent, suffering, and subject to change: this the wise in the world agree upon as existing, and I too say that it exists.

Here the Buddha talks about the reality of the emptiness of all phenomenal things emphasized in Mahāyāna teachings. Nothing is substantial or permanent; therefore everything is subject to change. If we think that this body is permanent, we attach to it, and from this attachment spring our desires. This mistaken idea comes from ignorance, and from ignorance greed, anger, and hatred arise. According to the Buddha, this is the source of suffering in samsara. Not only the body, but feelings, perceptions, formations, and consciousness—all five skandhas—are impermanent and without any fixed self-nature. To see the five skandhas (our body and mind) as impermanent and unstable, subject to change and decay, is the way we free ourselves from attachments and liberate ourselves from the three poisonous minds.

According to the Buddha, to see all beings as fixed is the delusion that causes suffering. On this point there is no difference between early Buddhism and Mahāyāna Buddhism. So we should see the reality of all beings as impermanence, the way the Buddha sees all beings.

Then the Buddha goes on: "Bhikkhus, just as a blue, red, or white lotus is born in the water and grows up in the water but having risen up above the water, it stands unsullied by the water, so too the Tathāgata was born in the world and grew up in the world, but having overcome the world, he dwells unsullied by the world."[68]

The Buddha was born in this world as the lotus was born in the muddy water and grew in this world as the lotus grows in the water. But the Buddha "rises to the surface." This is a metaphor of the Buddha's teaching and way of life. The Buddha was never separated from the muddy water, from this world, and yet he was not defiled by the worldly way of doing things or mundane, selfish desires.

The verse we are discussing says, "The mind is pure and goes beyond." The mind goes beyond the muddy water of the dusty world. The Buddha does not escape the world, but the purity of the Buddha's mind goes beyond the world. It is said that the Buddha and bodhisattvas do not stay in this world because of wisdom and never leave this world because of compassion. The Buddha is here and at the same time not here because of wisdom and compassion. So we venerate the most venerable one.

One of the basic teachings of the *Avataṃsaka Sutra* is that there are no differences between the Buddha, the mind, and living beings. These three are one, and there can be no discriminating between them. This is a verse of praise for Buddha. In this verse "the mind" also refers to the nature of bodhisattvas. In the not-yet-matured stages, bodhisattvas are, like us, ordinary human beings. Even though we have aroused bodhicitta, received the bodhisattva precepts, and taken the four bodhisattva vows, we live in the muddy water. We harbor many delusions and fundamental ignorance, and we are not yet completely free of greed, anger, and hatred. We are still defiled in many ways. Our perception is defiled and conditioned. Each of us usually thinks, "I am most important." We judge things to be good, useful, or valuable to the extent that we find them important, useful, or attractive to us. This is the worldly, conditioned way of viewing things, which is contrary to the Buddha's teaching. Our individual perspective is empty, so we cannot use it as a yardstick to measure the value or meaning of things. But we do. This is our basic delusion, and we cannot live without it.

Because all of us measure things with our own yardsticks, we get into arguments. If I think something is important, and you don't, we have to argue about who is right. If both of us think an object is important, we might fight about who owns it. When we live based on our own yardstick, this becomes a world of competition and argument.

If we cannot depend on anything man-made or conditioned, how can we live within this society with other people and their yardsticks? One way is to see that my own yardstick is limited. When I recognize my limitations, I create the space to consider that other people have other yardsticks and measure things differently. I can open my heart to them. This is how we can live in muddy water with other people in peace and harmony. This is our practice of letting go of self-centered thoughts. When we live in this way without attachment to objects or to our conditioned way of viewing and judging things, the lotus flower can bloom in our lives.

For me, this is the meaning of our practice of zazen: letting go of thought. Letting go of thought is letting go of my yardstick. But this doesn't mean I should discard this yardstick, because it's all I can use. Letting go doesn't mean it disappears; it is still there, but we know that it is relative and limited. That is the way we can see things in a broader perspective. Our minds become more flexible. The Buddha is the model for us bodhisattvas, children of the Buddha, and we make prostrations to this Buddha. This means we give up clinging to our own personal yardsticks. To make prostrations to the Buddha means to let go of our system of values and to trust in the reality of all beings.

The verse ends with "Thus we bow to Buddha." The original

expression is "Ki shu rin bujōson." *Ki shu rin* is the deepest bow or prostration, called *gotai-tōchi* (*lit: gotai*, five parts of the body; *tōchi*, are cast on the ground) We place our forehead and both knees and elbows on the floor. We hold our hands upward at the height of our ears. This means we receive the Buddha's feet on our hands. This is a most humble way to show respect to the Buddha. Our head is the highest point of ourselves, and the Buddha's foot is the lowest point of the Buddha, *bujōson*, the most venerable one. We make prostrations to the Buddha to become free from our egocentricity, our clinging, and our selves. We open our hands and venerate the reality of all beings that is the Dharmakāya Buddha.

When we understand the meaning of these verses in the meal chants and wholeheartedly practice, our meals become an essential practice of the Buddha's teaching.

MAHĀPRAJÑĀPĀRAMITA HṚDAYA SUTRA

Avalokiteśvara Bodhisattva
When practicing deeply the prajñā-pāramitā
Perceived that all five skandhas are empty
And was saved from all suffering and distress.

"O Śāriputra, form does not differ from emptiness;
Emptiness does not differ from form.
That which is form is emptiness;
That which is emptiness, form.
The same is true of feelings, perceptions, impulses, and
    consciousness.

"O Śāriputra, all dharmas are marked with emptiness;
They do not appear or disappear,
Are neither tainted nor pure,
Do not increase or decrease.

"Therefore in emptiness, no form,
No feelings, no perceptions, no impulses, no consciousness;

No eyes, no ears, no nose, no tongue, no body, no mind;
No color, no sound, no smell, no taste, no touch, no object
of mind;
No realm of eyes and so forth until no realm of mind
consciousness;
No ignorance and also no extinction of it, and so forth until
no old age and death and also no extinction of them;
No suffering, no origination, no stopping, no path;
No cognition, no attainment.
With nothing to attain
The bodhisattva depends on prajñā-pāramitā
And the mind is no hindrance.
Without any hindrance no fears exist;
Far apart from every perverted view the bodhisattva dwells
in nirvana.

"In the three worlds all buddhas depend on prajñā-pāramitā
And attain unsurpassed, complete, perfect enlightenment.

"Therefore know the prajñā-pāramitā
Is the great transcendent mantra,
Is the great bright mantra,
Is the utmost mantra,
Is the supreme mantra,
Which is able to relieve all suffering
And is true, not false.
So proclaim the prajñā-pāramitā mantra,
Proclaim the mantra that says:
Gate, gate, pāragate, pārasamgate! Bodhi, svāha!"

THE *Mahāprajñāpāramita Hṛdaya Sutra*, one of the most well known sutras, is commonly called the *Heart Sutra*. Most people who are interested in Buddhism have heard of it and many recite or chant it regularly. More than a hundred commentaries have been published, and many are available in any Japanese bookstore. Despite its popularity, I think the *Heart Sutra* is very difficult to understand.

I first read this sutra when I was sixteen years old. I was interested in everything related to religion, philosophy, and literature, and so I was interested in Buddhism. One of my uncles, a Shingon Buddhist priest, lent me a commentary on the *Heart Sutra* from his library. I read it but couldn't understand it. Even so, I found it very attractive, so I learned it by heart, memorizing all 268 Chinese characters. School didn't interest me, so during class I would write out the sutra although I didn't really understand what it meant. When I took a walk, I enjoyed chanting this sutra without thinking about the meaning. That was my first encounter with the *Heart Sutra*.

When I studied the teachings of early Buddhism at Komazawa University, I was surprised by what I learned about this sutra. It says that Avalokiteśvara saw that the five skandhas—the five mental and material elements of which we are composed—are empty and do not exist. It also says that the eighteen elements of our consciousness do not exist. This refers to the six sense organs, their six objects (color and shape, smell, sound, taste, touch, and objects of mind), and the six perceptions that arise when the six sense organs interact with their objects.

The sutra continues, "No ignorance and also no extinction of it, and so forth until no old age and death." Ignorance is the first of the twelve causes of suffering, and old age and death is the last. The sutra denies the existence of all twelve. Next it says, "No suffering, no origination, no stopping, no path." It claims that these four noble truths, the basic teachings of the Buddha, do not exist. The *Heart Sutra* denies the existence of the five skandhas, the eighteen elements of our experience, the twelve links of dependent origination, and the four noble truths. Yet it claims to be the true teaching of the Buddha. I was amazed and confused. How could the author of this sutra negate the Buddha's teachings and still call himself a student of the Buddha? After studying Mahāyāna Buddhism as a philosophy I understood the meaning of this sutra in an abstract sense. Only in the last few years have I understood its significance for my own practice. This question of why the *Heart Sutra* negates the teachings of the Buddha is essential to its understanding.

While I was in Japan, I had a chance to give a series of lectures on Dōgen's *Shōbōgenzō* to a group of Japanese Catholic laymen. I intended to talk first on "Genjōkōan" (Actualization of Reality), the first and most popular chapter of *Shōbōgenzō*. The second chapter of the seventy-five-volume version of *Shōbōgenzō* is "Maka Hannya Haramitsu" (Mahā Prajñā Pāramitā), a commentary by Dōgen Zenji on the *Heart Sutra*. Since my audience knew nothing about Buddhism, I needed to talk about the *Heart Sutra* before discussing Dōgen's commentary. While preparing these lectures I studied "Genjōkōan," "Maka Hannya Haramitsu," and the *Heart Sutra* together. It was then that I first realized that the *Heart Sutra* is very important to an understanding of Dōgen Zenji's "Maka Hannya Haramitsu" and "Genjōkōan." If we have a deep understanding of the *Heart Sutra* and "Maka Hannya Haramitsu," we can see that "Genjōkōan" is a clear and practical expression of prajñā-pāramitā.

The sutra's full title is *Mahāprajñāpāramita Hṛdaya Sutra*. *Mahā* means "great" or "vast." It also means "absolute" in the sense of beyond comparison or discrimination. *Mahāyāna* means "great vehicle," which can transport not just one person but many. Mahāyāna is also used as a synonym of "one vehicle" (*eka yāna*), which includes the three vehicles (*śrāvaka-yāna*, *pratyekabuddha-yāna*, and *bodhisattva-yāna*).[69] *Prajñā* means "wisdom." Wisdom and compassion are the two main aspects of Buddhism and must always go together. Without wisdom, compassion doesn't work, and without compassion wisdom has no meaning; it's not alive. This sutra is about the wisdom that sees emptiness.

Hṛdaya means "heart." In this context it means a part of our body and also the essence or most important point. The heart is the most important part of our body. If it stops, everything stops, and the whole body dies. Today many consider the brain to be more important. They believe that when the brain stops a person is dead, and their organs can be transplanted. But historically for Buddhists the heart is the basis for judging whether a person is alive or not. In Japan brain death is not recognized, and so heart transplants are still very uncommon. To remove a heart before it has stopped has been considered murder. There is a serious controversy among Japanese doctors over the proper way to determine death.[70] Since "heart" means the most important or essential point, the *Heart Sutra* is very short. The *Prajñāpāramitā Sutra* cycle is a six-hundred-volume collection of sutras. It's said that the *Heart Sutra* is the essence of those six hundred volumes.

Sutra means scripture or written expression of the Buddha's teachings. *Pāramitā*, usually translated as "perfection," is a word that is vital to an understanding of Mahāyāna Buddhism. The title of this sutra is usually translated as "Perfection of Great Wisdom." According to Chinese Buddhist philosophers, perfection or pāramitā means to cross the river to the other shore. It implies that we are living on this shore of samsara, and there is a river we must cross to reach nirvana. On this shore we transmigrate through the six realms of samsara: the realms of hell, hungry ghosts, animals, asuras (fighting spirits), human beings, and heavenly beings. We transmigrate according to our deeds. Nirvana is beyond these realms. Pāramitā, reaching the other shore, is a transformation of our way of life. The six pāramitās are commonly considered to be the method for transformation, but sometimes they are considered to be the transformed way of life instead of the means to reach there.

In samsara, our lives are based on desires. We chase after happiness. We want satisfaction, so we pursue our desires. We run after things we want and away from things we dislike. Sometimes we succeed and we are happy. Sometimes we fail and we are unhappy. This constant up-and-down is samsara.

Many people believe in transmigration from one lifetime to another. I don't believe in this, but I know we transmigrate within this life. Sometimes we feel like heavenly beings, sometimes like hell dwellers. Often we are like hungry ghosts, craving satisfaction, constantly searching for more. When our stomachs are full and we have nothing to do, we become sleepy and lazy like animals. Sometimes we are like asuras or fighting spirits. As human beings we work to acquire fame and profit. Even when our stomachs are full, we are not satisfied. We need something more, such as fame or wealth. Heavenly beings are like millionaires whose desires are completely fulfilled. They look happy but I think such people are rather bored. There's no challenge for them because all their desires are fulfilled.

Within this constant transmigration there is no peaceful basis for our lives. This way of life is a vain attempt to satisfy our egos. A life based on this constant search for satisfaction is filled with meaningless suffering. Suffering means not just physical or mental pain but also meaningless effort. This is what the Buddha meant when he said, "Everything is suffering." This is the first of the four noble truths.

According to the Buddha, the reality of our life is impermanence and egolessness. Nothing is fixed, and there is nothing that doesn't change. In Buddhism, ego refers to the idea that there is something that is changeless. Our bodies and minds change continually from birth, and yet we believe there is something that doesn't change. When I was born in 1948, I was a tiny baby; since then I have gone through many different stages of human life: a boy, a teenager, a young adult, a middle-aged person, and then a senior citizen. The conditions of my body and mind have changed in each stage and yet I think, "That was me and this is me. There is something that doesn't change." For Buddhists, the ego as an unchanging entity that is the owner and operator of the body and mind is an illusion. The Buddha taught that there is no such thing, that ego is an abstract fabrication.

Buddhism is not pessimistic nihilism, because the Buddha also taught that there is a way to become free from this kind of life. There is a path that leads to liberation from this continual transmigration through samsara. We can make a peaceful, stable foundation for our lives. It's called nirvana. It is not a particular state or condition of our minds but rather a way of life based on impermanence and egolessness. In every moment we must awaken again to the impermanent reality of our lives. Everything is always changing, and there is no substance. In Mahāyāna Buddhism, this is called emptiness. The Buddha taught that there are two different ways of living. If we are blind to the reality of egolessness and impermanence, our life becomes suffering. If we waken to this reality and live accordingly, our life becomes nirvana. This awakening is called bodhi or enlightenment. The way of transformation from the life of suffering in samsara to the life of nirvana is the eight-fold noble path. This path is our practice. It is a change in the basis of our life from egocentricity to egolessness. This transformation is called pāramitā, or "reaching the other shore." This eightfold path taught by Shakyamuni Buddha consists of right understanding, right thinking, right speech, right action, right livelihood, right effort (diligence), mindfulness, and samādhi (meditation). Instead of the eightfold path, the Mahāyāna practice for bodhisattvas emphasizes the six pāramitās or perfections. The first of the six is generosity (*dāna*). We are generous because we understand there is no one who can possess and nothing to be possessed. Generosity should be based on the realization of empti-ness, egolessness, and impermanence. The second pāramitā, the pre-cepts (*śīla*), is the same as right livelihood in the eightfold path. We base our day-to-day lives on the Buddha's precepts or teaching. When we become Buddhists we accept the precepts as guidelines for our lives. We regulate our activities with the Buddha's precepts—no killing, lying, stealing, and so forth. The third, patience (*kṣānti*), is emphasized in Mahāyāna Buddhism because it is a practice designed for laypeople. In a monastery patience is not considered so important because monks are assumed to have similar values and aspirations. Laypeople are in greater contact with people who have different philosophies and ways of thinking. For this they need patience. For a bodhisattva, patience is one of the most important practices.[71] The last three pāramitās are dili-gence (*vīrya*), meditation (*samādhi*), and wisdom (*prajñā*). The *Heart Sutra* and all the other *Prajñāpāramitā Sutras* say that prajñā is the most important of the six pāramitās to the practice of bodhisattvas.

Without prajñā the other five pāramitās don't work. For example, generosity without wisdom can be harmful. We must understand what is really needed before we can help someone. If we give money or assis-tance without wisdom, the person may become dependent and have more difficulty as a result. This is also true of raising children. Too much protection will spoil a child. We need prajñā or wisdom to really help people grow. Without prajñā the precepts become no more than a lifeless set of rules. We may even discriminate between people on the basis of a particular set of precepts or customs. Each nation or religion has its own set of precepts and taboos. It's easy to see people who follow our precepts as friends and to believe that all the others will go to hell. This is an example of precepts without wisdom, a type of egocentricity of a group instead of an individual.

We need a deep understanding of a situation to see what is most helpful to everyone involved. Dōgen Zenji said in *Shōbōgenzō* "Bodaisatta Shishōbō" (Bodhisattva's Four Embracing Dharmas) that as bodhisattvas we should aim at activities that benefit both others and ourselves. We should try to see the whole situation and do what is best for everyone. If we aim only for patience, we may harm ourselves or others. Patience alone can be a kind of poison. It can make the situation worse.

The same is true of diligence. If diligence is misdirected, the harder we work, the farther we deviate from the correct path. Without the wisdom to see which way to go, our diligence is meaningless effort.

Wisdom is also essential to meditation. If we don't understand the significance or meaning of meditation, our practice of zazen becomes no more than an escape from a noisy society. It becomes a meaningless method to simply calm our minds and reduce our stress. If our life is harmful to others and we practice meditation to relax and gain more energy for self-centered activities, our practice has nothing to do with Buddhist teachings. So wisdom, real wisdom, is essential. This is the meaning of pāramitā. According to the *Heart Sutra*, prajñā-pāramitā is the essence of Buddhist teaching. It is necessary to the transformation of our life from samsara to nirvana.

THE SITUATION IN WHICH THE *HEART SUTRA* IS EXPOUNDED

One reason the *Heart Sutra* is difficult to understand is that it's not clear who is speaking. There are two versions of the sutra. The one we usually chant, which is printed at the beginning of this chapter, is the shorter of the two. The longer version describes the situation more completely. The opening lines of this version, translated from Sanskrit by Edward Conze, are:

> Thus have I heard at one time. The Lord dwelled at Rājagṛha, on the Vulture Peak, together with a large gathering of both monks and bodhisattvas. At that time, the Lord, after he had taught the discourse on dharma called "deep splendor," had entered into concentration. At that time also the Holy Lord Avalokita, the Bodhisattva, the great being, coursed in the course of the deep perfection of wisdom; he looked down from on high, and he saw the five skandhas, and he surveyed them as empty in their own-being.
>
> Thereupon the Venerable Śāriputra through the Buddha's might said to the holy Lord Avalokita, the Bodhisattva, the great being: "How should a son or daughter of good family train themselves if they want to course in the course of this deep perfection of wisdom?"[72]

"Thus have I heard," is the traditional beginning of a Buddhist sutra. The "I" is Ānanda, a longtime attendant of Shakyamuni Buddha who memorized all of his sutras.

> The Lord dwelled at Rājagriha, on the Vulture Peak, together with a large gathering of both monks and bodhisattvas. At that time, the Lord, after he had taught the discourse on dharma called "deep splendor," had entered into concentration.

"Lord" refers to the Buddha. I question the use of this word. The Buddha never called himself Lord. In fact, he said that he owned nothing. The original word used in the sutra is "Bhagavat," which is usually translated into English as World-Honored One. "Concentration" means zazen or samādhi. After he gave a talk on "deep splendor," he stopped speaking and started to sit zazen. This sutra takes place within the Buddha's zazen. This is a very important point.

> At that time also the Holy Lord Avalokita, the bodhisattva, the Great Being, coursed in the course of the deep perfection of wisdom; he looked down from on high, and he saw the five skandhas, and he surveyed them as empty in their own-being.

In this translation the name Avalokiteśvara is divided into two parts, "Avalokita" and "īśvara." *Avalokita* means "to see." *Īśvara* is usually translated as "freely." This is what the Chinese translation *Kanjizai* means. Here *īśvara* is translated as "lord," a free person who does not belong to anyone. "Great Being" is a translation of Mahāsattva, another word for bodhisattva. To "course in the course" is a Sanskrit expression for practice. So Avalokiteśvara was practicing deep prajñā-pāramitā. And from within his practice of deep wisdom, he looked down on this world in which all sentient beings are living.

"Looked down" is a translation from Sanskrit. In Japanese this is *shōken*. *Shō* means "to illuminate," and *ken* "to see" or "view." So *shōken* means "see very clearly," as if a scene were illumined with a bright light. The Sanskrit expression is "he looked down from on high." When we are on the same level as all other human beings we can't see distinctly, but from a high place like a mountain, one can see the whole clearly.

"And he saw the five skandhas": From his practice of deep prajñā, that is, zazen, he saw that all beings are collections of the five skandhas and nothing but the five skandhas. The skandhas are the elements that comprise all beings. The first, form or *rūpa*, refers to all material things. For human beings, this means our bodies. The other four are the functions of our mind. So Avalokiteśvara saw that everything in this world is an accumulation of the five skandhas.

"And he surveyed them as empty in their own-being": The bodhisattva further saw that these skandhas are empty.

"Thereupon the Venerable Śāriputra through the Buddha's might said to the holy Lord Avalokita, the Bodhisattva, the great being": Śāriputra was one of the ten greatest of the Buddha's disciples. It is said he was the most sharp-witted. Śāriputra asked Avalokiteśvara through the Buddha's might, so it's really the Buddha, not Śāriputra, who is speaking. Śāriputra's question was "How should a son or daughter of good family train themselves if they want to course in the course of this deep perfection of wisdom?" His question was how people should practice if they aspire to prajñā-pāramitā. Avalokiteśvara's answer to Śāriputra's question is the teaching of the *Heart Sutra*. The person who gives this speech is Avalokiteśvara, but this question and answer both take place within the Buddha's samādhi, that is, zazen. This is a description of the Buddha's zazen and of ours. This teaching in the *Heart Sutra* is not a philosophical discussion between the Buddha's disciple Śāriputra and a bodhisattva about the philosophy of emptiness in Mahāyāna Buddhism. It is about our practice of zazen.

This description of how the conversation begins helps us to understand what Avalokiteśvara says in this sutra.

WHO IS AVALOKITEŚVARA?

When I first visited MZMC in 1989 I attended morning service and we chanted the translation of the shorter version of the *Heart Sutra*. I was surprised by the translation of the last line of the following paragraph.

> Avalokiteśvara Bodhisattva
> When practicing deeply the prajñā-pāramitā
> Perceived that all five skandhas are empty
> And was saved from all suffering and distress.

This line was completely different from my understanding. The translation implies that Avalokiteśvara was suffering and distressed, but through the practice of prajñā-pāramitā he was saved and released.

It is important to understand who Avalokiteśvara is. According to Mahāyāna Buddhism there are two kinds of bodhisattvas. We ordinary humans, who aspire to study, practice, and follow the Buddha's teaching are one kind. We are all called bodhisattvas. The other kind of bodhisattva is not an ordinary human being. Great bodhisattvas like Avalokiteśvara, Samantabhadra, or Mañjuśrī are the symbol of some part of the Buddha's virtue. They choose not to enter nirvana, or not to stay there, in order to help other beings cross over to the far shore.

In the chapter of *Shōbōgenzō* titled "Kannon," Dōgen Zenji said that Avalokiteśvara is the father and mother of buddhas. In a past life Avalokiteśvara was a buddha called Shōbōmyō Nyorai (True Dharma Wisdom Tathāgata). *Shōbō* means "true dharma." *Myō* is "light," the symbol of wisdom. So he was a buddha called "the light of true dharma." But because of his vow to save all beings, he became a bodhisattva and appeared in this world. He wasn't in trouble. So I don't think the translation quoted above is accurate. I found Katagiri Roshi's translation of the *Heart Sutra* in a magazine. He translates this paragraph: "Avalokiteśvara Bodhisattva, when practicing the profound prajñā-pāramitā, by virtue of illuminated vision, saw the five skandhas as empty and passed beyond all sufferings."[73] He wasn't saved from suffering but rather passed beyond it. The original Chinese words are *Do issai ku yaku. Do* is a verb and is sometimes translated as "to save." Another meaning of the Chinese character *do* is "to cross over from this shore." This *do* is not passive. So he wasn't saved, but rather he saved (others) or crossed over. He saved all beings in trouble, all who are suffering and in distress. This meaning is quite different. In the Sanskrit version we have today, this final part of the sentence is missing. In that version the point is that Avalokiteśvara came to the realization of emptiness, and that was it. There's no statement as to whether this realization relieved his suffering or that of others. This sentence may have been added by the Chinese translator, Xuanzang (Jap., Genjō), who lived in the seventh century. He may have been working from a different Sanskrit version from the one we have. In any case, the text seems to me clearer and simpler without the last phrase. Avalokiteśvara saw the five skandhas are empty. This is prajñā-pāramitā, the perfection of wisdom.

As noted above, in the Chinese translation of the *Heart Sutra*, "Avalokiteśvara" is translated as Kanjizai Bosatsu. Avalokiteśvara is also called Kanzeon Bosatsu in Chinese. Kanjizai and Kanzeon have different meanings. *Kan* means "to see" or "observe." *Jizai* is the translation of the Sanskrit word *īśvara*, a person who can see freely without obstruction. This means one who is free from egocentricity and ignorance, one who sees things as they are without distortion by intellect, desire, or expectation. This is the meaning of Avalokiteśvara.

Kanzeon Bosatsu as a translation appears in the twenty-fifth chapter of the *Lotus Sutra*, "The Universal Gateway of the Bodhisattva Perceiver of the World's Sounds," translated by Kumārajīva. In this case the name "Avalokiteśvara" is interpreted as "Avalokita" (to see) and "svara" (sound). The name Kanzeon means "one who hears the sound of the world." Human beings make sounds when they suffer. Avalokiteśvara hears these sounds of suffering and appears in various ways and tries to help. Kanzeon Bosatsu represents the aspect of compassion and the work of helping others. Kanjizai Bosatsu emphasizes the aspect of wisdom or prajñā—seeing things exactly as they are, free of distortion. In the *Heart Sutra* the bodhisattva is called Kanjizai Bosatsu. As a symbol of the wisdom of seeing the reality of our life clearly, he/she is, of course, a creation of the imagination of Mahāyāna Buddhists, not a historical being.

This bodhisattva, although a buddha, yet came back to this world of delusion and suffering in order to help people, vowing not to become Buddha until all sentient beings are saved and become Buddha together. So Avalokiteśvara will remain in this world, on this shore, as long as there are deluded human beings. To the extent that we are deluded Avalokiteśvara is here now. This is a very important point. Avalokiteśvara is not a person but rather a force that reminds us to awaken.

Today you have come to the Zen Center to sit and to listen to my talk. It's not necessarily fun. But you're here. You could have gone anywhere. This is a beautiful morning and you could be having fun, but you decided to come here and sit in this posture. It's not necessarily a comfortable posture and my talk is not necessarily interesting. But you made a decision to come here. What made you decide to come to the Zen Center and sit zazen? Avalokiteśvara. This is the power that keeps us practicing and tells us to awaken. Avalokiteśvara is a power not just inside us but all around us, which leads us to awaken to the impermanence and egolessness that is the reality of our lives.

New leaves are coming out on the trees. They show us that time passes and everything changes; now winter to spring and soon spring to summer. Life always changes, is always new and always fresh. We see everything around us change and yet we believe that we do not. We believe that "I am": "I am the same person I was forty years ago, twenty years ago, or yesterday." "I will be the same person tomorrow." But the reality is that we are always changing. Our bodies and minds constantly change. So in the spring the leaves appear and birds sing to tell us, "Awake, awake to this reality. Everything is moving and changing." Everything is ever fresh each moment. That is Avalokiteśvara helping us see things clearly as they are.

Everyone we encounter is Avalokiteśvara. Our parents who took care of us, our friends, our competitors, or even enemies can be Avalokiteśvara. They are here to show us the reality of life. We should be thankful. We should appreciate ourselves, all people we encounter, and all things in this universe. All of this is Avalokiteśvara telling us to wake up and not be caught in egocentric delusion, encouraging us to become free from illusion and see our life force straight on. That is Avalokiteśvara. This sutra is speaking from our life force.

In "Kannon," a chapter of *Shōbōgenzō*, Dōgen Zenji wrote about Avalokiteśvara.[74] He quotes a very interesting koan, or question and answer between two Chinese Zen masters, Yunyan (Ungan) and Daowu (Dōgo).[75] The two practiced together for forty years with various teachers at different monasteries. Many of their conversations have been recorded. This koan begins with Yunyan asking Daowu, "What does the Great Compassion Bodhisattva do with so many hands and eyes?" (Yunyan refers to Avalokiteśvara or Kanzeon Bosatsu. It is said that Avalokiteśvara had one thousand eyes and one thousand hands. Eyes symbolize wisdom, and the hands work with compassion to help others.) In answer to Yunyan's question Daowu replied, "It is like a person groping behind his head for his pillow at night."

We all turn over during the night as we sleep. Sometimes we lose our pillows. Daowu describes looking for his pillow in the dark with his hands behind his back. Complete darkness is rare these days. Even if we switch off all the lights there is usually some artificial light from outside. But in ancient times nighttime was completely dark. Once I had the experience of walking in complete darkness. There is a famous mountain outside of Kyoto called Mount Hiei, where Dōgen Zenji was ordained. There is a huge Tendai monastery there. I was staying at Antaiji in the northwest part of Kyoto. We had a party after a five-day sesshin and drank lots of sake and beer. After the party I had a lot of energy and decided to hike up the mountain to see the sun rise from the top. It took me three or four hours to walk up to the top. Since it is near the city of Kyoto most of the path was dimly lit by the lights of the city. But there was one stretch of several hundred meters covered by evergreens that was completely dark. I couldn't even see my hand. It was very frightening. My feet and hands became my eyes. I took each step very slowly and carefully because at the edge of the path was a cliff.

Perhaps blind people have this experience frequently. It's amazing to me to see blind people walking with a white cane. Their feet, hands, and even their canes are their eyes. Their whole body is their eyes. At night our entire body serves as our eyes. When we try to find a lost pillow our whole being, our whole body and mind, becomes our eyes and hands. Darkness has a special meaning in Buddhism. It means nondiscrimination. In the dark we can't see anything, and so we can't discriminate between things. We see only one darkness.

This is a metaphor for our zazen. In complete darkness there is no discrimination. Our body and mind work together as one. The *Heart Sutra* says there are no eyes, no ears, no nose, no tongue, no anything. Because they are not independent, they work together as one, and there is no distinction between eye or nose or tongue. The whole body becomes an eye in the darkness. The whole body becomes a tongue when we eat. We don't eat and taste with our mouths and tongues alone. We see the food with our eyes, we smell it with our noses, we touch it with our hands. The whole body functions together as one in all our actions. So there are no eyes or ears independent of other organs—all work together. That is the reality of life. This is how our life functions like a person groping for a pillow in the night.

> Yunyan said, "I get it, I get it. I understand what you mean."
> "How do you understand it?" asked Daowu.
> "The entire body is hands and eyes."

Since eyes don't work in the darkness of nondiscrimination, the whole body becomes eyes and hands.

> Daowu answered, "Good, you expressed reality almost completely. But only 80 to 90 percent. There is something lacking."
> Yunyan asked, "That is my understanding. What about you?"
> Daowu replied, "The whole body is hands and eyes."

Yunyan used the Chinese "hen shin." *Hen* means "entire." Daowu's wording was "tsū shin." *Tsū* means "whole." "Entire body" and "whole body" mean the same thing. Their answers were exactly the same. This is Avalokiteśvara. We have many hands and eyes besides our own. Our hands and eyes are universal. Our hands and eyes, our entire body, is part of the whole universe. The whole universe works as one, just like our whole body. There are innumerable hands and eyes. What is this whole universe doing for us? It's telling us to awaken from our dream of egocentricity and open our eyes. Whether Yunyan's and Daowu's expressions are the same or not and why Daowu said Yunyan's answer was only 80 to 90 percent complete are the points of this koan.[76]

Avalokiteśvara is like a person groping for a pillow in the darkness, with body and mind working as one. There is no distinction between eyes, hands, tongue, ear, or nose. The universe functions as one. This is the meaning of egolessness and impermanence. Everything is always changing, but we are blind to all of this. We dream that "I" am here, and unless my desires are fulfilled, my life is meaningless. We try to be successful. We build a fence between our body and mind and other beings in the universe. We say, "This is me. This is my territory. This is my house." We try to keep things we value inside our territories and things we dislike outside. If we own a lot of valuable things, we consider our lives successful. Our lives are a constant struggle to increase our income and decrease our expenses. This is our way of life. It works because human society is based on artificial conventions to which we all agree in order to make our lives more convenient.

But outside social conventions this framework doesn't apply. When we face our death, strategies of accumulation and avoidance don't work. No matter how successful your life, when you face death, you have to leave everything. Your property, your fame, and all your accomplishments disappear. Avalokiteśvara helps us awaken. Until we wake up to reality our life is like a building without a foundation. The *Heart Sutra* is about transforming our way of life. It is about waking up to reality and creating a life based on the reality that exists before convention. For us, the practice of zazen is the turning point of this transformation. According to Dōgen Zenji, zazen itself is enlightenment or awakening. Of course, even in our zazen we have delusive thoughts, desires, and emotions. And so we let go of them. This letting go is transformation. Our life is no longer personal, and we live out the universal life force. This is the meaning of zazen.

BOTH SIDES

Avalokiteśvara Bodhisattva
When practicing deeply the prajñā-pāramitā
Perceived that all five skandhas are empty
And was saved from all suffering and distress.

Avalokiteśvara was practicing prajñā-pāramitā. We must be careful to remember that prajñā-pāramitā is something to be practiced. Prajñā (wisdom) is not simply a matter of how our brain works. In *Shōbōgenzō* "Maka Hannya Haramitsu," Dōgen Zenji refers to the "whole body's clear seeing."[77] He is reminding us that this wisdom should be practiced with our whole body and mind. Seeing with the whole body and mind means we become one with the emptiness of the five skandhas. These five skandhas are nothing other than our body and mind. When we sit zazen our whole body and mind becomes nothing other than the whole body and mind that is empty. The five skandhas become five skandhas that are completely empty. Zazen is itself prajñā. The five skandhas (whole body and mind) clearly see the five skandhas (whole body and mind). There is no separation between subject and object.

In early Buddhism body and mind are described as being made up of the five skandhas (aggregates) to emphasize that there is no fixed ego. The five skandhas are form (Skt., *rūpa*; Jap., *shiki*), sensation (*vedanā*, *ju*), perception (*saṃjñā*, *so*), impulse or formation (*saṃskāra*, *gyo*), and consciousness (*vijñāna*, *shiki*). The first, form, refers to material things that have shape and color. In the case of human beings, form is body. The other four skandhas are mental functions. When we encounter an object we receive sensory stimulation, which may be pleasant, unpleasant, or neutral. This stimulation caused by objects we call sensation. The Chinese character for *ju* means "reception." This received sensation creates images or representations in our mind. We call this perception. Impulse (*saṃskāra*) is the power of mental formation, that is, will or volition. Based on sensation, perception, and impulse, the object is recognized and judgments are formed. This is the function of the fifth skandha, consciousness.

The Buddha taught that since we are made up of these five constantly changing skandhas, there is no fixed ego, and we are impermanent. Later, in Abhidharma philosophy, Buddhist scholars believed that we are egoless but that these five skandhas exist in an independent, fixed way. Mahāyāna Buddhists criticized this theory. The *Prajñāpāramitā*

Sutras said that these five skandhas are also empty. This emptiness is another way of describing impermanence and egolessness.

We can be saved from suffering because the cause of suffering is our selfish desire based on an ignorance of impermanence and egolessness. We cling to our body and mind and try to control everything, but we cannot. When we truly see the emptiness (impermanence and egolessness) of the five skandhas of our body and mind, we see that there is nothing to cling to. So we open our hands. This is liberation from the ego-attachment that causes suffering.

The sutra continues:

> "O Śāriputra, form does not differ from emptiness;
> Emptiness does not differ from form.
> That which is form is emptiness;
> That which is emptiness, form.
> The same is true of feelings, perceptions, impulses, and
>   consciousness."

The five elements of our life are all empty, and emptiness is those five skandhas. The phrases "form is emptiness" and "emptiness, form" say that "since *A* is not different from *B*, and *B* is not different from *A*, then *A* is *B*, and *B* is *A*." This is very simple. But this sutra has a more complex meaning. The longer version of the *Heart Sutra* reads:

> "There are the five skandhas, and those he sees in their own-
>   beings as empty.
> Hear, O Śāriputra, form is emptiness and the very emptiness
>   is form;
> emptiness is no other than form, form is no other than
>   emptiness;
> whatever is form, that is emptiness, whatever is emptiness,
>   that is form."[78]

The first sentence says that there are five skandhas, and they are empty. This sentence is very important to our understanding of the *Heart Sutra*. The *Āgama Sutras*, a collection of early Buddhist discourses similar to the Pāli Nikāyas, say that all phenomenal beings are aggregates of causes and conditions without any fixed entity. According to the *Āgama Sutras*, the Buddha affirmed that there is no ego, and we are merely collections of five skandhas. "Ego" means something unchanging and singular that owns and operates this body and mind. The Buddha taught there is no such thing. In Sanskrit "ego" is called *ātman*. To express the reality of no-ātman (*anātman*) he stated that only the five skandhas exist, and these various elements form the temporal being that is a person. Later, Abhidharma philosophers believed that the ego or ātman doesn't exist but that the five skandhas exist as substance. They analyzed these five skandhas into seventy-five elements. A particular combination of elements enables this being to exist as a unique person, and when one of the elements changes, this body and mind changes or even disappears. It's like atomic theory. Science says this body, desk, or notebook can be divided into smaller and smaller pieces until we eventually come to something that cannot be divided. Greek philosophers called this the atom. The conventional concept of the individual is analogous to the Greek concept of the atom. In the last century we learned that the atom can be split. It is no longer the ultimate particle. The *Heart Sutra* says the same thing about people. It says that each being is made up of five skandhas, five categories of elements, and these are empty. This line in the sutra is a criticism of the Abidharma philosophy that maintained the five skandhas exist as fixed substance.

Mahāyāna Buddhists criticized the Abhidharma idea of the self-nature of the skandhas. They believed the five skandhas or elements are empty, that they don't really exist. The skandhas are dependent on cause and conditions and have no existence independent from other things. In fact, nothing exists except in relationship with all other beings. This fundamental teaching of the Buddha is called interdependent origination.

Nāgārjuna was one of the greatest Mahāyāna philosophers. His Examination of the Four-Fold Noble Truth in *Mūlamadhyamakakārikā* is helpful in understanding these lines. He identified two levels of truth. The Dharma as taught by the Buddha is not some kind of objective reality. It is the reality of our own lives based on two truths, relative and absolute. He said, "Those who don't know the distinction between the two truths cannot understand the profound nature of the Buddha's teaching" (24:9).[79] The profound nature of the Buddha's teaching is prajñā, the Buddha's wisdom. In order to understand the Buddha's wisdom, we have to clearly understand this distinction between absolute and relative truth.

Nāgārjuna continues, "Without relying on everyday common practices (i.e., relative truths), the absolute truth cannot be expressed. Without approaching the absolute truth, nirvana cannot be attained" (24:10). Here "common practices" means relative truth, the way we usually think in our day-to-day lives. For instance, "I am a man. My name is Shohaku Okumura. I am a Buddhist priest. I was born in Japan and came to America. I have two children." This is our everyday way of explaining who we are. As a teacher, I have responsibilities and now I'm giving a talk. This is common practice, a relative truth. When I say I am Japanese that means I'm not an American. "My name is Shohaku Okumura" means I'm not someone else. "I'm a man" means I'm not a woman. These definitions are relative.

Nāgārjuna says that the absolute truth cannot be expressed without relying on relative truth. The absolute truth is beyond words, which are relative. That is śūnyatā or emptiness. That is prajñā. Without approaching the absolute truth, nirvana cannot be attained. As long as we stay only in the relative truth, in conventional ways of thinking, we cannot move toward nirvana. Nirvana is the most peaceful foundation of our life. In the realm of relative thinking, this body and mind change with each new encounter or situation. We are always thinking about how to behave in this situation, always adjusting ourselves. Often a situation is competitive, and we have to be careful, either to defend ourselves or become aggressive. It's a restless way of life. Nirvana is beyond the relativity of subject and object, teacher and student, customer and shop clerk.

Nāgārjuna continues, "We declare that whatever is relational origination is śūnyatā. It is a provisional name [i.e., thought construction] for the mutuality [of being] and, indeed, it is the middle path" (24:18). "Relational origination" is a synonym for interdependent origination. Everything is interconnected, and because of certain linked causes and conditions this person or this thing exists for awhile. This is not a substance; it is called śūnyatā or emptiness. Because of relational origination, nothing exists independently. The elements of this provisional existence are called the five skandhas. The idea of the five skandhas as fixed and the idea of emptiness contradict each other. If the five skandhas exist independently and permanently, there is no emptiness; if all is really emptiness, there are no fixed five skandhas. This simple sentence in the *Heart Sutra* is important to understand.

Form, as we've seen, is one of the five skandhas. In the case of human beings, it means our bodies. To say this body is empty means it doesn't actually exist. In a sense, "form is emptiness" means that form is not form. "Emptiness" means there is no form, and "form" means there is form. So this is not a simple logic at all. Nāgārjuna says that whatever is relational origination is śūnyatā. Emptiness, like all words, is a provisional name without substance that can exist and has validity only in relation to other words.

Form, feelings, perceptions, impulses, and consciousness—all five skandhas—are provisional names: names without substance. They are thought-constructions created by our minds. Everything is simply a provisional name. "Shohaku" is a provisional name. "Priest" is a provisional name. "Japanese" is also a provisional name. All of these are simply provisional names for "the mutuality of beings." This mutuality of beings means that nothing can exist by itself, but only in relationship with other elements. This means everything is empty; everything is merely a provisional name that exists temporarily as a collection of the five skandhas. This way of viewing things, beyond the duality of "independent being" and "nonbeing," is the middle path.

Nāgārjuna stated there are two levels of truth: absolute truth (śūnyatā) and conventional truth (provisional being). He said we must see reality from both sides. We must see it as śūnyatā and as a provisional name. This is the middle path. By seeing reality from both sides we can see without being caught up in either side. The *Heart Sutra* says, "Form is not different from emptiness." This means form is a tentative or a provisional name. This person Shohaku Okumura is just a provisional name and doesn't actually exist. That means emptiness. So form is not different from emptiness. This is one way of seeing. This is negation of form, negation of this being. This being looks like existence but isn't.

By negating independent being, we become free from attachment to this body and mind. This is a most important point. If we don't see the reality of emptiness, we cannot become free from clinging to this tentative being that is defined by relative concepts. Through the wisdom of seeing this being as empty and impermanent, we can free ourselves from clinging. This is the meaning of "form is emptiness." To see that form is emptiness means to negate attachment to this collection of five skandhas. Even though we cling to this body and mind, sooner or later it is scattered. If we really see the reality of emptiness, we are free from ego attachment. This is the meaning of the sentence "Form does not differ from emptiness." This is the way to negate our relative perceptions and open our eyes to absolute reality.

However, freedom from attachment to this body and mind is not enough. Once we see the absolute reality that is emptiness, we must return to tentative reality. This is the meaning of "Emptiness does not differ from form." When we really see the emptiness, we become free from this body and mind. That's okay, but then how shall we live? We cannot live within the absolute truth because without distinctions there is no way to choose. Without making choices we cannot live. To choose a path, we have to define who we are and what we want to do. To accomplish things, to go somewhere, we have to make distinctions. If we have no direction, there is no way to go. So to live out our daily lives we have to return to relative truth.

Nāgārjuna also said, "A wrongly conceived śūnyatā can ruin a slow-witted person. It is like a badly seized snake or a wrongly executed incantation" (24:11). If we don't understand emptiness as the middle path, we can become irresponsible. Freedom and irresponsibility can be the same thing. But the Buddha's compassion means to be free and yet responsible to everything. It is compassion without attachment. Through wisdom we see that everything is empty. Through compassion we return to relative truth. We must think, "How can I take care of this body and mind to keep them healthy so I can help others?" This is what the Buddha taught. To be responsible to whatever situation surrounds us, we have to become free from emptiness. We have to come back to the relative truth of everyday activities and take care of things. So this is not just a formal, simple logic, *A* is *B* and *B* is *A*. When we say form is emptiness, we negate this body and mind. When we understand that emptiness is form, we negate emptiness. Negate means to let go. To let go of thought means to become free from both sides. Then we can see reality from both perspectives without being attached to either. The wisdom of Avalokiteśvara is the Middle Way that includes both sides. It is not something in between this side and that. From the middle path we see reality from both views, relative and absolute. We simultaneously negate and affirm both sides. To let go of thought means to become free from both perspectives and simply be in the middle (reality).

According to Dōgen Zenji, sitting in zazen posture and letting go of thought is itself the Buddha's wisdom, prajñā. So prajñā is not a particular state of mind or way of thinking. To express this Middle Way, Dōgen Zenji paraphrased the *Heart Sutra* in the chapter of *Shōbōgenzō* called Mahāprajñāpāramita. He said, "Form is emptiness, emptiness is form. Form is form, emptiness is emptiness." When we say, "Form is emptiness," there is still separation between form and emptiness, between relative and absolute. When we really see the middle path we don't need to say, "Form is emptiness" or "Emptiness is form." When we see form, emptiness is already there. We don't need to say, "Form and emptiness are the same." When we say so, we are still comparing form and emptiness and thinking these two are one. This is still a relative way of thinking. So Dōgen Zenji said, "Form is form and emptiness is emptiness." This is our practice of zazen based on Mahāyāna philosophy.

For us as practitioners, a mere understanding of this philosophy is not enough. We must apply this understanding in our everyday activities. We see that we cannot do anything completely by ourselves. We cannot live alone; we are always living with other people and other beings. To work together and live together with other people and beings, we have to negate ourselves. We have to negate this person to see what other people are doing or thinking. This means that we negate the five skandhas and see śūnyatā as it is. When we interact with our environment, we have to express the things happening inside us through our lives. We have to do something. We have to respond to situations and make choices. As Dōgen Zenji said in "Genjōkōan," "To study the Buddha's Way is to study the self. To study the self is to forget the self." To forget the self means to negate this one. By negating this one we see others more clearly. When we negate our egocentricity or personal point of view, we can see things more objectively. We can see the situation as a part of ourselves, and at the same time we see ourselves as a part of the situation. We can choose what to do right now, right here, as this person who is a part of the total situation. That's how we can be responsible to the situation.

This attitude applies to more than our daily lives. Dōgen Zenji said in Shōbōgenzō "Shōji" (Life and Death), "To clarify life and death is the most significant point of practice of the Buddha's students." We see our life and death from both sides and see reality as the Middle Way. Our body and mind is just a collection of five skandhas that is empty and will someday disappear. Sooner or later we will die. To negate the five skandhas is to see emptiness, egolessness, and impermanence. And yet if we see only in this way we may become nihilistic, pessimistic, or irresponsible. We will not live with compassionate hearts. We might think that if sooner or later it will all disappear, why should we strive to accomplish anything? That is the sickness of emptiness.

Then we must return to the relative truth. Although we are empty and sooner or later we disappear, right here and now we are living as reality. We exist right now as a tentative collection of five skandhas. We choose to be responsible to this life at this moment. So there must be some way to live. There must be some direction to follow. This is an important point of our practice. We see reality, the middle path, from both sides and become free from attachment to either. Therefore Dōgen Zenji said in *Shōbōgenzō* "Shōji,"

> When we speak of life, there is nothing other than life; when we speak of death, there is nothing other than death. Therefore, when life comes we just face life. When death comes we just face death. We should not be used by them or desire them. This present life-and-death is the Life of buddha. If we dislike it and try to get rid of it, we would lose the Life of buddha. If we desire to remain [in life-and-death] and attach ourselves to it, we would also lose the Life of buddha.[80]

This is almost impossible for an ordinary person. But that is the path the Buddha or Avalokiteśvara saw and tried to show us. It is very difficult simply to become free from ego attachment. To become free from emptiness is even more difficult. Yet to follow this way of life is our direction as Buddhist practitioners. This is our vow. Somehow I cannot help but follow this way of life. It is my practice. And when I see another person living this way I feel encouraged. If even one person is inspired or encouraged by my practice, I am really happy.

EMPTINESS IN THEORY

The third paragraph of the *Heart Sutra* says:

> "O Śāriputra, all dharmas are marked with emptiness;
>   They do not appear or disappear,
>   Are neither tainted nor pure,
>   Do not increase or decrease."

First I will discuss the philosophical aspects of this passage and then its practical meaning. This passage is very important to Mahāyāna

Buddhism. If we read it superficially, we might think there is something that neither appears nor disappears, is neither tainted nor pure, and neither increases nor decreases. We might think that this passage refers to something that exists beyond the phenomena we see. We think the purpose of our practice is to realize this something beyond phenomena. But this is not Buddhism. There is nothing beyond this phenomenal world in which things are always changing, appearing and disappearing. There is nothing that never appears or disappears. That is the Buddha's teaching.

What does this mean? To understand these lines I think it's helpful to look at Nāgārjuna's dedicating verse in the *Mūlamadhyamakakārikā*. Here he elaborated and refined the philosophy of emptiness. At the very beginning of this piece he wrote:

> I pay homage to the Fully Awakened One,
> the supreme teacher who has taught
> the doctrine of relational origination,
> the blissful cessation of all phenomenal thought
>   constructions.
> (Therein, every event is "marked" by):
> non-origination, non-extinction,
> non-destruction, non-permanence,
> non-identity, non-differentiation,
> non-coming (into being), non-going (out-of-being).[81]

The fully awakened one, the supreme teacher, refers to Shakyamuni Buddha. "Buddha" literally means "awakened one." Relational origination, we've seen, is the same as interdependent origination. It means nothing exists independently, but only in relationship with other things, causes, and conditions. Nothing has substance, self-nature, or independent being. Everything is impermanent, egoless, and always changing. These teachings of Buddha are the same in early Buddhism and Mahāyāna Buddhism.

"Thought constructions" means idle discussion or argument about metaphysical philosophy, the meaning of life, or of this world. The teaching of relational origination, according to Nāgārjuna, puts an end to all idle arguments. "Non-origination" has the same meaning as "not appear" (*fushō*) in Chinese. "Non-extinction" is the same as "not disappear" or, for human beings, birth and death. Nothing can be destroyed and nothing is permanent. Nāgārjuna lists five pairs of dichotomies: birth and death, one and many, identity and differentiation, coming and going, delusion and enlightenment. We could add any dichotomy to the list, and Nāgārjuna would put a "no" in front of it.

This is because we can only think about one side of things. When we think about something we take a point of the view. We form an opinion. We think, "This exists," or "This doesn't exist." We may think, "I am deluded" or "I am enlightened" or "There must be something eternal" or "There is nothing eternal." These are opinions. To form our way of thinking we have to take a side. We cannot function in society without a point of view. If we adopt different points of view at the same time, we are seen as inconsistent and untrustworthy. But according to Nāgārjuna these are all phenomenal thought constructions, idle or meaningless arguments. Whichever side you take it's only a half of reality. Reality is there before taking a view.

According to Nāgārjuna things do not appear or disappear, are neither tainted nor pure, do not increase or decrease. This means we should not think that these things appear at a certain time in the past and stay in this moment and then disappear sometime in the future. For instance, I was born on June 22, 1948. Before that day I didn't exist. On that day I started to exist. I will exist for a certain period of time and then I will disappear. This is a very common way of thinking. It's not a mistake on a conceptual level. But in reality if we look closely at this being, there is nothing that can be called Shohaku. I am no more than a collection of five skandhas, different elements.

This body and mind is like a waterfall. A river flows past a place where there is a change of height, and a waterfall is formed. Yet there is no such thing as a waterfall, only a continuous flow of water. A waterfall is not a thing but rather a name for a process of happening. This body and mind is like a waterfall. We cannot distinguish where the waterfall starts and ends because it is a continuous process. Since there is no "I," no substance called Shohaku Okumura, I cannot say "I" will disappear. This is the meaning of "do not appear or disappear." It refers to this body and mind and to all beings. It is not about mysterious beings beyond the phenomenal world. This is very clear, ordinary reality, and yet we cannot define it, so it is strange and wondrous. We see things happening every moment, and yet we cannot grasp them. That is the meaning of wondrous dharma. We cannot grasp it, and yet it is not mysterious. It is ordinary things happening every day. For instance, this is a book, this is a desk, this is my robe, and this is Shohaku Okumura. These are like definitions we can find in the dictionary. We think these things exist in a fixed way because they are defined in the dictionary, but it's not true.

In another part of *Mūlamadhyamakakārikā* Nāgārjuna says, "Those of low intelligence [i.e., inferior insight], who see only the existence and nonexistence of things, cannot perceive the wonderful quiescence of things."[82] By "low intelligence people" he means people who lack wisdom. Existence and nonexistence is the same kind of dichotomy he referred to in the dedicatory verse and in the *Heart Sutra*. This is our usual way of thinking: good or bad, right or wrong, rich or poor. But wonderful quiescence is the reality of all beings before being processed by our conceptual thinking.

Pingala, a late third- or early fourth-century Indian scholar, wrote a commentary on *Mūlamadhyamakakārikā*. We know nothing about who Pingala was, but Kumārajīva translated Nāgārjuna's *Mūlamadhyamakakārikā* together with Pingala's commentary and gave it the title "Zhonglun" (Jap., Chūron, The Thesis of the Middle). In it he says, "When people have not yet attained the way, they don't see the true form of all beings. Because of causes and conditions of attachment to their own limited views, they engage in various meaningless arguments."[83] Our views are always shaped and limited by our experiences, and we are very attached to them. For example, if we have an experience with someone that leads us to believe this person is not honest or trustworthy, we make a judgment and decide this is not a good person. We then cling to this definition or preconception. We form stereotypes about people, countries, everything. These stereotypes are the basis of our usual way of seeing things. Nāgārjuna believed that these phenomenal thought constructions were the basis for meaningless arguments.

Pingala continues, "When they see something appear they call it 'being' and take it as existence. When they see something disappear they think it perishes and call it nonexistence." When we encounter something we form a view, idea, or conception. This is our usual way of life. It is not a matter of good or bad, but rather the way we are. So it follows that "When a wise person sees something appear, he extinguishes the view of nonexistence. When a wise person sees something disappear he extinguishes the view of existence." We usually form a view when we experience something. But Pingala says that when a wise person meets someone or experiences something he extinguishes, or lets go of, his preconceptions. So each encounter becomes an opportunity to transform our preexisting ideas and to set aside our biases and preconceptions. Each experience becomes an opportunity to see a fresh new world. This is an important point. The difference between ordinary and wise is not a difference in the quality of a person's intelligence. It's a difference in the attitude with which they meet things in their daily lives. We form ideas that become fixed as the basis of our identity. This identity, this way of thinking or system of values, becomes a limitation and we are imprisoned by it. It's difficult to open our perception again because it becomes very stiff, and we become very stubborn. To be a wise person, according to this commentary, we must negate, break, or open up our premade system of values every time we experience something. This is not something mysterious. It's very clear.

"Therefore, although a wise person sees all beings, the person sees them as phantoms or dreams," says Pingala. Ordinary beings and wise people see things in the same way, but their attitude is different. Nothing is fixed. No one is necessarily a bad person (always bad) or a good one (always good). There is no fixed nature because we are always changing. In a sense, each time we meet a person, we meet a different person. Because I am changing, and the other person is also changing, we can appreciate each meeting as a fresh new one.

An important phrase that conveys the spirit of having tea together in the tea ceremony is "Ichi go ichi ye." The phrase *ichi go* means "one time," "one occasion," or "one life." *Ichi ye* means "one meeting." Each meeting or encounter happens only once. We cannot meet with the same person twice. Each meeting, each moment, is very significant and precious because it is unique. To see things as phantoms or dreams doesn't mean they are not important. Because reality is like a phantom or dream, we have to appreciate it. Since everything is changing, since nothing stays forever, this is the only time we can meet. We have to savor each moment.

Pingala says, "A wise person extinguishes even a view of the undefiled way." "Undefiled way" refers to the Buddha's teaching. A wise person extinguishes, negates, and goes beyond any view, opinion, or understanding of the Buddha's teaching. This point is crucial to an understanding of the next part of the *Heart Sutra*, which appears to negate almost all of the Buddha's teaching. To negate means to free oneself from any view, even a Buddhist one. If we take the Buddha's teaching as an opinion or view, it's no different from the preconceptions we have about other things. In Buddhism it's said that ordinary people are bound by iron chains. If we liberate ourselves from these iron chains, we are still bound by the gold chain of Buddhism. We are still not free. We have to become free even of the Buddha's teaching, even of enlightenment. That is the Buddha's teaching.

This is the reason Dōgen Zenji says we shouldn't seek after enlightenment. In "Fukanzazengi" (Universal Recommendation of Zazen) he says that when we sit, we should give up even our aspiration to become a buddha. This is important. It's not a matter of delusion or enlightenment but attitude. It's a matter of whether we are caught by our desires, expectations, and fixed ideas. To become free from these things is our zazen. To extinguish our views is to let go of thought.

Pingala's conclusion is that "unless one sees the Buddha's peaceful dharma by extinguishing views, we see being and nonbeing." The Buddha's peaceful dharma is reality itself free of all dichotomies. This reality is blissful and precious. We don't usually see reality itself but only our preconceptions: things we like or dislike, something useful or useless, something desirable or undesirable. We divide reality into categories, running after things we desire and trying to avoid those we detest. Our life becomes a matter of chasing and escaping. That is our usual way of life. In this kind of life there is no stable foundation, no peace, because we are always escaping from or chasing after something. There's no time to rest, to just calm down and be right here. Letting go of thought in zazen for ten minutes or for a day or for five days is very precious. The blissful dharma, true reality, is revealed when we let go and become free from our fixed views. When the *Prajñāpāramitā Sutra* says things do not appear or disappear, are neither tainted nor pure, do not increase or decrease, the sutra doesn't refer to things outside us. It means that when we refrain from viewing and judging things in dualistic ways, our attitudes toward external things are transformed. The relation between things inside of us and our perception of the world is changed. The perceptions of the external things cease to be the objects of our desires and self-centered views. We are released from the habitual association between subject and object. Then things begin to reveal themselves as they are. When our attitude toward each thing in the world is shifted as Pingala described, our way of life is transformed. The *Heart Sutra* does not say that there is something mysterious which neither appears nor disappears, is neither tainted nor pure, neither increases nor decreases.

My teacher, Uchiyama Roshi, wrote a poem about life and death when he was about seventy years old and very sick. For fifty years he had tuberculosis. He'd been living with sickness almost all of his life. Several times a year he bled from his lung. He was facing death. He felt that was his practice. Facing life and death is the most important challenge for the Buddhist practitioner. This is one of his poems.

SAMĀDHI OF THE TREASURE OF RADIANT LIGHT

Though poor, never poor.
Though sick, never sick.
Though aging, never aging.
Though dying, never dying.
Reality prior to division.
Herein lies unlimited depth.

Radiant light is a metaphor or symbol of the Buddha's life. Uchiyama Roshi was poor. He never worked just to earn money. He contrasts dichotomies—life and death, poverty and wealth, sickness and health—with the unlimited depth of reality prior to division. Our practice is to deepen our understanding and experience. This is what we do in zazen by letting go of thought. Our sitting practice is the practice of prajñā-pāramitā, which enables us to actually transform our way of life. If our lives are based on dichotomies like good and bad, we chase after good things and run from bad things. We are concerned about whether we are good or not. If we think we are good, then life is worth living. If we think we are bad, then life is just a mistake. This dualistic thinking makes our life rigid and narrow.

No matter what mistakes we make, we can start over because everything is impermanent. We can change. We can change the direction of our life. That is the way we transform our life, our thinking, and our views. According to Dōgen Zenji, sitting in zazen and letting go of everything is the key to shifting the basis of our life. By sitting and letting go we become free, even from the Buddha's doctrine. We are not deluded, and we are not enlightened. So we just keep practicing. That is the meaning of shikantaza, or just sitting. If you feel good or enlightened in certain conditions, and you cling to this experience, you are deluded. You are already stagnating in enlightenment. So we open our hands and keep practicing. This is the meaning of just sitting, of continuous practice. There is no one who is deluded or enlightened.

Sitting is itself enlightenment. This is why Dōgen Zenji said that we need to arouse bodhi-mind, moment by moment, billions of times.

EMPTINESS IN PRACTICE

> "O Śāriputra, all dharmas are marked with emptiness;
> They do not appear or disappear,
> Are neither tainted nor pure,
> Do not increase or decrease."

This paragraph was discussed above in relation to Nāgārjuna's sayings in *Mūlamadhyamakakārikā*. It refers not to something outside ourselves but rather to the way we see things, the way we grasp things using our intellect. Nāgārjuna says that our usual way of seeing and thinking is based on mental formations or thought constructions that he describes as meaningless argument. This is an important point in Mahāyāna philosophy that is difficult to understand. I will discuss it from the perspective of my own experience.

Buddhist teachers from Shakyamuni Buddha to Nāgārjuna to Dōgen Zenji address the reality of our life, the true form of all beings. The problem is that when we think about this reality, when we try to grasp it, we lose it. We live inside reality. We are never apart from it, and yet we almost always lose sight of it. To discuss something we have to take a particular point of view. This is the problem.

A long time ago I read a book on logic that included many famous paradoxes. One of the most interesting was a story about a king who told his retainers that no liars should be allowed into his kingdom. He built a barrier at the border. The guard asked everyone who wanted to enter the kingdom whether he was a liar or an honest person. Since everyone wanted to get into the country, they all said they were not liars, except for one who admitted, "I am a liar." The guard didn't know what to do. If this person really was a liar, then his statement was true; he was telling the truth and therefore he was not a liar. If he was not a liar, his statement was false, which meant he was a liar. Either way there could be no conclusion. Our usual way of thought presents a similar paradox. It doesn't really fit reality, so we often make poor decisions.

This story is an example of emptiness. Before we decide whether someone is a liar or an honest person, we have to define these terms. A liar is a person who tells lies, of course, and yet this is not enough. A liar is a person who *always* lies, and an honest person *always* tells the truth. This is the basic definition of a liar and an honest person. When we use these definitions, we should be consistent. A liar always lies. If a liar tells the truth, "liar" doesn't apply. But in reality there is no one who always tells lies. We tell lies to deceive other people but if we speak only lies, we cannot deceive anyone. If someone always lies, I'll know that the opposite of what he says is true. In fact, there is no one so honest he never tells a lie. If we think someone is weird, we don't say, "You are weird." We might say instead, "You are unique." No one speaks only lies or only the truth.

In reality there are no liars and no completely honest people. Thinking based on such definitions is an example of a thought construction, or meaningless argument. Such thinking misses the reality that we all lie to some degree. And yet there are some really honest people, and there are some liars. As Buddhists, we have to try to avoid lying because it is one of our precepts. If we interpret the precept of not lying with strict logic, we cannot be Buddhists. We can never completely follow the Buddha's precept. So we have to inquire deeply into reality. This is not a matter of pure logic but of our attitude. This is our way of life, the Buddha's truth, and the true form of human beings. In Buddhism the true form of all beings, the reality of our lives, is not based on simple logic. The wisdom of seeing emptiness is to see both sides. There are no liars and no honest people, and yet we try to avoid lying. There are two sides, and to see things from both is prajñā.

Our thoughts, values, and attitudes are based on our work, education, and experiences. We must have some yardstick to live in society. But this yardstick is not absolute. I was born in Japan and grew up in Japanese society and cannot be completely free of a Japanese way of thinking and behaving. I don't think that I have to become American, or that you should become Japanese. We have to understand that neither the American nor the Japanese way of thought is absolutely right. There is another way of thinking, of acting, of valuing things. It is the way of letting go of thought.

This is what we do in our zazen. We become flexible. We have to let go of our evaluations and discriminations, or we cannot really connect with people from other traditions or cultures. In the past there were separate cultures that didn't meet on a daily basis. Our modern world is becoming one society. Here in the United States many different kinds of people live together. If we hold on to our yardsticks and negate other people's ways of doing things, we will fight. We will feel that we have to eliminate those who don't agree with us. But when we let go of our way of thinking and become even a little bit free of our yardsticks, we have room to accept other ways of thinking. Our lives become broader and richer.

The United States is the only foreign country I have lived in so far. Japan and America are special countries for me. My ideas about America have changed many times. I was born three years after World War II. My first memory of America is when I was about four or five years old and was told that my family lost all its wealth when the Americans bombed Osaka in March 1945. My family had lived in the center of Osaka for three hundred years, and they had accumulated some wealth. In one night we lost everything. I remember the only thing we had after the bombing was a statue of the Buddha, quite a large one for a lay family to own. I heard that my family had a shrine for this statue. I never saw it, but it must have been a large building. I also knew that my uncle was killed during the war. In my mind these memories created anger, hatred, and fear. In elementary school I heard that Japan was very poor and survived only because of help from America. America was a very prosperous country, while ours was very poor. America seemed like paradise, and we hoped to follow the American way. I then had two completely different, almost opposite views of America. America became something very positive, something we had to study as an ideal of democracy, science, technology, and materialistic consumer culture.

My generation studied the American way of life, production, and system of values. Japan became much too American, almost more American than America. When I was a high school student during the Vietnam War, the Japanese mass media presented American imperialism as the enemy of humanity. This was another completely different idea. Later, when I studied history, I learned that the Japanese army did terrible things in China, Korea, Taiwan, and other Asian countries during World War II. My understanding deepened. Anger, hatred, and fear turned into a kind of sadness about humanity. All human beings have the same problems. America, Japan, all nations, and all individuals have the potential to do terrible things. To see things from different points of view is good. Finally I came to America to live in 1975. I lived in Massachusetts for about five years and experienced the American way of life. I found that there are many kind people and some who are not so kind, just as in Japan. People smile, laugh, cry, and scream the same ways in Japan and America. I think there is no big difference.

To deepen our understanding we must negate our concepts. When we negate our beliefs and preconceptions we can see things from other points of view or a wider perspective. We should try to avoid grasping with our ready-made preconceptions or prejudices. If we open our hands and perceive things carefully, closely, then we can see other perspectives. This is opening the hand of thought. This is what we do in our zazen.

This practice of letting go of thought enables us to see people and things with fresh eyes. Right now we have many flowers outside. When we see them we think they are beautiful. But when we look closely at a flower, it's more than beautiful, it's something really wondrous. Why is this flower so beautiful? Why does this flower bloom like this? Why is it that I can appreciate this beauty? There is surprise when we encounter things with fresh eyes. When we see the flower without thinking "This is beautiful" or "What is this flower called?" we really meet the flower itself. When we see the flower without thinking, we find that our life, this body and mind, and the life of the flower are the same life. There's no separation. We can say, "I am blooming there as a flower." To extinguish our views, to let go of thought, or to negate our own way of thinking is not negative. It makes our life very vivid and dynamic.

To return to the passage:

"O Śāriputra, all dharmas are marked with emptiness;
They do not appear or disappear,
Are neither tainted nor pure,
Do not increase or decrease."

If we read this carelessly, we may think dharma is somehow beyond appearance and disappearance, beyond taint and purity, or increase and decrease. We might assume there is something formless beyond phenomena. But the passage shouldn't be understood in this way. For example, this bookstand was made in the past by someone using pieces of wood and today it exists as a bookstand. Someday it will break and disappear. This is a temporal form, a phenomenon. When we hear "since all dharmas are marked with emptiness, they do not appear or disappear," we might imagine there is "something" beyond the phenomenon, in this case, the bookstand. We might believe this something is a noumenon which does not either appear or disappear, something that is permanent. We imagine this something beyond form is the true nature of this tentative phenomenon, and that to see this true nature of emptiness is enlightenment. In other words, we think emptiness is separate from form. This is not what is meant by the *Heart Sutra*. Emptiness is simply how form is. This bookstand is itself emptiness. We should not seek emptiness beyond this concrete bookstand.

"Neither tainted nor pure, do not increase or decrease" should be understood in the same way. This bookstand is neither tainted nor pure. We should not think that there is something neither tainted nor pure that exists beyond this bookstand. Some people think that enlightenment is to see and become one with something formless and permanent beyond concrete things which have form and are impermanent. But the *Heart Sutra* says, "Form is emptiness, emptiness is form." We should not look for emptiness beyond form. There is nothing beyond phenomena. Phenomena are emptiness.

In "Genjōkōan," Dōgen Zenji says, "Conveying oneself toward all things to carry out practice-enlightenment is delusion. All things coming and carrying out practice-enlightenment through the self is realization."[84] Delusion and enlightenment depend on the relationship between ourselves and other beings. We cannot say this individual person is either enlightened or deluded because there is no person without relationship to others. Practice-enlightenment is not some mysterious experience. It is as clear and obvious as everyday reality.

"Genjōkōan" continues, "When the Dharma has not yet fully penetrated body and mind, one thinks one is already filled with it. When the Dharma fills body and mind, one thinks something is [still] lacking."[85] When we are not filled completely with Dharma we grasp our self as the center of the world. We think this self is an absolute person who can see things objectively and understand them as they are. This belief occupies some part of our being, so the Dharma cannot completely permeate this body and mind. Therefore, we have to empty ourselves. Then the Dharma suffuses us and starts to fill the Dharma itself. When the Dharma completely pervades this body and mind, we feel something is lacking. Our way of thinking, our yardstick, is not complete or absolute, so we feel inadequate. We search more deeply. This is prajñā, to become free from our own yardstick and see things from a broader or deeper perspective. This is the wisdom that sees emptiness. There is nothing we can hold on to, nothing we can grasp. We open our hearts.

Dōgen Zenji used an analogy: "For example, when we sail a boat into the ocean beyond sight of land and our eyes scan [the horizon in] the four directions, it simply looks like a circle. No other shape appears. This great ocean, however, is neither round nor square. It has inexhaustible characteristics. [To a fish] it looks like a palace; [to a heavenly being] a jeweled necklace. [To us] as far as our eyes can see, it looks like a circle. All the myriad things are like this. Within the dusty world and beyond, there are innumerable aspects and characteristics; we only see or grasp as far as the power of our eye of study and practice can see.

When we listen to the reality of myriad things, we must know that there are inexhaustible characteristics in both ocean and mountains, and there are many other worlds in the four directions."[86]

The ocean is not merely round. It has many other characteristics and aspects. In Buddhism it is said that the heavenly beings see water as jewels. There are many ways to perceive a single thing. The ocean is just one example of the myriad things we encounter in our lives. All people and things exist in ways other than how we see them. The phrase Dōgen Zenji uses is *san gaku gen riki*, meaning the power of the eye attained through practice. We develop the ability to see things clearly, closely, and deeply through the practice of letting go of thought. In Dōgen Zenji's writing, practice means zazen.

This is a very concrete description of emptiness in our practice. According to Dōgen Zenji our practice of zazen is the practice of prajñā that sees emptiness. Empty means ungraspable. We open our hand and see things from other perspectives by letting go of our own personal yardsticks. The Mahāyāna Buddhists who wrote the *Prajñāpāramitā Sutras* considered the *Heart Sutra* to be a sutra of transformation of the self. This is the way we transform ourselves, transform our way of life, enabling us to be flexible and see things without attachment. It is not mere insight or wisdom but rather a practice. Practice in the form of zazen is the foundation of our life. But since we cannot sit twenty-four hours a day, we have to learn how to encounter all things in our daily lives. We have to learn about the self, about our body and mind. We have to practice together with others. To live and practice together with all beings is the bodhisattva Way. This practice enriches our lives.

DONGSHAN'S NOSE

"Therefore in emptiness, no form,
　No feelings, no perceptions, no impulses, no consciousness;
　No eyes, no ears, no nose, no tongue, no body, no mind;
　No color, no sound, no smell, no taste, no touch, no object
　　of mind;

No realm of eyes and so forth until no realm of mind
consciousness."

This is one of the most popular parts of the *Heart Sutra*. It says there
is nothing. I started to study Buddhism when I entered Komazawa
University. The first thing we had to do was to memorize the dharma
numbers. For instance, there are the five skandhas: form, sensation, perception, impulse, and consciousness (in Japanese, *shiki ju sō gyō shiki*).
Also, there are six sense organs—eyes, ears, nose, tongue, body, and
mind. The eye senses shape and color; the ear hears sound; the nose
smells; the tongue tastes; with our skin we touch. Each of these six
sense organs has sense objects, and these two sets of six are called the
twelve sense fields.

When sense organs encounter objects, something happens within
our mind. These interactions are called the six consciousnesses, *roku
shiki*. The sutra uses the word "realm." For instance, the realm of the eyes
is eye-consciousness, or *genshiki*. I think "realm" is not a good word here.
The word used is *dhātu*, which in this case means element, not realm.
When the eye encounters shape or color, eye-consciousness arises but
initially no judgment is made. It's just a sensation, which then becomes
a perception. Impulse or formation is a process of making definitions,
conceptions, and judgments, which finally become consciousness.
Each sense organ and object gives rise to a corresponding consciousness. These are called the eighteen dhātu, the eighteen elements of our
lives. So there are five skandhas, twelve sense fields, and eighteen dhātu.

In the next sentence the *Heart Sutra* says, "No ignorance and also
no extinction of it, and so forth until no old age and death and also no
extinction of them." These are the twelve links of causation. "Ignorance"
is the first link, "old age and death" is the twelfth, and the phrase "and
so forth until" simply means that all the intervening links are likewise
negated. Next, "No suffering, no origination, no stopping, no path."
This refers to the four noble truths.

These dharma numbers were the first things I learned when I began
studying Buddhist teachings at the age of nineteen. But the *Heart Sutra*

seemed to contradict what I had learned. It said there are no such things. I was surprised and confused. What did this mean? If the people who wrote the *Heart Sutra* wanted to negate the Buddha's teaching, they should have said they were not Buddhists. But they claimed to be true Buddhists. Now I realize that this was a childish opinion. If you study the history of Buddhism, especially Mahāyāna Buddhism, you see that this really is the Buddha's teaching. But as a nineteen-year-old I didn't understand at all.

Later I read the biography of a Chinese Zen master, Dongshan Liangjie (Tōzan Ryōkai). Dongshan was the founder of the Caodong (Sōtō) school in China. This is a translation from *Denkōroku* (*The Record of Transmitting the Light*) by Keizan Jōkin.

> While still young, [Dongshan] read the *Heart Sutra* with a teacher. When he reached the place where it said, "There is no eye, ear, nose, tongue, body, or mind," he suddenly felt his face with his hand. He asked his teacher, "I have eyes, ears, nose, tongue, and the rest. Why does the scripture say that they do not exist?"[87]

That was Dongshan's original question. His biography says that Dongshan's first teacher was amazed by his question and knew immediately that he was an unusual person. The teacher knew he couldn't be this boy's teacher and sent him to a better instructor. I was happy to know that Dongshan had the same question that I did. It's true we have a nose, eyes, and so forth. Why does the *Heart Sutra* say we have no such things? This is a very simple, childish question, but if you don't understand this point the *Heart Sutra* is incomprehensible.

The longer version of the *Heart Sutra* I introduced above begins:

> At that time also the Holy Lord Avalokita, the Bodhisattva, the great being, coursed in the course of the deep perfection of wisdom; he looked down from on high, and he saw

the five skandhas, and he surveyed them as empty in their own-being.[88]

So the five skandhas exist. Avalokiteśvara saw them. But he didn't see the self or ego. In our everyday lives we think, "I have a body and mind." But what is this "I"? Where is this "I" that thinks it is the owner and operator of this body and mind? Avalokiteśvara saw that there is no "I," only the five skandhas. When the *Heart Sutra* says Avalokiteśvara saw only the five skandhas it means there is no ego, no "I," no self. Only the body and the functions of mind exist.

The *Heart Sutra* also said that Avalokiteśvara saw that the five skandhas are empty. To understand this statement we have to understand something about the history of Buddhism. Three or four hundred years passed between the life of Shakyamuni Buddha and the beginning of Mahāyāna. During this period Buddhist monks studied Buddhist philosophy and established the system called Abhidharma. In Abhidharma philosophy there is no ego, no "I," only the five skandhas and the other elements. There are several ways to categorize these elements. One way is into twelve sense fields, another is into eighteen dhātu. The system of Abhidharma philosophy established in the school known as Sarvāstivādin categorizes dharma into seventy-five elements. As a student of Buddhism, I had to memorize this system. There is another system called Yogācāra that analyzes the dharma into one hundred elements. I tried to memorize them all, with their definitions. Traditionally that's how we studied Buddhist philosophy in Japan.

In the Abhidharma philosophy there is no ego, no substance. Only the dharmas or elements exist, and they never change. The ego or self is just a collection of elements. Abhidharma philosophers believed that the seventy-five dharmas, which cannot be further divided, have existed in the past, exist in the present, and will exist in the future. In the *Heart Sutra* or *Prajñāpāramitā Sutra*, Mahāyāna Buddhists said that even those elements are empty. That is a philosophical way of understanding this passage. There are no eyes because eyes are empty. The objects of eyes, such as color and shape, are empty. Empty means they cannot be grasped. There is no self-being or self-nature, so we cannot grasp the self.

For instance, we think there is something in front of our eyes when we see a notebook. But our eyes are limited. We can see light waves only between ultraviolet and infrared lengths. This is a small part of the spectrum, but other animals can see a broader range. To them this world looks totally different. Our ears can hear only sounds of certain frequencies; dogs hear higher ones. What we think is quiet could be very noisy for dogs. What we see and hear really depends on our capabilities. We believe that what we see exists just the way we see it, but this is an illusion.

Our picture of the world is our reality, but we should understand that it is distorted. This is the meaning of emptiness. Our mind is emptiness. Our sense organs are emptiness. Things outside us are also emptiness. Everything is just illusion. The fact that we live with illusion is our reality. When we really understand this and see how illusion is caused, we can see reality through the illusion. Whatever we see, whatever we grasp with our sense organs and consciousness, is illusion. When we see this we are released from attachment to our limited view, to what we have, to what we think we own. We may not become completely free, but we become less restricted by our limitations.

In our zazen we sit in an upright posture and breathe quietly, smoothly, and deeply into our abdomen. We let go of whatever comes up in our mind. In front of our eyes is nothing but a white wall. This letting go of thought means to become free from what we are grasping, from the objects to which we attach ourselves. This letting go is prajñā or wisdom. It means to become free of our picture of the world caused by our karma. In this way our view becomes a bit broader and deeper. We keep practicing this zazen, sitting and letting go of thought, trying to see things in the most flexible way. This doesn't mean we negate our delusions. We can never negate them; they are our life. But so long as we fail to see that they are illusory and grasp them as reality, we cannot be free. When we really see the emptiness of subject and object, we can be free from grasping, clinging, and greed.

Dōgen Zenji described zazen as *shin jin datsuraku*, or dropping off body and mind. He recorded his conversation with his teacher, the Zen master Rujing (Nyojō), about *shin jin datsuraku* since it was originally Rujing's expression. Rujing explained that "dropping off body and mind" means to become free from the five desires caused by the five objects (eyes, ears, nose, tongue, and body)—he didn't mention mind.

When the five senses encounter an object, desire arises to grasp or hate it. We think, "I want this," "I don't like this," or "I don't care." These are all desires caused by an object contacted through the five sense organs. We are like kids. We see something good, something attractive, and we want it. We try to grasp it. When I go to the supermarket with my kids they run to the toys and take whatever they want and just put it in the cart. When I try to take it back to the shelf, they scream. They are very honest.

We are not so honest. We pretend that we are not attached to things, but deep in our hearts we cling to what we encounter. We are still childish. We cling not to toys but to wealth, reputation, or to very subtle things in our minds. We want to get these things. Sawaki Roshi called this grasping our thief-nature. We also have buddha-nature. All human beings have both buddha-nature and thief-nature. Depending on our actions, we become a thief or a buddha. When we let go of thought and become free from the five desires, we are buddhas.

We must see the emptiness of the subject, of things outside us, of our sense organs, our minds, and the delusions or desires caused by the encounter between the sense organs and objects. When we really truly see the emptiness of all this, we become free from the five desires. We don't get rid of delusion or illusion, but we understand that illusion is illusion and delusion is delusion. We see that we don't have to satisfy all our desires.

Even if we are dissatisfied, that's okay. Just let it go. We can still live. We don't need to satisfy all our desires. We think that when all our desires are satisfied we will be happy, but if not, we can still be happy if we feel oneness with other people and other beings. Other people's happiness then becomes my happiness, other people's pleasure my pleasure, other people's sadness my sadness. Together we can feel a synthesis called in Japanese *hōraku*, joy or delight in the Dharma. It is not a pleasure caused by fulfillment of our individual desires.

Dharma embraces the reality that we are living together with all beings. We are all connected, so there is nothing to gain and nothing to lose. Everything is coming and going in a natural circulation. But human beings create fences or walls between themselves. We calculate how much we gain for our side and how much we lose. When income is greater than expenses, we feel happy. This is a fiction, but in human society it works. We don't need to break or destroy these rules. They're okay. In human society each person should be independent. But in reality all beings are interdependent. Our life has two layers.

We usually see only the surface, where we appear independent. We should keep our record of income and expenses. That's all right. But if we see only this level, our life is no more than a calculation of how much we acquire, how much we lose, and whether we get more or less than others. On a deeper level we are all living together. There are no walls that separate us from other beings. This is seeing emptiness, no separation. The wall is a useful illusion in human society, so we shouldn't negate or destroy it. Still, we should see that this barrier is just a useful fiction, a means to live together with other people. I think this is a practical definition of seeing emptiness.

In his "Maka Hannya Haramitsu" (Mahā Prajñā Pāramitā) commentary on the *Heart Sutra*, Dōgen Zenji quotes his teacher Rujing's poem about a wind bell hung in a Japanese or Chinese temple. I included it in chapter 5, but here it is again:

The whole body is like a mouth hanging in empty space.
Not questioning the winds from east, west, south, or north,
Equally with all of them, speaking of prajñā:
Ding-dong-a-ling ding-dong.[89]

This whole body of the wind bell is ourselves. The winds come from all directions, yet the wind bell never discriminates among them. There are many kinds of wind. Spring brings pleasant breezes. In winter a cold north wind blows. In summer the wind is hot. Wind has a different meaning in each situation, each season. All different kinds of wind come to the wind bell, yet the wind bell never discriminates. It abides "Equally with all of them, speaking of prajñā." The wind bell expresses the prajñā or wisdom that sees the reality of our life. The empty wind bell is hanging in emptiness. When wind comes it makes sound that is prajñā. The last line of the poem, "Ding dong a ling ding dong," is the sound of the bell. This is our practice of zazen. We are empty, but when we encounter others we make a sound that is prajñā. Together with all beings we express prajñā. This poem is an expression of the reality of our zazen and our lives.

No Buddhism

"No ignorance and also no extinction of it, and so forth until
    no old age and death and also no extinction of them;
No suffering, no origination, no stopping, no path."

As we saw above, these lines refer to the twelve links of dependent origination, the four noble truths, and the eightfold noble path. Dependent origination is one of the essential teachings of the Buddha. It can be expressed as follows:

All things arise from a cause.
He who has realized the truth has explained the cause,
And also how they cease to be:
This is what the great samana has taught.[90]

The twelve links of dependent origination are the final and most complete form of the teaching of dependent origination. This teaching does not refer to objective beings in the phenomenal world around us, but rather to the causes and extinction of suffering in our lives. In early Buddhism, it is called dependent origination, but in Mahāyāna Buddhism after Nāgārjuna, it is called interdependent origination. This is for a reason. In the early Buddhist teachings cause and result flow in one direction only. Ignorance is the cause of action, action is the cause of consciousness, and birth is the cause of old age and death. Old age and death depend on birth, but birth does not depend on old age and death. In Nāgārjuna's and other Mahāyāna teachings, however, all things are interdependent on each other.

This teaching does not refer to the objective beings in the phenomenal world around us but rather to the causes of suffering in our own lives and the extinction of them. In the *Heart Sutra* only the first cause (ignorance) and the last condition (old age and death) are mentioned. The other ten causes and conditions are referred to by the words "and so forth until," as we saw above. The phrase "No ignorance and so forth until no old-age and death" is therefore a negation of all twelve causes and conditions. They are listed in an order that parallels transmigration through samsara. The sutra also negates the extinction of all twelve causes from ignorance to old age and death, a progression that parallels movement toward nirvana. In one phrase, "No suffering, no origination, no stopping, no path," the *Heart Sutra* denies the causes and conditions of both samsara and nirvana!

The *Heart Sutra* thus appears to deny the core of the Buddha's teaching. This negation of Buddhism points beyond Buddhism. In other words, Buddhism negating Buddhism is still Buddhism. The *Heart Sutra* says that to truly live the Buddha's teaching, we must negate it. A true student of the Buddha must go beyond the study of his teachings as recorded in the scriptures. When we directly see and experience the Buddha's truth in our own lives, his teachings and the scriptures are irrelevant. The truth becomes a vivid reality. Seeing the reality of our lives with our own eyes through our practice is the wisdom that sees emptiness. This is the wisdom that is called prajñā. This is why prajñā is called the mother of buddhas.

What did the Buddha teach with the twelve links of dependent origination and the four noble truths? Why does the *Heart Sutra* negate all of them? We will start with the four noble truths. The first truth is that everything in samsara is suffering. Suffering (Skt., *duḥkha*) is categorized into eight kinds. The first four are birth, aging, sickness, and death. The fifth is the suffering we feel when we meet someone we don't like. The sixth is what we feel when we are separated from people we like. The seventh results when we can't get what we want. These don't need explanation because we all experience them often in our daily lives. The last kind of suffering is a result of the fact that our life, a collection of the five skandhas, is itself suffering. This is different from the usual sorts of suffering which are the opposites of pleasure, joy, and happiness. It occurs because we can never make the world completely conform to our desires. Because of continually changing causes and conditions, the world around us must change. These constant changes in the world and our lives are not designed to fulfill our desires. Reality is impermanent and egoless, but we are blind to this and strive to satisfy our egocentric desires. Often reality doesn't cooperate with our plans. We cannot really control even our own bodies and minds. Even if we are very lucky and successful, eventually we die and lose everything. This is simple reality.

The second truth is that the basic cause of suffering is desire or "thirst" (Skt., *tṛṣṇā*). It's as if we are thirsty and looking for water. There is always a feeling that something is lacking, and we try to fill that emptiness. We believe that if we get the right thing, we will be satisfied. We constantly search for and run after the things we desire. There is no end to our desires. Even when they are temporarily fulfilled, we suffer because we are afraid of losing what we have. The Buddha's teaching doesn't make sense until we realize that this constant search for satisfaction is itself suffering. When we see that a life spent in pursuit of something better is empty and meaningless, we begin to seek a spiritual path; we begin to practice.

For those who have begun this search, the Buddha taught a third truth—the cessation of suffering. We can live without being pulled about by egocentric desires. How? The fourth truth is the path that leads to cessation of suffering, or nirvana. It is called the eightfold noble path and consists of right view, right thinking, right speech, right action, right livelihood, right effort, right mindfulness, and right meditation.

The lessons of the four noble truths are straightforward. We spend our lives trying to fill the emptiness we feel. When we succeed we are happy and feel as if we are in heaven. When we fail we are miserable as if we are in hell. Our life is a continuous transmigration through the six realms of samsara. The Way leading to release from this suffering is the eightfold noble path.

The twelve links of dependent origination explain the first two of the four noble truths in more detail. In short, our lives become suffering because we act (create karma) based on ignorance and desires. This is the teaching of the four noble truths and the twelve links of dependent origination. Why does the *Heart Sutra* seem to negate all of them? A serious Buddhist practitioner might be offended by this. I don't think the early Mahāyāna Buddhists wrote this to insult other Buddhists. They felt they had to negate these things to sincerely practice the teachings of the Buddha.

There are two reasons for this. First, this negation is a criticism of the Buddhist monastic orders of the first century CE, when Mahāyāna Buddhism emerged. These monks believed that to eliminate ignorance and desire, they had to study and practice in quiet monasteries. In ordinary society they would encounter difficult situations that could cause anger, hatred, or competition. This could lead to transmigration through samsara. To become emancipated from ignorance and desire, monks primarily lived apart from the rest of society. They made no great effort to help laypeople who needed their spiritual guidance. To Mahāyāna Buddhists these monks who studied and practiced the Buddha's teachings only for their own liberation may seem somehow selfish because they appeared to do little for others who were seeking the Way. Mahāyāna Buddhists felt this selfish attitude contradicted the spirit of Shakyamuni Buddha's practice. Many of the Jātaka stories say Shakyamuni Buddha practiced as a bodhisattva for many lifetimes for the sake of all living beings. And the historical Shakyamuni Buddha walked all over India for forty years teaching.

Mahāyāna Buddhists referred to the monks who practiced for their own sake as *Hīnayāna* (the smaller vehicle). Mahāyāna Buddhists believed that practice for the sake of others was more important than eliminating one's own desires. The theoretical basis for this belief is the prajñā of emptiness. "No ignorance and no extinction of it" means the same as "Ignorance is emptiness and emptiness is ignorance." The latter expression is used to negate the five skandhas. Since ignorance and other causes are empty from the beginning, there is no possibility of eliminating them. We should not think of them as enemies and spend our lives trying to kill them. The bodhisattva vow to save all beings is more important. Eliminating the negative is less important than nurturing the positive. We can be free from selfish desires without fighting against them when we are trying to help others. This is a more joyful way to practice.

The second reason is more existential. If we seriously practice the four noble truths and the twelve links of dependent origination, we are faced with a self-contradiction. We begin to study and practice Buddhism when we realize that a life spent pursuing our desires is meaningless. We set forth with an aspiration to find a better way of life and achieve emancipation from the suffering of samsara. This aspiration is called bodhi-mind. When we practice with this Way-seeking mind we are confronted with a terrible contradiction. The aspiration that motivates us to find a way of life free of suffering is merely another selfish desire. We substitute a desire for emancipation or enlightenment for the desire for fame and wealth. The object of desire is different but what is happening inside us is the same. We feel dissatisfaction and are driven to find something to remedy it. Spiritual ambition may be a more sophisticated form of desire, but it's the same principle. When we seriously devote ourselves to practice this becomes a crucial question: Isn't the desire to eliminate ignorance caused by ignorance? In the practice of zazen we have to ask ourselves, "Isn't this practice like pulling the cushion on which we sit from under us?" We can't quit practice and go back to our earlier life of chasing worldly desires because now we know it's useless and hollow. We can go neither forward nor backward. We are at a dead end.

I faced this problem when I returned to Japan in 1981 from the Valley Zendo in Massachusetts. I was thirty-three years old. I had been ordained by Uchiyama Roshi when I was a university student in 1970. After graduation I had practiced with Uchiyama Roshi at Antaiji until 1975 when he retired. There our practice was focused on sitting. We sat nine periods daily for more than a year. We had a five-day sesshin each month except February and August. During sesshin we sat fourteen periods a day for five days. We had no ceremony, no chanting, and no lecture. We just sat.

In 1975 I went to Massachusetts. We bought about six acres of land to establish a small practice center in the woods of western Massachusetts. We built a house and zendo by ourselves. When I first went there the house was still incomplete. We survived the winter with a wood stove but had no electricity on the second floor. We sat and studied by the light of a kerosene lamp. For the first three years three Japanese monks from Antaiji lived there together. We sat four periods daily. We had a one-day sesshin every Sunday and a five-day sesshin each month. We cut trees, pulled out stumps, and made a green garden, all with hand tools. We dug a well with shovels. We used a huge amount of firewood for cooking and heating. Since we had no financial support from Japan, we harvested blueberries and potatoes for local farmers. Later we worked in a tofu factory to support our practice. After five years, I had pain in my neck, shoulders, elbows, and knees from the hard physical labor. I couldn't work, and sitting sesshin was very difficult. I had no health insurance or money for medical treatment. I had to return to Japan.

When I got back I was completely alone. My body was half broken. I had no money, no job, and no place to live or practice. I stayed at my brother's apartment in Osaka for several months while he traveled in the United States. Then I moved to Seitai-an, a small temple in Kyoto, where I lived as a caretaker for three years. Seitai-an is near Antaiji's original site. There I had a monthly five-day sesshin with one of my dharma brothers and cotranslator, Rev. Daitsu Tom Wright, and a few other people. I couldn't practice as I had before because of my physical condition. This was the first time I had lived and practiced alone after ten years at Antaiji and Valley Zendo. I had to give up medical treatments. Initially I did takuhatsu (begging) to raise money for them. But during takuhatsu we hang a *zudabukuro* (a bag) from our necks. This aggravated my neck injury, and my chiropractor said it wouldn't get better if I continued to do takuhatsu. It was a vicious circle. Finally I gave up both takuhatsu and the treatments. I did takuhatsu only a few times a month to survive. When I had extra income I spent it on books.

I had a hard time for several months while I was staying at my brother's apartment before moving to Seitai-an. I was bewildered and didn't know what to do. My biggest problem was that I couldn't practice as I had for the last ten years because of my physical condition. In my twenties I had committed my entire life-energy to practice. Nothing else had seemed important to me. I didn't know how to live outside that way of practice.

While in this situation I read a Japanese translation of *Buddha-carita*, a biography of the Buddha written by the famous Indian Buddhist poet Aśvaghoṣa. When describing the Buddha's experience of seeing the old, sick, and dead outside the gates of his palace, the author refers to the "arrogance of youth and health." This expression hit me. I realized that my belief that practice was the best and most meaningful way of life was nothing more than the "arrogance of youth and health." That's why I was at a loss when I could no longer practice that way because of my health. My previous practice had been an attempt to satisfy a need for status and benefit. I wanted to live a better life than ordinary people. Ever since I read Uchiyama Roshi's book as a high school student and began practicing according to Dōgen Zenji's teachings, I knew that I should not practice zazen for gain. Sawaki Roshi, Uchiyama Roshi's teacher, said that zazen is good for nothing. Dōgen Zenji says that we should practice Buddha Dharma only for the sake of Buddha Dharma, with no expectations. That is shikantaza, or just sitting. I knew all of this and thought I had been practicing with the correct attitude.

Now, when I found myself unable to continue that practice, I was perplexed and depressed. I didn't know what to do. I discovered that I had relied on a practice that was possible only for the young and healthy. I used the teachings of the Buddha, Dōgen Zenji, Sawaki Roshi, and Uchiyama Roshi to fulfill my own desires. This discovery completely broke my "arrogance of youth and health." I saw clearly that my practice had not been for the sake of Buddha Dharma but for my own self-satisfaction. I knew I couldn't continue to practice with this attitude. Nor could I stop practicing and go back to an ordinary life. I was stuck in this situation for some time.

One day something made me sit on a cushion. I had no desire, no reason, no need to sit, but found myself sitting at the apartment by myself. It was very peaceful. I didn't sit because of the Buddha's teaching. I didn't need a reason to sit; I just sat. There was no need to compete with others or with myself. Thereafter I didn't need to sit as often as I had before. I could sit just as much as my physical condition allowed. Finally I felt free of my understanding of the Buddha's teachings and my desire to be a good monk. I felt free to be myself and nothing more. I was still a deluded, ordinary human being with ignorance and desires. But when I just sat and let go of thoughts, I was—or more precisely, my zazen was—free of ignorance and selfish desires.

Even though we may understand all this intellectually, we cannot sit without hope for gain unless our "arrogance of youth and health" is completely broken. This is what Dōgen Zenji meant when he said in "Genjōkōan," "Conveying oneself toward all things to carry out practice-enlightenment is delusion. All things coming and carrying out practice-enlightenment through the self is realization."

Was my previous practice meaningless? I don't think so. In "Sesshin-sesshō" (Expounding Mind, Expounding Nature), a chapter of *Shōbōgenzō*, Dōgen Zenji wrote:

After we arouse bodhi-mind and wholeheartedly practice the difficult practice, even though we practice, we cannot hit the mark even once out of one hundred times. And yet, we can hit the mark while we practice with our teachers and with scriptures. Hitting the mark at this present moment is enabled by the strength of the one hundred attempts which were off the mark. One hundred practices which were off the mark enable us to become mature.[91]

As we continue to practice wholeheartedly, even with a shallow understanding, we become mature enough to see our own shallowness and stupidity. As we see our shallowness, we go deeper into the dharma. To the extent that we struggle to eliminate our ignorance and desires, we are still within our karmic self based on ignorance and desire. We create an endless feud between two sides of ourselves. If we think we can become completely free from ignorance and desire as a result of an enlightenment experience, we have not yet thoroughly seen ourselves. As we awake to the reality of ourselves, we see more clearly that we are deeply deluded.

"No ignorance and also no extinction of it, and so forth until no old age and death and also no extinction of them," the *Heart Sutra* tells us. From the beginning, ignorance does not exist as a fixed entity, and yet it will never die out. This expression arises from a profound understanding of the reality of ourselves and the dharma.

And then: "No suffering, no origination, no stopping, no path." This denial of the fundamental beliefs of Buddhism is the expression of a truth that can be seen only by those who actually practice these teachings, instead of merely understanding them intellectually.

No Attainment

"No ignorance and also no extinction of it, and so forth until no old age and death and also no extinction of them;

No suffering, no origination, no stopping, no path;
No cognition, no attainment."

After listing the twelve links of dependent origination and the four noble truths, the *Heart Sutra* negates each of them. It then concludes, "No cognition, no attainment." No cognition means no person. No attainment means there is nothing to attain. There is no one to realize or understand the dharma. There is no dharma or enlightenment we can attain. This is the meaning of "No cognition and no attainment."

When we start to practice we almost always have a problem. Something is bothering us. We want to find a better way of life. We feel something is lacking or not quite right. That's why Shakyamuni Buddha left his home. He was a crown prince, and yet he left his palace and became a beggar to search for the truth of life. When we start to practice or study we have the same problem. We are looking for the truth. This is good. This is called bodhi-mind or Way-seeking mind. We are seeking after the truth or reality of our life. We are trying to find the best way of living. Without this bodhi-mind, the mind that seeks the Way, we cannot practice.

Shakyamuni Buddha found that the cause of suffering, of the trouble we have in our worldly lives, is clinging or thirst. He found that thirst, clinging, greed, and hatred resulted from ignorance of the reality of our lives. This is what the Buddha discovered and what he taught. He showed us the way to become free from clinging, greed, hatred, and ignorance. He showed us the four noble truths. The Buddha's students devote themselves to this very difficult practice.

We have to see deeply inside of ourselves, both the positive and negative sides of our psyches. We have to control our desires and delusions. This is the Buddha's practice. It is called nirvana. We practice to become free of self-delusion and ego. For many hundreds of years the first Buddhists practiced in this way. But Mahāyāna Buddhists felt there was a problem with this type of practice. Our usual way of life based on delusion, likes and dislikes, is samsara. We transmigrate in the six realms from hell to heaven, always moving up and down, up and down. This is our usual way of life. We want to find a more peaceful, stable way of life. The four noble truths are the way to transform our life in samsara to a life of nirvana. And yet if we really practice in this way we discover a deep, basic contradiction. Without bodhi-mind or a desire to practice, we cannot practice. But this desire is itself a cause of suffering.

The desire for truth and the desire for fame or profit are not so different. We feel something is lacking, so we try to get it. When we are poor we want more money. We want to become famous, and we want to become free from desire. These are different goals but the inner thirst is the same. We feel emptiness and we try to fill it with something. Life in samsara is characterized by the first two noble truths: suffering and desire (the cause of suffering). The Buddha taught the third and fourth noble truths: transformation is possible through practice. We try to transform our lives from samsara to nirvana, a life based on the Buddha's teaching. This is our practice. Yet if we separate samsara and nirvana, we miss the path. If we imagine that we are here in samsara and desire to get over there to the path or the Buddha's Way, this desire or aspiration itself creates another type of samsara. It is almost impossible to become completely free from our desires, so we have to put our whole energy into practice. We have to pay attention to each of our activities. We have to examine our motives. Even when we help other people, we have some egocentricity. If we really practice hard and sincerely, we cannot ignore this egocentricity. Even in our practice, even in our good deeds, we have some delusion and self-clinging.

To the extent that we try to negate life in samsara and live in nirvana we create a deep separation. We perceive a chasm between samsara and nirvana, and no way to cross it. Mahāyāna Buddhists felt that because of emptiness, the division between samsara and nirvana is a dream. The five skandhas have no self-nature. Suffering is caused by the five skandhas, so suffering, ignorance, clinging, greed, and hatred are all delusions. They don't exist as substance. Mahāyāna Buddhists found that egocentricity itself is illusion.

There's no separation between samsara and nirvana, or between delusion and enlightenment. "No ignorance and no extinction of it" means that ignorance and extinction are both without substance. Ignorance is always there, but it's an illusion. This means there is no separation between samsara and nirvana. It's a contradiction, and yet that is our life. We have to practice life within samsara. Samsara and nirvana are one. There are no steps, no separation between our usual, ordinary, deluded, material life and an enlightened, Buddhist, sacred, holy life. We are living in a single reality, and within this one reality, many things are happening. The continuous interaction between the self and the conditions surrounding the self creates our life and our karma.

Our practice is not to escape from delusion or samsara but to practice right in the middle of them. We try to manifest nirvana within samsara. Ignorance, greed, hatred, all negative emotions, intellection, and misunderstanding exist. We want to be free of all this. But to become free of something and to eliminate it are two different things. Our bodhisattva practice is not to eliminate delusion or the three poisons of ignorance, greed, and hatred. We shouldn't negate anything. We should accept everything and try to work with it. This is how to make our world nirvana.

Our world always has the potential for both samsara and nirvana. We are responsible for what we create. It all depends on our attitude toward life. There's no objective samsara and no objective nirvana. We create our own world. Delusion never disappears. Delusion is delusion; it never exists as substance, and it never disappears. Delusion is like a movie. Different scenes appear on the screen, but they are not reality. Seeing the scenes as a movie is reality. Delusion remains delusion, and yet the fact that we are deluded, that we are living in delusion, is reality. Our brain is always producing something, perhaps a totally deluded projection or maybe a very pure, lofty, peaceful illusion of the Buddha land or enlightenment. These are all delusions or illusions. We don't need to destroy them. What we have to do is see them as illusions. This is the meaning of letting go of thought. Thought is delusion, but it is a necessary part of the reality of our lives.

When we sit we let go of all illusions, good and bad, all emotions, and all philosophical understanding. We just let them go. We just open our hands. This is the way we accept reality without separating it into negative or undesirable parts and positive or desirable parts. When we stop this escaping and seeking, reality is right there. We are living in reality. We never left. This is what we do in our zazen. This is the basis upon which we have to create our way of life. We must be free from the illusions that arise from both sides, samsara and nirvana, and just work right here and now.

In bodhisattva practice we try to see the reality before separation. When we see the reality of our life, we find that we are not living as an individual substance but are more like a phantom, a bubble, or a flash of lightning, as the *Diamond Sutra* says. We are phenomena caused by many different elements and factors. We live with the support of all beings. This dynamic interpenetration works constantly. Nothing exists independently. We live together in this universal movement. Our existence is movement. We have to accept this ever-changing reality as our self.

When we see this reality it's very natural to try to be kind, friendly, and helpful to others. This is the bodhisattva vow. It's not something special. This way of life arises spontaneously from a realization of the reality of our life. It's not an order from the Buddha or God. When we see this reality we cannot avoid taking the bodhisattva vow.

Mahāyāna Buddhism identifies three kinds of nirvana. In Japanese, the first is *uyo-nehan*. An example of uyo-nehan is Shakyamuni Buddha. After he became enlightened and attained nirvana he lived forty years. He still had his physical body and mind and could suffer. The second type of nirvana is *muyo-nehan*. *Muyo* means "without anything extra," specifically, without body or mind. *Muyo-nehan* means that at the moment of his death, Shakyamuni became free of his physical body. This is called *parinirvana*, or perfect nirvana.

Lastly, Mahāyāna Buddhism names a nirvana called *mujūsho-nehan* for bodhisattvas. *Mu*, again, means "no." *Jūsho* means "place to live or stay." *Mujūsho* thus means "no dwelling" or "no place to stay" and refers to nirvana. This means that a bodhisattva doesn't stay in samsara because of wisdom and doesn't remain in nirvana because of compassion for others. A bodhisattva always practices in this world of desires and helps others but never dwells on either side. It is said there is a river between this shore of samsara and the other shore of nirvana, and a bodhisattva operates the ferry, traveling freely between shores but not abiding on either.

This third kind of nirvana is the basis of our practice. We don't practice to reach the other shore. We always practice on this shore. In fact, we don't separate this shore from the other. Both shores are right now, right here. If we separate this shore from the other, we generate dualism and contradiction. There's no way to escape this shore and attain the other. In reality there is no separation. We practice in this world, in this society; to carry out the bodhisattva vow, to walk with all living beings, to help and support each other. Then we can find nirvana right here within samsara. We vow eventually to transform samsara into nirvana without escape.

Our practice is not an escape from a worldly life of desire and delusion. It is not a method to "attain" enlightenment or wisdom. We just sit in the absolute reality that is before separation into enlightenment and delusion. They are both here. We negate nothing. We accept everything as reality and work together with it. There is no one to attain enlightenment and no enlightenment to be attained. The *Heart Sutra* says this is wisdom or prajñā. To see that there is no separation between delusion and enlightenment or between ignorance and wisdom is true enlightenment, true wisdom. This prajñā is often called the wisdom of nondiscrimination. It means to see both sides as a whole and create our own way of life based on this absolute reality. This is what Dōgen Zenji called shikantaza, just sitting.

Shikantaza doesn't mean that we are okay as long as we are sitting or that we don't need to do anything else. Just sitting really means just sitting, with no attempt to escape from or chase after anything. Just settle down right now, right here. This is just sitting. It doesn't mean we should sit exclusively, without doing anything else. Just sitting means just settling down right now, right here, and working on the ground of this absolute reality before the separation of samsara and nirvana.

Samsara and nirvana are one. That is prajñā. That is wisdom before separation or discrimination. It's easy to talk about but very difficult to practice.

I first studied Buddhism at Komazawa University. I liked studying, but studying books about Buddhism is like studying recipes without cooking or tasting. When I decided that was not what I wanted to do, I visited Uchiyama Roshi and asked to become his student. Since I had studied hard in school, I knew a lot about Buddhism. When I started to practice at Antaiji we sat a lot. We sat three fifty-minute periods in the morning and two in the evening. We had five-day sesshins every month. During these sesshins we sat fourteen periods each day. We did nothing but sit—no chanting, no lecture, no working, nothing but sitting. I believed that this practice of just sitting, taught by Dōgen Zenji, was the Way. I kept up this practice for many years until eventually I was unable to continue. Zazen became very painful for me. I had no money. I was thirty-one years old. I had no place to live. My body was broken so I couldn't work. I had no group to practice with. I was completely alone.

It was a really good situation in which to see myself. It was a very hard time, and I thought a lot about what I had been doing. I could no longer devote myself to practice as before. Dōgen Zenji taught there's nothing to attain. Sawaki Roshi said our practice of zazen is good for nothing. I knew that I shouldn't expect anything from practice. I had thought I was practicing without expectation, but when I couldn't practice in the way I had, I felt I was good for nothing. I thought I had been doing things without desire, but when I was unable to continue I felt useless and empty. I finally realized that I felt worthless because I was unable to fulfill my desire to practice in a certain way. I finally understood that the purpose of our practice is not to fulfill our desires, even our desire for the dharma.

If we practice in order to fulfill our desires, sooner or later we lose those things that fulfill our desire. We all lose our youth and eventually our health. If we believe that a certain style of practice is the Buddha's true practice and makes a person a real Buddhist, we are not good

Buddhists. This is samsara. Sometimes we are good, sometimes we are not. I realized that to the extent my practice was based on a distinction between good and bad, there was no nirvana for me. The way I practiced before I was thirty really was good for nothing. I was practicing in samsara, not nirvana. I was unable to continue practicing, but if I stopped and started doing something else, I would create another samsara. So I tried to just stop everything. I started doing takuhatsu to survive. I lived on about three hundred dollars a month, just enough for food. I had to give up any treatment for my body. I quit everything. I also quit practice based on desire, on my idea of what practice should be. I practiced as much as my physical and financial situation allowed. I found that I didn't need to compete with other people or with myself. I didn't need to compete with who I was or who I thought I should be. I had to accept reality with a half-broken body in a very hard situation. When I did, there was nothing to seek after, nothing to escape from. I didn't need to sit fourteen periods a day for five days. I simply had to settle down in the present moment.

This was the turning point of my practice. I became free of my own practice. I became free of my teacher's teaching and the Buddha's teaching. I just settled down in the reality where I was and practiced as much as possible. This is a really peaceful practice. You don't need to compete. Just settle down. If I hadn't had physical problems, I don't think my practice would have changed. I thought I was a great Zen master, but fortunately or unfortunately that didn't happen. Adverse experience gave me a broader perspective on the dharma. I am really grateful for that. This is bodhisattva practice. Although our capability is sometimes severely limited, we can find the compassionate Buddha that allows us to practice, even if only a little. That is enough. I think this is real nirvana. We don't need to find nirvana in a special place or state of mind. Nirvana is right now, right here.

This nirvana is not something special, just an ordinary way of life. I think the *Heart Sutra* is trying to show us this way of life. Just accept the reality of this body, mind, and world as it is and practice as much as possible. This is bodhisattva practice.

No Hindrance

"The bodhisattva depends on prajñā-pāramitā
And the mind is no hindrance.
Without any hindrance no fears exist;
Far apart from every perverted view the bodhisattva dwells
in nirvana.

"In the three worlds all buddhas depend on prajñā-pāramitā
And attain unsurpassed, complete, perfect enlightenment."

The sutra up to this point has talked about the emptiness of all beings. Emptiness means everything is impermanent, so there is no unchanging self-nature. Seeing impermanence and egolessness is the wisdom called prajñā-pāramitā. A consequence of this prajñā is there is no one to see reality. No one is there. There is nothing we can gain through wisdom. Actually there is no wisdom. If wisdom existed, our practice wouldn't be really empty. The conclusion of wisdom, of prajñā, is that there is no one who gains and nothing to be gained.

This section of the *Heart Sutra* talks about our wisdom and the practice of that wisdom. It says, "With nothing to attain, the bodhisattva depends on prajñā-pāramitā." The present translation says "the bodhisattva" but doesn't specify a particular bodhisattva. Rather, it refers to each one of us as a bodhisattva. As we see in the longer version of the *Heart Sutra*, Avalokiteśvara here is responding to Śāriputra's question about how people who wish to practice profound prajñā-pāramitā should train themselves. And this sutra is Avalokiteśvara's answer. Therefore, "the bodhisattva" refers to any person who has aroused bodhi-mind, including ourselves. Originally, "the Bodhisattva" referred to Shakyamuni before he became the Buddha. Shakyamuni aroused bodhi-mind, Way-seeking mind, or aspiration to find the truth. When he attained the Way or enlightenment, he was called the Buddha. Before he became the Buddha he was called the Bodhisattva, the person who is seeking the truth. Later in the Buddhist literature, especially in Mahāyāna Buddhism, there are many bodhisattvas, such as Mañjuśrī and Avalokiteśvara. They are very great bodhisattvas. Avalokiteśvara, who is preaching this *Heart Sutra*, is not seeking to attain enlightenment, and not choosing to become a buddha. Out of compassion for others Avalokiteśvara stays in this world as a bodhisattva and yet is considered the teacher of buddhas. So in Mahāyāna Buddhism "bodhisattva" doesn't necessarily mean a person who is practicing to become a buddha. There are bodhisattvas who vow not to become buddhas because of their compassion.

The important point in Mahāyāna Buddhism is that all of us, not just great bodhisattvas like Mañjushrī, Avalokiteśvara, or Maitreya, are bodhisattvas if we awaken the bodhi-mind that seeks the Way or reality. As bodhisattvas we try to see the emptiness in which there is no one who sees reality and nothing to be seen. No wisdom: this is the meaning of "nothing to attain, no one who attains, and nothing which is attained." The Japanese for "with nothing to attain" is *mushotoku*. Mu means "no" or "nothing" and *shotoku* means "income," so *mushotoku* means "no income." We have no income. This is prajñā—no gain and no loss. There's nothing coming in or going out because there is no place where anything can come to or go from. There is no border, no separation, just a flow of energy. This is reality beyond our conceptual and calculating way of thinking.

We are born as human beings and we gain nothing. We will die sooner or later and lose nothing. We are born with nothing but this body and mind. While we are living we think we attain, gain, or accomplish something. But when we die we leave everything behind, so only this body and mind die. We really attain nothing and lose nothing. This is the reality of our life. But we don't see this because we are always calculating our income and expenditures. When we have more coming in than going out we think our life is secure and successful. But if we understand that nothing comes in and nothing goes out, we actually have a much more secure foundation for our lives. We don't need to worry so much about income and expense, success and failure, poverty and wealth. It's not a real problem. As bodhisattvas we rely on this wisdom.

A bodhisattva's mind has no hindrance. "Hindrance" here means something that covers our mind, or an obstacle that prevents us from seeing reality as it is. A hindrance is something that makes it impossible for our mind to be natural. The Chinese expression is *keige*. *Kei* and *ge* both mean difficulties through which we can pass. These impediments are within us. Something covers or constrains our mind so we cannot be free. We are limited and made rigid by our knowledge and ways of thinking. Life is always moving. It's soft and flexible. When you put a big rock on a plant it tries to move through or around the obstruction and continue to grow. This is the flexibility of the life force. If we have an idea that we have to be this way or that, we have something very heavy sitting on our life. We cannot grow. We think our life is a failure and that we're in trouble. But the life force is flexible. There is always some other way to live, to grow, and to manifest our life force.

We should try to see the hindrances in our minds, the obstacles that block our free growth. As bodhisattvas we are freed from hindrances by seeing emptiness. We see that nothing exists as substance, so there is nothing to prevent our growth. Obstacles are illusions, delusions, and creations of our thought. We fear because of our desires. We think they must be fulfilled, and we're afraid that's impossible. We think there is only one way to live even though there are many ways. So our desires, our ideas, our values become hindrances, and we are not free. This is the meaning of fears. But if we remove our imagined obstacles we can grow in many different ways.

The sutra tells us that the bodhisattva dwells "far apart from every perverted view." The expression in Japanese is *ten dō musō*. Here *mu* means "dream" and *sō* means "thinking." *Musō* then literally means "thought in dream." *Tendō* means "upside-down." Our attitude, or understanding of our thought, is upside-down. We cannot wake up. We are thinking in a dream. We create our own picture of the world depending on our karma or experience. Our experience is very limited, and yet we think it is the whole world. So we are like the frog in the well. We can see only a small circle of sky, but we think we are seeing the whole universe. Even seeing emptiness doesn't allow us to see the whole universe, but it enables us to realize that our view is limited.

In our zazen we see that we are deluded. This is enlightenment. We see that we are deluded and limited, so we let go of thought. We become free from our limited views. This doesn't mean we can see the whole universe. That's impossible because we always have a particular position or point of view. When I look in this direction I can see this side of the world. I cannot see the half behind me. I know it's there because of my memory. But it's just a memory. We are seeing only half the world, but because of our assumptions and memory we think we can see the whole. We even think that we can see how other people see the world. But since we each have a unique perspective, we can never see the world in the same way. In fact, each of us has a different perspective, a unique way of seeing, thinking, feeling, and valuing things. We become flexible when we free ourselves from our fixed views. This is prajñā.

"Perverted" literally means "upside-down." We usually assume that our thoughts operate our body and mind. Our body and mind serve the emperor, thought. This is really upside-down. Thought is just one part of our life, but we so often live on the basis of our thinking. This is really an upside-down way of seeing things. If we turn it over, then we are living. We all have life force. Part of it is our power of thought. We don't need to discard this power, but we should realize that what we think is not reality. Once we really accept that thought is only a part of our life, most of the fear and other problems caused by our thoughts will disappear. We want to be secure. If we can't support ourselves we are afraid. It's very natural. But we can think too much. We can think about ten, twenty, or thirty years in the future. We even worry about the world after our death. It's okay to think about the future, but if worrying about it prevents us from living in this present moment, it's too much. Bodhisattva practice is about this present moment.

Within this present moment there is a direction to the future. We usually think what we are doing right now is a preparation for the future or a step to accomplish something. But this is an upside-down way of seeing things. Our effort, work, or study at this present moment brings about the future. We can think about it but we don't need to worry. Worry dilutes our effort and it's not healthy. So just be right now, right here, and put your whole energy into what you are doing. This is prajñā. It is very difficult. Moment by moment we have to let go of worry and fear and return to this moment. That is our practice of mindfulness, sitting in zazen, letting go, and coming back to this moment. This letting go is the practice of prajñā.

The next two lines of the sutra are:

> "In the three worlds all buddhas depend on prajñā-pāramitā
> And attain unsurpassed, complete, perfect enlightenment."

The three worlds here are the past, present, and future. The Japanese for "three worlds" is *sanze*. *San* is "three" and *ze* means "generation" or "time." "Unsurpassed, complete, perfect" means "absolute." There is nothing relative. There is no separation between self and others or between self and all beings. That is enlightenment. Here the *Heart Sutra* tells us that through prajñā-pāramitā we can liberate ourselves. We can transform ourselves from slaves of thought, slaves of the ego, into bodhisattvas. We use our thoughts, delusions, and desires as the seeds of prajñā, which we nurture with our practice. We make them function as the Buddha's work. Prajñā is called the Buddha's mother. This is the way of life the *Heart Sutra* and Mahāyāna Buddhism encourage us to follow.

To become free from all perverted views or upside-down ways of seeing things means to turn the foundation of our life over, to see reality and live based on it. Reality means impermanence and egolessness. Nothing stays forever unchanged. There is nothing substantial. Everything is changing, and everything is supported by everything else. We are all connected, one universal life force.

As we've seen, in Dōgen's teaching mushotoku—no income, no attainment—is essential. In *Shōbōgenzō* "Zuimonki," a record of his informal talks, he says:

Now if you wish to practice the way of the buddhas and ancestors, you should practice the way of the previous sages, as well as the conduct of the ancestors with no (expectation of) profit; expect nothing, seek nothing, gain nothing. Although you should quit seeking and give up expectations of buddhahood, if you stop practicing and continue engaging in your former evil deeds, you will still be guilty of seeking and will fall back into the old nest.

Without having the slightest expectation, maintain the prescribed manner of conduct. Think of acting to save and benefit living beings, earnestly carry out all good deeds, and give up former evil ones. Do this solely for the sake of becoming the foundation of happiness for human and heavenly beings. Without stagnating in good deeds of the present, continue practicing your whole lifetime. An ancient called this practice "breaking the bottom of the lacquer pail." The way of the life of the buddhas and ancestors is like this.[92]

Here Dōgen admonishes us to be mushotoku, without expectation of income. It's very strict. Our zazen, study, work, all the activities of our daily lives are our practice. We should do them as the practice of this moment without expectation of result or reward in the future. Just put our whole energy into this moment and results or fruits will grow naturally. We simply need to trust the life force itself.

When we hear this teaching we might think to practice is to seek after enlightenment. If so, it sounds like Dōgen Zenji is saying you shouldn't practice. He, however, continues, "*Although you should quit seeking and give up expectations of buddhahood, if you stop practicing and continue engaging in your former evil deeds, you will still be guilty of seeking and will fall back into the old nest.*" Evil deeds mean karmic deeds, activities based on our personal desires. So if we stop practice to avoid seeking buddhahood, we are still seeking. We become just ordinary human beings. So we have to continue practicing without expectation. It's really difficult.

"Without having the slightest expectation, maintain the prescribed manner of conduct." Here he's talking about monks living in a monastery. They should follow the schedule and devote their whole energy to daily practice. In the case of laypeople, taking care of our families, living in communities, and working is what we do.

"Think of acting to save and benefit living beings, earnestly carry out all good deeds, and give up former evil ones. Do this solely for the sake of becoming the foundation of happiness for human and heavenly beings." In each activity we should think of how we can benefit all living beings. That is our vow. We try to practice skillfully to create a foundation of happiness for all beings. That means we try to make this world better, even if only in small ways. We have many problems in this world today. We should do what we can to make it a better place for those who follow us. That too is our vow. Each of us has different capabilities and each of us can do something, even something small to improve this world. That is true bodhisattva practice.

"Without stagnating in good deeds of the present, continue practicing your whole lifetime." If we think we are doing good, we already have a problem. If we think we are good people because we try to make the world better, we have a problem. This is a judgment. We think that we are good and that those who don't follow us are bad. This is a problem. If we think in this way we ignore emptiness. Even though we are doing good deeds, we should not think of ourselves as good people. We are doing what we choose to do or feel we should. It's just a natural function. This is a subtle point. Our good deeds can make us arrogant. Fighting is often caused by this kind of arrogance. We think, "We are doing good and they are not, so they are our enemy. We have to eliminate them to make the world a better place." Then we really have a problem. Many wars are caused this way. The wisdom of emptiness is a way to avoid conflict based on concepts of justice.

Just keep doing. This is the meaning of *shikan*. Dōgen Zenji's most famous phrase is "just sitting," or shikantaza. We may think that just sitting means it's okay if we merely sit, that we don't need to do anything else. But shikantaza doesn't mean that. It means just sit for now, without any expectation for the future, without thinking that we are doing good or practicing well. Just sit.

"*An ancient called this practice 'breaking the bottom of the lacquer pail.'*" This is a common expression for becoming enlightened. For Dōgen Zenji enlightenment means just sitting or just doing good. Just keep practicing without any expectation.

"*The way of the life of the buddhas and ancestors is like this.*" This is the way buddhas and ancestors practiced. When he mentions just sitting, Dōgen Zenji is talking about the practice of prajñā. He's talking about becoming free of even the Buddha's teaching. This is the Buddha's practice, or prajñā-pāramitā.

Nāgārjuna says something very similar in *Mūlamadhyamakakārikā*: "Those who delight in maintaining, 'Without the grasping, I will realize nirvana; nirvana is in me,' are the very ones with the greatest grasping" (16:9).[93] We believe that we are letting go of thought, opening our hands, and grasping at nothing; we think that we are completely free from self-clinging and that we are in nirvana or nirvana is within us. Nāgārjuna says that those who think this way are the very ones with the greatest grasping. We must open our hand even concerning our practice, even about opening our hand. Nāgārjuna continues, "Where nirvana is not (subject to) establishment and samsara not (subject to) disengagement, how will there be any conception of nirvana and samsara?" (16:10). We don't have to establish nirvana or eliminate samsara. There is no separation between them. This is a koan. There is no answer, so we have to keep opening our hands. If we think we are okay because we open our hands, then we are grasping. So what? This is our practice.

GREAT BRIGHT MANTRA

"Therefore know the prajñā-pāramitā
Is the great transcendent mantra,
Is the great bright mantra,
Is the utmost mantra,

Is the supreme mantra,
Which is able to relieve all suffering
And is true, not false."

In this section the sutra says that prajñā-pāramitā is the wisdom to see impermanence and interdependence. This body and mind exist as a result of many factors. When these elements change, we change. Consequently, there is no fixed self-nature within us, nothing substantial. To see this reality is prajñā-pāramitā. It is a difficult reality to face moment by moment. We often forget about it because our way of thought in daily life is very different.

In our usual thinking we use concepts and words. Each word has a certain meaning or definition that doesn't change. A word should always mean the same thing. If the meaning changes, we have no basis for consistent communication. I'm always Shohaku Okumura, always Japanese, always a man, always a Buddhist priest. But in reality my body and mind are always changing. On a conceptual level, however, I'm always Shohaku Okumura, and it's difficult to see these changes. When the two levels of our life, conceptual thought and life force, harmonize, we have no serious problems. But sometime our thinking contradicts reality.

For instance, I still think of myself as a young man when in fact I am getting older every day. One of my son's favorite games was to sit on my shoulders and beat my head like a drum. He did this often.[94] One day I was sitting on the sofa when he jumped onto the back of my neck. I had no pain that day but the next morning I couldn't move my neck. I was in bed for two days and missed Thanksgiving dinner. Pain is so realistic, always fresh. It's very difficult to accept the reality that I am getting older and unable to do some things and that my son is getting bigger every day. If I try to move something too heavy, it's difficult. These are examples of how our conceptual thinking and self-image often diverge from the reality of our lives. When there is too great a gap between reality and our thinking we run into trouble. Prajñā-pāramitā is the wisdom to see both sides. It's not simply a negation of our thought or a particular way of thinking. It is seeing the limitations of our usual logic. Our day-to-day thought is unable to see the reality of constant change.

The *Heart Sutra* says that this prajñā or wisdom which sees the reality of impermanence, egolessness, and interdependence is a mantra. *Mantra* was originally a term used in the Vedic tradition of ancient India commonly called Brahmanism, and later it became an essential part of Hinduism. The practice of chanting mantras was much older than Buddhism. One of the oldest of the many sacred scriptures of ancient India is called the *Rig Veda*. In the Vedas there are many gods much more powerful than human beings. The basic idea of a mantra was that if Brahman priests uttered the proper words and conducted the right rituals, the gods would comply with their requests. These mantras supposedly had the supernatural power to move the gods. Originally Indian Buddhist monks didn't use mantras. But Mahāyāna Buddhism was strongly influenced by Hinduism and began to use them. The word "mantra" is used commonly in Vajrayāna Buddhism, which arose around the seventh century as the final development of Indian Buddhism. In the Vajrayāna school (such as the Shingon school in Japan), prayers serve a particular purpose. For example, on certain occasions the priest builds a fire inside the temple, sits in full lotus, makes a particular mudra, and chants mantras. Then Vairocana, the main Buddha in Vajrayāna, is supposed to help them. This is the basic idea of the Vajrayāna or Shingon school of Buddhism.

On Shikoku, one of the major Japanese islands, there are eighty-eight destinations for pilgrims. As Shingon practitioners visit each temple, they often chant the *Heart Sutra*. This sutra is also used as a mantra in Vajrayāna Buddhism. For Zen Buddhists, however, reciting the *Heart Sutra* doesn't mean that we believe it's a mantra that can influence the gods. For instance, right now I have pain in my neck, but I don't believe that reciting the *Heart Sutra* will relieve it. Although the sutra has the phrase "relieve all suffering," I don't believe it works as a kind of pain-killer. Instead it enables us to change the way we view our lives and ourselves. It allows us to see the deeper meaning and broader reality of our life. Our way of thinking is limited by our experience, education, culture, and values. Our picture of the world is narrow. This wisdom of prajñā-pāramitā enables us to break through these fixed systems of value and see reality from a wider perspective.

The *Heart Sutra* concludes:

"So proclaim the prajñā-pāramitā mantra,
   Proclaim the mantra that says:
   Gate, gate, pāragate, pārasamgate! Bodhi, svāha!"

Since this is a mantra, the words themselves are believed by some to have divine power and so are not translated. Depending on the translator, the meaning is, "Gone, gone, gone beyond" or "Gone altogether beyond. Oh, what an awakening!" *Bodhi* means "awakening" and *svāhā* means "all hail." "Gone" points to a reality beyond our system of values, beyond the boundary of our ready-made picture of the world and ourselves. This mantra enables us to break through our internal limitations and see a deeper reality inside us. The Buddha taught us to wake up to this deeper meaning in our daily lives.

Some of my time in Japan I lived on takuhatsu, religious begging. Usually I walked the street and stopped in front of each shop. I would stand there and say, "Hō." In Japanese this literally means "bowl," and figuratively it means "dharma." In Osaka there is a large temple called Shitennōji.[95] Here, on the twenty-first of each month, people observe *en'nichi*, a kind of a memorial day for Kōbō Daishi, the founder of the Japanese Shingon school. Thousands of people visit the temple. Whenever possible I went to that temple on the twenty-first and did standing takuhatsu. I stood from about ten o'clock in the morning until about four in the afternoon. For six hours I didn't move. I just stood with a begging bowl and recited the *Heart Sutra*. It takes about three or four minutes to recite the whole sutra, so I would chant it more than a hundred times. Usually when people do takuhatsu they chant *Enmei-jukku-kannon-gyō*. This is a very short sutra, too short to repeat for six hours, so I recited the *Heart Sutra* instead. Chanting kept my mind from darting here and there in distracted thinking.

The people who visit the temple are mostly older people who are very religious in the traditional sense. They are very sincere Buddhists and give generous donations, sometimes a small amount of money, sometimes ten yen or a hundred yen, about one dollar. When they made a donation they did gasshō and bowed to me. I also bowed while I was chanting. I saw many people who were poor but more generous than the rich. It was apparent to me that they were suffering. Some were in wheelchairs. Chanting the *Heart Sutra* was a very powerful practice. I could see people's suffering. It's not something mysterious, but there was a special realm in which we were living together, sharing our suffering. Although we didn't talk we communicated on a profound level. I felt dharma joy. The *Heart Sutra* was a mantra that enabled us to relieve suffering.

Suffering is more than just pain. Suffering is pain plus something mental. Pain alone is not such a big problem because it will end sometime. For example, I had pain this morning and knew I had to give a talk. That made my pain suffering. Still, I was able to come and speak. Chanting this mantra, this *Heart Sutra*, enables us to communicate with each other deeply without speaking. For this reason chanting is a really good practice.

At some Zen centers in the United States, we chant in both Japanese and English. Some ask me why we chant in Japanese. They think it doesn't make sense. Chanting is first of all a practice of breathing. When you chant you use your *hara*. In a Japanese monastery one is taught, "Chant with your hara, your abdomen, not with your mouth." Chanting is a practice of deep breathing with your abdomen. Next we are taught, "Chant with your ear, not with your mouth." That means we should listen to what other people are chanting. We should be together with all beings when we chant. We shouldn't chant alone. When we chant with others, the chanting of all people should be one, like a chorus or orchestra. Chanting enables us to be right now, right here at this moment. We have to put our whole body and mind into chanting and let go of other things. When we are chanting we should not think about sitting or eating or errands we have to do. Just be right now, right here,

100 percent. In this way chanting is a mantra. The meaning is not so important. Of course, it's better to understand the meaning, but the meaning is not really the point. Chanting can be prajñā-pāramitā if we put our whole time and being into it. It can open our eyes to reality, not to an intellectual reality but rather to our life energy. When we chant wholeheartedly, our voice is the sound of emptiness, exactly like the sound of the wind bell in Rujing's poem. It is the sound of the wind, the bell, our ears, our mind, the entire universe.

7

ALL IS ONE, ONE IS ALL:
MERGING OF DIFFERENCE AND UNITY

SANDŌKAI

The mind of the great sage of India
Is intimately communicated between east and west.
People's faculties may be keen or dull,
But in the path there are no "southern" or "northern"
    ancestors.
The spiritual source shines clearly in the light;
The branching streams flow in the darkness.
Grasping things is basically delusion;
Merging with principle is still not enlightenment.
Each sense and every field
Interact and do not interact;
When interacting, they also merge—
Otherwise, they remain in their own states.
Forms are basically different in material and appearance,
Sounds are fundamentally different in pleasant or harsh quality.
"Darkness" is a word for merging upper and lower;
"Light" is an expression for distinguishing pure and defiled.
The four gross elements return to their own natures
Like a baby taking to its mother;

Fire heats, wind moves,
Water wets, earth is solid.
Eye and form, ear and sound;
Nose and smell, tongue and taste—
Thus in all things
The leaves spread from the root;
The whole process must return to the source;
"Noble" and "base" are only manners of speaking.
Right in light there is darkness, but don't confront it
    as darkness;
Right in darkness there is light, but don't see it as light.
Light and dark are relative to one another
Like forward and backward steps.
All things have their function—
It is a matter of use in the appropriate situation.
Phenomena exist like box and cover joining;
Principle accords like arrow points meeting.
Hearing the words, you should understand the source;
Don't make up standards on your own.
If you don't understand the path as it meets your eyes,
How can you know the way as you walk?
Progress is not a matter of far or near,
But if you are confused, mountains and rivers block the way.
I humbly say to those who study the mystery,
Don't waste time.[96]

THE TITLE of this poem, "Sandōkai," is composed of three characters. The first, san (cen in Chinese) means "difference," "diversity," "variety." In this poem it is used as a synonym for ji, which indicates the concrete, phenomenal aspect of our life. The second character, dō (tong in Chinese), means "sameness," "equality," "commonality." Here it is used as a synonym of ri, the absolute or ultimate reality of emptiness beyond discrimination. Kai (qi in Chinese) means "promise," "agreement," or "tally." In ancient times when merchants made a contract, they wrote it on a tally (a wooden board), which they then broke into halves. When they actually exchanged goods, they put the two halves of the tally together to confirm the agreement. *San-dō-kai* refers to both aspects of our lives: the concrete, comprised of many specific situations, ideas, evaluations, and things; and the absolute, based on universality, emptiness, and nondiscrimination. These are like the halves of a tally. These aspects work together as one seamless reality. Hence, "Sandōkai" can be translated as the "Merging of Difference and Unity."[97]

THE MIND OF THE GREAT SAGE OF INDIA

The mind of the great sage of India
Is intimately communicated between east and west.
People's faculties may be keen or dull,
But in the path there are no "southern" or "northern"
    ancestors.

The first four lines of this poem by the Zen master Shitou Xiqian (Sekitō Kisen) are an introduction to what follows. To understand this, we need to know the situation in Shitou's time.

"Southern" and "Northern" Ancestors

Shitou lived in eighth century China, from 700 to 790. He practiced with the sixth ancestor, Dajan Huineng (Daikan Enō, 638–713) when he was young, perhaps as a teenager. After Huineng died he practiced with one of Huineng's disciples, Qingyuan Xingsi (Seigen Gyōshi, 660–740). Shitou became Qingyuan's dharma successor, thus a second-generation disciple of the sixth ancestor. It is said that earlier, under the fifth ancestor Daman Hongren (Daiman Kōnin, 602–675), Zen had divided into two schools, Southern and Northern. Huineng's lineage was called the Southern school, while the Northern school was founded by Yuquan Shenxiu (Gyokusen Jinshū, 606–706), one of Huineng's dharma brothers. There is a famous story about the dharma transmission from the fifth ancestor Hongren to Huineng.

According to the *Platform Sutra* of the sixth ancestor, Huineng was practicing at the fifth ancestor's monastery. He had not yet been ordained and was still a lay practitioner working at the monastery. Shenxiu, the founder of the Northern school, was the head monk and a very experienced practitioner. He was the oldest student of the fifth ancestor. The fifth ancestor was getting old and looking for a successor. He assembled his students and asked them to write a poem to show their understanding of the dharma. All the other monks, convinced that Shenxiu would be chosen as the fifth ancestor's successor, declined to compose poems. Shenxiu alone wrote one, as follows:

> The body is the bodhi tree,
> The mind is like a bright mirror's stand.
> At all times we must strive to polish it
> And must not let dust collect.[98]

This body, our human body, is the bodhi tree. *Bodhi*, as we've seen, means "awakening," so this body is the tree of awakening or enlightenment. Original wisdom is like a clear mirror. But there is usually dust on the mirror, so it doesn't reflect things as they are. We have to continually polish the mirror of our mind to keep it clean. This was Shenxiu's understanding of the dharma, human beings, and the meaning of practice. Our body and mind is original enlightened reality itself, but the dust of desire and ignorance cover it. When we polish it, the mirror becomes bright and functions as wisdom.

Huineng couldn't read or write. Even though he was not well educated, when he heard people reciting Shenxiu's poem he must have thought, "That is not deep enough." So Huineng asked one of the students to transcribe a poem for him, which he posted next to Shenxiu's poem. His poem was:

> Bodhi originally has no tree.
> The bright mirror also has no stand.

Fundamentally there is not a single thing.
Where could dust arise?[99]

Huineng said that enlightenment has no tree and the mirror no shape or form. Nothing exists. Since everything is completely empty, there is no place for dust to land. There is nothing that can be called desire or delusion. Our enlightenment or reality is always clear. There is nothing we have to polish and nothing we have to eliminate. That was Huineng's understanding.

The fifth ancestor secretly gave dharma transmission to Huineng in the night and let him leave the monastery. Shenxiu's teaching, the Northern school, was called "gradual" enlightenment because Shenxiu held that we become enlightened after a long period of practice, polishing the mirror. In this school people practice to eliminate delusion based on ignorance. Huineng's teaching was called "sudden" enlightenment. According to the Southern or "sudden" school realization is attained suddenly, without any stages of gradual practice. People realize reality beyond the discrimination between delusion and enlightenment. For example, the story of Huineng's first realization experience—which happened before he began to study Zen when he heard someone chanting the *Diamond Sutra*—was taken to illustrate the idea of sudden enlightenment.

The two schools separated under the fifth ancestor, and Shitou was a dharma grandson of Huineng. This is what Shitou refers to when he says that in the path, the Buddha's Way, there are no "southern" or "northern" ancestors. Even though he was a dharma grandson of Huineng, the founder of the Southern school, he says that there is no distinction between southern or northern, which means between sudden or gradual enlightenment. Shitou wrote this poem to show the fundamental reality and go beyond the distinction between the factions of schools. This is a traditional understanding of the history of Chinese Zen in the eighth and ninth centuries.

Historical Reality

To understand Shitou's position in the history of Chinese Zen Buddhism and also what he wrote in "Merging of Difference and Unity," it might be helpful to understand the historical background of Zen in the eighth and ninth centuries. The actual reality was probably much more complex than we usually imagine. Guifeng Zongmi (Keihō Shumitsu, 780–841) was a famous Zen master and Buddhist philosopher who was born eighty years after Shitou. He was a scholar of the Kegon School, a Buddhist philosophical school based on the *Kegon Sutra* (*Avataṃsaka Sutra* or *Flower Ornament Sutra*). Feixiu (Haikyū, 797–870), a government minister, was very interested in Zen but was confused because there were so many different Zen groups at that time. He couldn't understand how such diverse groups could have a common origin. When he questioned Zen practitioners, their answers were paradoxical. They said nothing logical. Since Zongmi was a scholar as well as a Zen practitioner, the minister asked him to explain the origin, tradition, and history of Zen, and how the many different methods of teaching related to this tradition. Zongmi explained the lineages of Zen from Bodhidharma in a short treatise. He wrote that at the time there were six schools of Zen, not just the Southern and Northern.

The first one was called Niutou (Gozu, or Oxhead) school, named for the mountain where the founder lived. This school was headed by Niutou Farong (Gozu Hōyū, 594–657), who is said to have been a disciple of the fourth ancestor. So there was a division in Zen even before the fifth ancestor.

The second, the Northern school, was Shenxiu's school. It was particularly popular in the imperial court. Shenxiu himself and a few of his disciples became teachers of the emperors. This school was attacked by Heze Shenhui (Kataku Jinne, 668–760) in the first half of the eighth century and lost popularity within a few generations.

The third and fourth were two smaller groups, the Jingzhong (Jōshū) school founded by Jingzhong Wuxiang (Jōshū Musō, 684–762) and Baotang (Hotō) school started by Baotang Wuzhu (Hotō Mujū,

714–774). Those were the streams that branched from the fifth ancestor. Zongmi did not say much about these two minor schools.

The fifth and sixth were "Southern" schools derived from Huineng's lineage. The fifth was called the Hongzhou (Kōshū) school founded by Mazu Daoyi (Baso Dōitsu, 709–788). Nanyue Huairang (Nangaku Ejō, 677–744) was a disciple of Huineng, and Mazu was Nanyue's disciple and of the same generation as Shitou. Mazu was also Huineng's dharma grandson.

The last school, the Heze (Kataku), was founded by one of Huineng's disciples named Heze Shenhui, who attacked the Northern school and claimed that his teacher, Huineng, was the legitimate dharma heir of the fifth ancestor.

Zongmi didn't talk about Shitou's group at all, probably because it wasn't big enough. He did discuss the similarities and differences between the Niutou school, the Northern school, and the two divisions of the Southern school, Hongzhou and Heze. Zongmi himself claimed that he belonged to the Heze school, whose teaching he considered the highest of all. However, modern scholars think Zongmi had no connection with this lineage. Shenhui was one of the most active of Huineng's disciples and probably created the story of the dharma transmission from the fifth ancestor to Huineng. As Huineng's disciple, Shenhui wanted him to be seen as greater than Shenxiu and recognized as the sixth ancestor. Shenxiu's Northern school was more powerful and popular in the capital, in the north of China, whereas Huineng came from the southern countryside, was not well known, and may have lacked credibility because of his youth.

In a sense, the history of different groups of Zen before Zen became established in Chinese Buddhism shows the meaning of "merging of difference and unity." The groups were different and yet they were all considered as Zen practitioners.

One Mind

Zongmi compared the four schools on the basis of their understanding of difference and unity. Difference is a translation of *ji* and refers to the phenomenal or relative aspect of our life. Unity refers to the absolute aspect. Originally these two concepts, difference and unity, the phenomenal and absolute aspects of our life, are discussed as the two aspects of the One Mind.

Shitou uses the phrase "the mind of the great sage of India." The idea of a One Mind originated in the *Awakening of Faith in Mahāyāna*, one of the most important texts on the theory of *tathāgata-garbha*, or buddha-nature. It begins:

> The revelation of the true meaning [of the principle of Mahāyāna can be achieved] by [unfolding the doctrine] that the principle of One Mind has two aspects. One is the aspect of Mind in terms of the absolute (*tathātā*, suchness), and the other is the aspect of Mind in terms of phenomena (*samsara*, birth and death).[100]

Samsara is the aspect of life into which we are born, live for a while, and die. It refers not only to the psychological mind but also to the functions of our lives. During the period between birth and death, our minds and lives constantly change, and we are limited by our particular time and place. We are conditioned by our unique experiences, education, and culture. Delusive desires function within this aspect because we can't perceive reality as a whole. We have to make choices based on our limited perspectives.

The *Awakening of Faith* continues, "Each of these two aspects embraces all states of existence. Why? Because these two aspects are mutually inclusive." They completely interpenetrate each other. According to the text, we live a universal, eternal life as the absolute aspect of the Mind, and yet, as the phenomenal aspect of the same Mind, our life is individual and limited by that individuality. The Buddha addressed the relationship between these two aspects. He taught that life is suffering and the cause of this suffering is our desire, which arises out of ignorance. He taught that we have to transform our way of life into nirvana. This is the Buddha's basic teaching. To realize nirvana we have to practice, to walk the eightfold noble path leading out of samsara. In the *Awakening of Faith*, samsara and nirvana are really two aspects of One Mind. The basic idea here is that both are embodied in the reality of our individual lives. Even though the reality of one life is beyond discrimination and delusion, from a relative or phenomenal perspective we are deluded and egocentric. We have delusive desires that bring suffering to our lives. So what should we do? How can we live in nirvana? The various answers to this question are the basis of the many different teachings and schools.

Zongmi's Comments on the Four Schools

Zongmi discussed the four schools, although he wasn't completely objective because he felt that his was the best form of practice. He used the interesting analogy of a *mani* jewel, the bright, transparent gem that symbolizes buddha-nature or One Mind. He explained that this jewel has no color, so when it is illuminated by light of a particular color, it takes on that color. A transparent jewel placed on a black sheet of paper becomes black. On a red sheet it appears red. These apparent changes were used as an analogy for individual or relative aspects of situations in our lives. If our life becomes really black, full of delusion and desire, the jewel of One Mind appears black. The bright jewel takes on the color of each situation. Yet the jewel itself is transparent and does not change.

Zongmi said the Northern school taught that the black color is false. To become enlightened, to reveal the bright jewel, we have to remove the black. Our practice is to erase the darkness of our delusions. We have to polish the bright jewel to remove the colors that arise from particular situations. This requires constant practice.

Mazu's Hongzhou school maintained that everything we do, whether we are enlightened or deluded, is the function of the bright jewel. They taught that without color—black, white, or red—there is no bright jewel. We don't need to eliminate a particular color to reveal the jewel. Buddha-nature doesn't exist independently of particular situations. Even deluded actions are nothing other than the function of buddha-nature. So we don't need to polish anything or engage in any particular practice. We just accept everything as reality, as a function or movement of buddha-nature.

Zongmi made another analogy to explain Mazu's beliefs. He compared buddha-nature to the flour used in cakes and bread. One can bake many types of bread and cake with different shapes and tastes, but the same flour is used to make them all. So it is with buddha-nature in the myriad situations of our lives. Mazu believed that there is nothing other than buddha-nature and that we need to realize that everything is buddha-nature. Zongmi may have exaggerated Mazu's beliefs, as a way of criticizing Mazu. We cannot be sure whether this is what Mazu and his students really thought. But according to Zongmi, those who followed this form of practice/enlightenment felt that it is enough to believe that everything is a manifestation of the absolute. They believed that we don't need any particular form of practice and can live freely.

Zongmi explained that while Mazu's school taught that everything is a manifestation of buddha-nature, Niutou's teaching maintained that everything is empty. Not only the jewel's color, but even the transparent jewel itself is empty, like a dream. So we should not grasp anything. Delusion is empty and without substance, as is the bright jewel. Our practice then is not to attach ourselves to anything. This is a complete penetration of emptiness. There is nothing we can achieve, nothing we have to eliminate. We must see both delusion and buddha-nature as empty. We have to realize the emptiness of all things. Zongmi criticized the Niutou school for its failure to recognize the permanent essence of One Mind and its mistaken belief that the One Mind is also empty.[101]

Finally, the Heze school, as interpreted by Zongmi, believed that each of the other schools was partially correct. They asserted that the individual colors caused by various conditions are false, an imperfect reflection of reality. This means our discriminations are false, empty delusions. At the same time, they believed that the One Mind is not empty. We cannot grasp it, but it is here, clear and bright, and it is not empty. We must realize this oneness and see this bright jewel covered with delusions and then practice to free ourselves from delusions through sudden enlightenment. Thus this school combined the elements of gradual practice and sudden enlightenment. [102]

Shitou's Lineage

Our lineage, the Sōtō school, was also transmitted by the sixth ancestor, Huineng. Qingyuan Xingsi was Huineng's dharma heir and Shitou's teacher. Shitou transmitted the dharma to Yaoshan Weiyan (Yakusan Igen, 751–834). Yaoshan taught Yunyan Tansheng (Ungan Donjō, 780–841). The founder of the Chinese Sōtō school, Dongshan Liangjie (Tōzan Ryōkai, 807–869), was Yunyan's disciple. This lineage was not well known by the other Zen schools at the time of Zongmi, who was a contemporary of Dongshan. This was perhaps because Mazu's Hongzhou school was overwhelmingly larger and more popular. It was called the "one-stop shop," like a supermarket that had something for everyone. Shitou was a contemporary of Mazu. In comparison with Mazu's style of practice, Shitou's school was called the "real-gold shop." His form of practice was considered very pure, and since the school offered only real gold, it was small. Yaoshan's sangha was in fact very small, fewer than twenty people. Yunyan was a very quiet person. He didn't think of himself as enlightened. After the time of Dongshan and his disciples, this lineage finally became popular and the sayings of these five masters were recorded.

"Sandōkai" is Shitou's attempt to record his understanding of the relationship between buddha-nature—the absolute aspect of our life—and the relative or phenomenal aspect of our life, in other words, between enlightenment and delusion. He does this by contrasting the beliefs of the various schools. The Northern school emphasized difference and tried to transcend it through unity. In Mazu's Hongzhou school, unity is found only in difference. Since there is no unity outside of difference, they believed we must accept difference. In the Niutou school difference and unity are both empty, and we are taught to strive to become free from such distinctions. Finally, the Heze school focused on recognizing that differences are empty, while unity is not. Shitou suggested that we must try to see the relationship between difference and unity clearly. He emphasized neither, but instead tried to see reality as a merging of difference and unity. I think this is what "Sandōkai" (Merging of Difference and Unity) expresses.

Shitou says, "People's faculties may be keen or dull, but in the path there are no 'southern' or 'northern' ancestors." He means there is no difference between sudden and gradual enlightenment. People have different capabilities. Some understand suddenly and some more gradually, but in reality there is no such distinction. For Shitou, any division of the dharma or discussion of which approach to it is superior is senseless. Instead he tries to show us the One Mind, "the mind of the great sage of India" before separation. This One Mind embraces two aspects: a spiritual source and branching streams.

SPIRITUAL SOURCE AND BRANCHING STREAMS

> The spiritual source shines clearly in the light;
> The branching streams flow in the darkness.
> Grasping things is basically delusion;
> Merging with principle is still not enlightenment.

As we've learned, in Shitou's time Buddhism was separated into schools that argued about basic issues like the nature of enlightenment and the best method of practice. Shitou's response was to describe the mind of the great sage of India. He wasn't talking about psychology, but rather about the reality of life that includes both the absolute and phenomenal aspects in terms of the relation between the self and other things as objects.

As Dōgen Zenji said in Shōbōgenzō "Genjōkōan," "To study the Buddha's Way is to study the self. To study the self is to forget the self. To forget the self is to be verified by all things. To be verified by all things is to let the body and mind of the self and the body and mind of others drop off."[103] The study of the Buddha's teaching is the study of this body and mind, of who we are. Shitou's teachings on difference and unity, two different understandings of the Buddha Way, are really about seeing our lives from two different perspectives as one seamless reality.

In Buddhism the concept of seeing one reality from two angles origi- nated in Nāgārjuna's teaching. In *Madhyamikakarika* Nāgārjuna said, "Without relying on everyday common practices (i.e., relative truths), the absolute truth cannot be expressed. Without approaching the abso- lute truth, nirvana cannot be attained" (24:10).[104] Here he distinguishes between relative truth, our day-to-day way of thinking, and absolute truth. In this way he introduces the idea of seeing one reality in two ways, which is the origin of the idea of difference and unity. The *Awak- ening of Faith* says, "The revelation of the true meaning of the principle of Mahāyāna can be achieved by unfolding the doctrine that the prin- ciple of One Mind has two aspects."[105] Here "One Mind" is the same as one reality, or "the mind of the great sage of India." This One Mind has two aspects, absolute truth and relativity or phenomena. One Mind can be seen from two perspectives. This is the origin of the idea of difference and unity called *ji* and *ri* in Chinese Buddhism. As we've seen, *ji* liter- ally means "event" or "thing," something very particular and concrete. It can also mean phenomenon, material, or something individual and independent. *Ri* means "principle" or "law," something abstract that has no shape or form, something universal. These two aspects are not two parts of one thing. Both aspects are included in reality, the One Mind. From one side, One Mind is a collection of individual things, and from another side, this whole reality is simply one. There is no distinction or separation within this one reality. And yet, individuality does not dis- appear. Individuality is there without separation. This means we don't discriminate between individuals.

One Hand and Five Fingers

For example, if I hold up my hand you might see it as a hand. And yet you can also see it as five fingers. One hand has five fingers, and there is no hand beyond these five fingers. Five fingers and one hand are the same thing: two aspects of one reality. Within this collection of five fin- gers, each finger is different and even has a different name. In Japanese the thumb is called *oyayubi*, or "parent." The index finger is called *hito-sashiyubi*, the finger to point at something. The middle finger is called *nakayubi*, which literally means the finger in the middle. The ring finger is called *kusuriyubi* because sometimes a doctor would use this finger to check medicine. The fifth finger is called *koyubi*, "child." Each finger differs in name, function, and shape. Each is independent, and yet when we call them a hand, the individuality of each finger disappears. *Ji* and *ri* are two ways of viewing things—as independent beings and as a whole. In the same way, the hand is a part of our body, which has many more parts. Each part—hand, head, foot, and billions of cells—is different, and yet this body works as one thing, a body.

Form and Emptiness

The phrase "the spiritual source" refers to unity or *ri*; "branching streams" refers to plurality or *ji*. The spiritual source is one and the branching streams are many. In "Sandōkai" *ji* is first translated as "things." Later the same word is translated as "phenomena." In the phrase "merging with principle," principle is a translation of *ri*. So "things" is *ji* and "principle" is *ri*.

In the *Heart Sutra* the terms "form" and "emptiness" correspond to *ji* and *ri*. "Form" refers to an individual being with a beginning and end; it is born, stays for a while, and disappears. Transient beings or entities without permanent self are said to have form. The *Heart Sutra* tells us that form is emptiness. This means that nothing exists as a truly independent being with a fixed self-nature. We appear to be independent but in reality are supported by all beings. I cannot survive as a human body or mind without the support of air, water, food, and so forth. The *Heart Sutra* also says that emptiness is form. Emptiness does not exist outside of form. We are a merging of difference and unity. From one perspective we are independent, but at the same time we are completely interdependent. As Buddhists we try to understand this contradiction by seeing it as two perspectives on a single reality. This is the basic idea of difference and unity, or ji and ri.

Light and Darkness

In the sentence "The spiritual source shines clearly in the light," light symbolizes ji or difference. The original word for "shines clearly" is *kōketzu*. *Kō* means "white," and *ketzu* means "clear and undefiled." This evokes an image of a full moon. But the moon shines in the darkness, not in the light. This sentence confuses us by saying the moon or the spiritual source shines in the light.

In the phrase "branching streams flow in the darkness," darkness represents ri. I didn't understand these two sentences for a long time because the spiritual source is ri, unity, and light is ji, or difference. This sentence means that the spiritual source (or unity) shines clearly in the light (or difference). Similarly the "branching streams," a symbol of ji or difference, "flow in the darkness," a symbol of ri or unity. The statement that unity shines in difference and difference flows in the unity is a paradox. It points out the dynamic interpenetration of discrimination and nondiscrimination.

We Are Separate but Together

We should try to understand this as a whole. Unity and difference are not two different things; they merge. From the perspective of ji or difference, we are independent people, separate individuals. I am not you; you are not me. Yet we cannot live completely alone. We live with other people and things; they are part of the reality of our life. Even so, I can't feel your pain, and you can't feel mine. My wife has pain in her teeth, but I have never had pain in my teeth. I have never even been to the dentist. I can't feel her pains, but I have different pains of my own. I have pain in my lower back that she cannot feel. The reality is that we are completely separate individuals. We can't even share pain. We are born alone, and we die alone. No one can be born for me, no one can live for me, and no one can die for me. From birth we are alone: we live alone, completely independent, and when we die we are really alone.

And yet we can never be completely alone. We cannot be born without a mother and father. We cannot grow up without support from our parents, family, and society. There are two aspects of our lives:

independent and interdependent. This is not a matter of separate parts of our life. Our whole life is individual, and at the same time our whole life is 100 percent interdependent. There is no separation of the two. This is an important point. We should see both aspects of our life at the same time. This is how we wake up to the reality of our life. This seems contradictory, and it causes problems when we think about it. These two aspects become separate things, two principles: individualism and socialism. If we don't understand, if we are unable to awake to reality, we become unhealthy. If we cling to the principle of individuality, we live on the basis of "I am I, I am not you, and you are not me." We live in isolation from the rest of the world. On the other hand, if we cling to the aspect of unity or wholeness, individuality is ignored. Then the individual lives only to serve society, and that's not healthy either.

In American society, individualism is a problem. In Japan, however, until recently the family was most important, and each person lived for the sake of the family. Either extreme is unhealthy.

Just Sitting Is Itself Merging of Difference and Unity

Often the practice or study of Zen or Buddhism involves an attempt to negate or go beyond individuality. We try to become one with universality, or buddha-nature. I disagree with this approach. For example, the Chinese master Sheng-yen wrote in a commentary on "Merging of Difference and Unity," "The first line of this couplet refers to light or brightness. The second line refers to darkness. Lightness represents enlightenment, and darkness represents vexation, or the condition of sentient beings before enlightenment."[106] In his interpretation, darkness is delusion, and we are deluded human beings because we don't see the unity. He says that enlightenment is to perceive the unity. However, Shitou is saying that delusion is grasping ji, that is, grasping independent things. I believe this is true. Shitou goes on to say, "Merging with principle is still not enlightenment." To merge with principle means to transcend individuality and become one with unity. It means to see the emptiness of all things. But Shitou says, "Merging with principle is still not enlightenment." Neither individuality nor unity is enlightenment.

Zen is often understood as a series of steps. We start out egocentric, completely deluded, clinging to ourselves. Through study and practice we try to become free from egocentricity. To be free from ego-clinging, we have to see the emptiness of all beings. This is called kensho or satori. But this is not final enlightenment. We have to return to individuality. This is a common way of explaining the steps of practice, but it is not consistent with my understanding of dharma or practice based on Dōgen Zenji's teachings.

Dōgen taught that there are no steps in practice. He said that practice and enlightenment are actually one. If there were steps, there would be deluded people and enlightened people, and there would be a step from the deluded to the enlightened stage of mind. There would be a separation between delusion and enlightenment, and between deluded and enlightened people. This separation is itself delusion, because in the absolute realm there is no such step, no discrimination between delusion and enlightenment. Discrimination between enlightenment and delusion only exists in ji; there is no distinction in ri. In unity or emptiness, delusion and enlightenment are not different, nor are samsara and nirvana, or deluded human beings and buddhas. That's the teaching of emptiness. Our practice does not proceed step by step. With this body and mind we sit in both individuality and universality. We are often pulled by our egocentricity. When we sit in this posture and let go of thought in our zazen, we have no technique. We have no object of meditation or contemplation. We don't concentrate our mind on anything particular. We don't even pay special attention to our breathing. We don't count breaths. We don't visualize anything. We just sit in this upright posture, breathe through the nose, quietly, deeply, and smoothly, and let go of thought. To let go of thought means to allow whatever comes in to go out. We let any idea, desire, or imagination come up and then go free. Nothing stays forever. We don't try to control our mind. We simply keep our body straight, breathe quietly, and let go of thought. This is our zazen based on Dōgen Zenji's teachings.

Within this zazen individuality is not lost. This is my practice; no one else can sit for me. My sitting is mine alone. And yet within this sitting practice we let go of our egocentricity. To let go of thought means to let go of our egocentricity. This body and mind is really part of buddha-nature, not something separate. Within this zazen, both ji and ri are manifested; neither is negated, neither affirmed. Both sides arise naturally in this simple practice. That's the meaning of Dōgen Zenji's expression "practice and enlightenment are one." Practice is my own individual practice, and enlightenment is universal. There is no separation between my enlightenment and your enlightenment, but practice is individual. I cannot practice for you. Practice is my personal activity, which manifests the universal reality of life. This zazen is itself the merging of difference and unity, not a step-by-step meditation practice. When we sit, we just sit. We express completely difference and unity, individuality and universality. To let go of thought is, I think, the most important point of our practice of zazen.

Practice in Day-to-Day Activities

We cannot let go of thought in our day-to-day activities. For example, when we prepare a meal we have to read the recipe. We have to use the correct ingredients in the proper way. Since we cannot let go of thought, we have to practice with our thoughts, with what we are doing now. We have to be clear about what we are cooking. We need to discriminate. Salt and sugar look very similar but are completely different, so we must discriminate between them. We need discrimination, and yet, as a practice when we are cooking, we let go of thought. In this case to let go of thought means to let go of all thought that is not needed for cooking. This means we are completely mindful of what we are doing right now, right here, at this moment. We use our whole mind to concentrate on our day-to-day activities.

Cooking also involves serving others. To prepare a meal for others is to make an offering. Our life becomes part of another person's life. This is the concrete meaning of interdependent existence. Through our activities we can become one with other beings. Oneness of subject and object is not a matter of philosophy, contemplation, or belief but a result of concrete action. Through an activity like cooking for others, our energy becomes the meal, and the meal becomes other people's energy. Our day-to-day activity, not only at the zendo but also at home and work, should be based on our zazen, on a merging of difference and unity. Our practice is not to kill our individuality. Of course, our practice is not to become more egoistic, but neither is it to simply become one with unity, with all beings. Our practice is to manifest the merging of difference and unity completely in every activity, including zazen. We try to live and act on this basis. We don't rely on others and yet we practice together with others. This is difficult but it is the healthiest way of life. We can be independent and not rely on others but still help them. Yet we often go astray. To be natural is the most difficult thing for us human beings.

SUBJECT-OBJECT: INTERACT AND NOT INTERACT

> Each sense and every field
> Interact and do not interact;
> When interacting, they also merge—
> Otherwise, they remain in their own states.

Each line in the original Chinese poem consists of five Chinese characters. In these four lines Shitou uses only fifteen different Chinese characters, fifteen words to express the whole of reality. This is incredible to me. I could write a whole book about these four lines.

Six Sense Organs and the Six Objects

The first phrase, "each sense," is a translation of the Chinese expression *monmon. Mon* means "gate," "entrance," or "exit." This expression refers to each of the six sense organs. These are called gates because stimulation from outside comes to us through them, and we express our thoughts and emotions through them to the outside. The next phrase, "every field," is a translation of *issai no kyō. Issai* means "all," and *kyō* in a Buddhist context means "objects or things outside of ourselves." This refers to the six objects of the sense organs. The object of the sixth sense organ, the mind, is something that we cannot touch, see, hear, smell, or taste but can imagine. Abstract concepts like love, numbers, and things that do not exist such as "the hair of a turtle" or "the horn of a rabbit" can be objects of mind. We cannot perceive these things, and yet we can think about them.

The sense organs and their objects are the totality of our life. Our life consists of subject (self, body, and mind) and objects (all beings as the objects of our sense organs). The objects of our sense organs are outside of our body and do not belong to us. Common sense tells us that there is a separation between the six sense organs and their objects. We, with our bodies and minds, relate to the objects outside us. We consider some things valuable or useful, others we don't. So we judge and evaluate, discriminate and categorize. When we encounter an object, we put it into a category and think we understand it. That's our usual way of seeing.

The six sense organs and their six objects appear in the *Heart Sutra*: "No eyes, no ears, no nose, no tongue, no body, no mind; / No color, no sound, no smell, no taste, no touch, no object of mind." The sutra says that such categories are not real. In fact, it says there is no independent thing called "I" to establish these categories. There are no independent entities called eyes, ears, nose, tongue, body, or mind. Nor are there independent entities called color, sound, smell, taste, touch, or objects of mind. In reality there are no independent entities at all, either inside or outside us. Instead, eyes, ears, nose, tongue, body, and mind work together as one body and mind, as one self. Color, sound, smell, touch, taste, and objects of mind also work together. This is the meaning of emptiness or dependent origination. Everything supports everything else; nothing has independent self-nature. As a result everything permeates everything else.

We Exist Supported by All Things

Without food, water, and air, we cannot live. We cannot maintain our bodies and minds. Food is made of other beings; when we digest, we incorporate them into ourselves, into our bodies. Our life is supported by all beings. This is the meaning of dependent origination. We are also supported by things from the past. I can use this glass to drink water today because someone made it and someone put water in it and served it to me. Everything in this present moment, in the past, and also in the future, supports everything else. It all works together as one function. This is the meaning of śūnyatā, emptiness, or dependent origination.

Sense Organs Work Together

In the sentence "Each sense and every field interact and do not interact," "field" refers to the object of each sense working together with the sense organ. There is no separation from the universal view. And yet we cannot say that the eye and ear are the same. Eye is eye, ear is ear, and nose is nose. They have different functions and shapes. They cannot replace each other. If we lose our eyes, we can't see. If we lose our nose, we can't smell. But in a universal sense they are not independent; none of them have self-nature. They are really interdependent. And yet in our common sense way of seeing the world, eye is eye, nose is nose, tongue is tongue. Individuality and universality always coexist, and neither side should be negated or ignored. We should always try to see reality, all beings, and our lives from both perspectives.

Interact and Not Interact

In the phrase "interact and do not interact," the Japanese for "interact" is *e-go*. *E* means "turn around," and *go* means "each other" or "mutually." So *e-go* means mutually to turn, to influence, to work together, or to penetrate each other. Interaction is the aspect of unity—eye, ear, nose, tongue, body, and mind working together with no separation. The second half of the phrase, *fu e-go*, means "do not interact"; eye is eye, ear is ear, nose is nose, tongue is tongue. Everything is independent in its own function. This refers to individuality, independence, and difference, as in the title "Merging of Difference and Unity."

Consider an orchestra: Each person plays a different instrument. A violin is not a piano, and a piano is not a drum. They all make different sounds. They are independent and cannot replace each other. Yet when they work together, they make one musical whole. But even as we listen to an orchestra as one sound, there are still many independent musicians all playing their own parts. Both sides are always present. This is true of any community. For example, in this sangha there are different positions, each filled by a different person who carries out his or her own duties. But this sangha also exists as a whole, as one sangha, and in this sense there is no separation among us. "Interact" refers to everything working together and "not interact" describes everything having its own individual shape, function, and practice.

Harmony in Community

Community always includes both aspects. If we ignore either, the sangha, family, or body becomes sick and functions poorly. If we think only of one individual and lose sight of the community as a whole, the community doesn't work. But it's not healthy to put too much emphasis on the community and ignore individuals. When we go too far toward either extreme, we become sick. We have to try to find the Middle Way. This is one of the most important concepts in Buddhism. We find the Middle Way when we sacrifice neither the individual nor the community. In *Shōbōgenzō* "Bodaisatta Shishōbō" (Bodhisattva's Four Embracing Dharmas), Dōgen Zenji said, "Identity-action means not to be different—neither different from self nor from others."[107] This means we have to find a way for both self and others to be peaceful, harmonious, and beneficial as a whole. This is called compassion. It doesn't mean that I sacrifice myself for the sake of the community but that the community should include this self. We have to find a way that this community can include this individual self and be healthy. This is the bodhisattva Way.

Interacting and Not Interacting Interact

The next line of "Sandōkai" says, "When interacting, they also merge." "When interacting" as a translation of *e-go* is not quite accurate because it implies that things interact only at particular times. Actually all things are always interacting. The Japanese word for "merge" here is *wataru*.

The Chinese character for this word has two parts; one means "water" or "river," and the other means "to walk." Together, the two mean to cross the river, in this case to cross on foot a river with no bridge. Often Chinese or Japanese villages are separated by a small river. The river is a boundary that is crossed only when there is a problem to be resolved. This character thus means to negotiate, to meet in order to solve problems. It also means to see around the world, or to walk around the world and see things. So *wataru* means to cross borders and work together.

At the same time, it implies some independence, since people don't cross the boundaries between villages very often. Especially in ancient times, people who were born in a village died in the same village. One family might live in the same village for many generations. When I lived in a small farming village in Kyoto, Japan, there were about seventy families, most of whom had lived there more than five hundred years. In the temple there was a family grave that dated back to the sixteenth century. The villagers didn't get out much. But when there were problems they had to cross the boundary and meet, negotiate, and work together. That's the meaning of wataru. This kanji, or Chinese character, shows both individuality and collaboration. The interaction it describes is not tied to a special time or occasion but ongoing, among all beings and things. And yet at the same time all things have independence.

Not Interacting Within Interacting

The next line, "Otherwise, they remain in their own states," refers to noninteraction, which is also an ongoing aspect of reality rather than a specific time or circumstance. Eye is always eye, nose is nose. I am I, you are you. The Chinese character translated here as "state" has two parts. One means "human being or person," the other "standing." Together they describe a person standing in a certain place, meaning that each person has his or her own place or position. This refers not only to individuals but to the functions of each individual. All the senses and their objects are independent. Each has its own place, stage, rank, and function. They cannot combine. Both aspects, individuality and interaction, are always present. This seems contradictory but is in fact the nature of reality.

Wondrous Dharma

Dōgen Zenji's major work is *Shōbōgenzō*. *Shō* means "true," "right," or "correct." *Bō* is "dharma." *Gen* means "eyes." A *zō* is a storehouse or treasury. *Shōbōgenzō* thus means "treasury of the true dharma eye." This means that this reality, the reality of our life, is a treasury of the eye. In this case, "eye" stands for the wisdom that sees the true dharma. The Sanskrit for "true dharma" is *saddharma*. It is part of the title of the *Lotus Sutra*, *Saddharmapuṇḍarīka Sutra*, where it means "true reality or true teaching." The Chinese translation of this Sanskrit word is *myōhō*. *Myō* is an interesting character with two parts: one means *woman* and the other *young*. Literally, *myō* refers to the beauty of a young woman. It means beautiful, excellent, wonderful, strange, and always changing—something we can't grasp. *Myō* is sometimes translated into English as "wondrous," meaning excellent and ungraspable. We can't understand it with logic. So the reality of our life is excellent, wonderful, and yet strange and hard to understand. As explained above *hō* means dharma.

Reality itself is a question for us. There is no way to reduce the reality of our life to any logical system and completely understand it, because our life is so complex. Reality is always asking us, "What is this life? Who are we? What am I doing?" Somehow we have to answer with our practice. Practice doesn't necessarily mean sitting or studying the Buddha's teaching. Practice can mean the activities of our day-to-day lives. Even when we try to avoid answering reality's questions, that avoidance itself is an answer. If we try to deny reality, that's also an answer. So we can't avoid it. Each one of us has to engage this reality, including our self, body, mind, and situation. Our self and our situation work together. We have to accept this total reality as our self. Self is not a separate part of reality. Our life is the sum of all the things happening inside and outside us. We try to be peaceful, not only inside ourselves but throughout the whole universe. There may be no war within this country, but if there is fighting somewhere else this country cannot be peaceful, because everything is connected. We have to work together with things inside and outside ourselves. This attitude is bodhisattva practice.

These four sentences express the wondrous reality of our life; a life that has two aspects, interacting and not interacting, that also interact with each other. And yet each and every thing stays in its own dharma position. This expression "dharma position" is originally from the *Lotus Sutra*. Dōgen Zenji uses it in *Shōbōgenzō* "Genjōkōan," where he says that firewood stays at the dharma position of firewood, and ash stays at the dharma position of ash, and yet "before and after is cut off" by the fire. It's difficult to understand, but we have to work through this as a koan. *Genjō* refers to whatever is happening in this present moment as the dharma position. *Koan* means both "reality" and also "question." Reality asks a question, "What is this?" and we must try to answer. The answer is our practice.

DARKNESS AND LIGHT

Forms are basically different in material and appearance,
Sounds are fundamentally different in pleasant or harsh
    quality.
"Darkness" is a word for merging upper and lower;
"Light" is an expression for distinguishing pure and defiled.

Differences of the Objects

Here "forms" means the material objects of our sense field. Although this poem only mentions forms and sounds, it means all six objects of our sense organs (including mind, which senses mental formations). All things have varied natures and characteristics. We are all human beings and yet each of us looks different. Although we share a common nature or essence, we vary in appearance. All things have some aspects in common and also some unique qualities.

Shitou continues, "Sounds are fundamentally different in pleasant or harsh quality." There are many different kinds of sound, some pleasing, some terrible. We feel good when we listen to beautiful music, but if we are sitting in the zendo and someone turns on loud rock-and-roll, it's disturbing. The same song might make us feel good or bad depending on the situation. The effect of a song depends not only on the nature of the sound itself but also on the condition of this body and mind.

The same is true of taste. Delicious food and awful food might have very similar nutritional value. But we have likes and dislikes. Each thing has its own unique character, and we also respond to it in different ways. Sometimes we feel good, sometimes we feel bad. Even when we have delicious food in front of us, if we are not hungry the delicious food is the same as junk food. When we are really hungry, even junk food seems a feast. The appearance, quality, meaning, and value of things around us all depend on the properties of each thing and on the condition of our body and mind. Nothing has a fixed nature or value.

Darkness and Light: Nondiscrimination and Discrimination

Shitou goes on to say, "'Darkness' is a word for merging upper and lower; 'Light' is an expression for distinguishing pure and defiled." This is the same principle as *ji* and *ri*. *Ji*, it will be recalled, is the aspect of independence; each thing has its own characteristics. *Ri* is the aspect of universality or unity. For example, a hand is made up of five independent fingers, each with a different shape, function, and name. We cannot separate the fingers from the hand, and we cannot separate the fingers from the billions of cells that make them up. A cell is a collection of billions of atoms that cannot be separated. Each atom is also a collection of smaller particles. This one hand is a part of my body, which is a part of the human society, which is a part of the larger ecology of the earth. Earth is a small part of the whole universe. Nothing is fixed and yet each thing is really independent. This is really a wondrous way of being. This is what is meant in the *Heart Sutra* when it says, "form is emptiness and emptiness is form." Nothing is fixed, yet this hand is this hand. I am I, but this "I" doesn't exist independently. I can exist as a part of something or as a collection of things. Darkness, or *ri*, is the universal aspect of our life. Light, *ji*, is the individual, independent aspect of our life. In the dark, colors are indistinguishable. In the light, everything becomes clear. We can distinguish between red and blue, north and south, grass and water. We should see our life and world from both perspectives, light and darkness, differentiation and non-differentiation. We usually see ourselves as individuals, distinct from other people. I say this is me, and this is my opinion. I like this, I hate that. If someone else has a different opinion we may feel angry or sad. Many conflicts and problems arise from this difference. Yet when we see oneness or universality, we understand that we are living out the same life, supported by all beings. We realize that without others we cannot live. When we clearly, deeply understand this, many problems disappear naturally.

Nondiscrimination Is Not Enlightenment

Because of our upbringing, we can easily see our individuality. So the first thing we have to learn is to see the universality of our life. We need to be able to see that we share our life with other people, with all beings in the whole universe. That is the meaning of interdependence, one of the main teachings of the Buddha. But if we cling to that perspective and call it enlightenment, it's a mistake. The Buddha taught that we must see the reality of our life from both sides.

Our zazen practice is to awaken to the reality prior to separation. Ordinarily we see things from one perspective or the other. When we sit, we let go of thoughts and all particular perspectives. We don't grasp anything. That doesn't mean that we have to extinguish thought. Thought is always there as we experience our life, even when sitting in this posture. Our mind often seems busier than usual when we sit in a quiet place. In fact, our body and mind are busier and noisier in everyday life, but since our environment is also noisy, we don't notice the commotion inside ourselves. When we come to a quiet place, however, we hear even the smallest noise. When we sit in the zendo, we can hear the sound of the clock. The sounds our bodies make, coming from within us, become more noticeable, and it seems that our mind is noisier than usual. I think that's a good sign of our practice. We hear this noise because our mind is beginning to calm down. Of course, we should let go of the internal noise. We should neither cling to nor try to escape from the noise. We should just be awake and let it go. Let all thoughts, feelings, and daydreams simply come and go freely. Everything is moving; nothing stays forever. Just let everything be with you.

In zazen you should keep this upright posture, breathe quietly through your nose, and let go of everything. We don't try to control anything, just keep this posture and let go. That is how darkness and light manifest. Thought is still there. Yet we don't think. It's a difficult point to explain. It's like when you are driving a car and shift into neutral. The engine is moving but the car doesn't go anywhere. In our zazen we put our mind into neutral. Thought is there but we are not moved by it. My teacher Uchiyama Roshi said, "Thought is just a secretion from our brain." Thought is not a poison. But if you grasp and are controlled by it, it becomes poisonous. We actualize both darkness and light when we open our hand of thought and are not moved. That is sitting practice. Our zazen is not a method to contemplate reality which has lightness and dark. It is a way to manifest both darkness and light. We are not the observer but rather the reality itself.

FOUR GROSS ELEMENTS

> The four gross elements return to their own natures
> Like a baby taking to its mother;
> Fire heats, wind moves,
> Water wets, earth is solid.
> Eye and form, ear and sound;
> Nose and smell, tongue and taste—

The four gross elements are fire, wind, water, and earth. Here these four words refer not to the literal elements but to the elements of our life. For example, fire represents body heat; wind symbolizes breathing and moving; water denotes blood, tears, or other bodily liquids; and earth suggests bones, nails, hair, and other solids. In addition to these four, Mahāyāna Buddhism considers *ku*, which means "emptiness" or "space," the fifth gross element. In Chinese, space and emptiness are represented by the same character, which means "sky." Everything occupies space, so space is, in a sense, another element.

Each element has its own nature: fire heats, wind moves, water is wet, earth is solid. These elements cannot be confused. But at the same time the five elements combine to form one body, one mind, one person. Not only this one person but everything in this universe is composed of these five elements. Everything is just a collection of those elements, and yet each being, each thing, maintains its independence. It's really wondrous and yet this is reality.

Shitou continues, "Eye and form, ear and sound; nose and smell, tongue and taste." This is a list of some of the sense organs of the body and mind and their objects. They are independent and yet work together to create the world. When we sit in this space, the space and my sitting become one. When I cook in the kitchen, this body, my self, the ingredients, the water, the fire, the utensils, and the space called the kitchen become one being working together. When we play baseball, this whole universe becomes the world of playing baseball. Our activity and the universe become one. It all works together. If we become angry, this whole world becomes the world of anger. Everything around us makes us crazy, angry. When we have a competitive mind, this entire world becomes the world of competition. All other beings, all other people, become competitors. Our body and mind work together with our environment to create one world. In this sense our mind is very important. A change in our mind could change the whole world. Our practice is important because it is not just the practice of our mind; it influences the whole universe.

ROOT AND LEAVES RETURN TO THE SOURCE

Thus in all things
The leaves spread from the root;

The whole process must return to the source;
"Noble" and "base" are only manners of speaking.

The Source Gives Birth to the Root and the Leaves

Here Shitou uses the expression "leaves and root" in the same way as "spiritual source and branching streams." This too is a symbol of individuality and universality. The leaves represent individuality and the root symbolizes oneness. I question the translation of the next phrase, "The whole process must return to the source." The Japanese word used for "whole process" is *hon matsu*. *Hon* means "original" or "foundation," and *matsu* means "twigs and leaves." *Hon* can also mean "root." From the root or foundation all individual beings arise. And this sentence says that both *hon* (root) and *matsu* (twigs) must return to the source. A better translation would be, "Unity and individuality must return to the source."

This "source" is different from the "spiritual source" mentioned near the beginning of the poem. "Spiritual source" refers to the root (oneness). In contrast, this "source" is a translation of the Chinese word *zong* (Jap., *shū*), which means "essence" or "origin." This is a very Chinese expression of reality. In Chinese thought, individuality emerges from oneness. It is often said that Zen Buddhism is a mixture of Indian Buddhism and Chinese philosophy—in this case Taoism. The idea that individual beings spring from oneness is a typically Taoist way of thinking. Lao Tzu said, "Return is the movement of the Tao. Yielding is the way of the Tao. All things are born of being. Being is born of nonbeing. The Tao is nowhere to be found. Yet it nourishes and completes all things. The Tao gives birth to One. One gives birth to Two. Two gives birth to Three. Three gives birth to all things."[108] This means that myriad independent things flow from oneness. This oneness in turn derives from the Tao of nothingness, or *mu*. Ultimately both difference and unity return to the source (*shū*), which is nothingness (*mu*).

Unlike the Chinese, Indian Buddhists didn't believe that emptiness is the source of form. They believed that form is emptiness and emptiness is form but not that emptiness is the source of form. In this poem, we can see a mixture of Indian and Chinese philosophy. Some modern Buddhist scholars conclude that because Zen is a mixture of Chinese and Indian thought, it is not true Buddhism. I think the situation is more complex. Chinese Buddhism is Buddhism influenced by Chinese culture. Japanese Buddhism is Buddhism influenced by Japanese culture. We could also say that Japanese Buddhism is Japanese culture influenced by Buddhism. In the same way, we can say that Chinese Buddhism is Chinese culture influenced by Buddhism. We can look at either from two different directions. We can think of American Buddhism as American culture influenced by Buddhism or as Buddhism influenced by American culture. To judge a practice as true Buddhism or not based on the national and cultural background of the practitioner's understanding does not make much sense to me. We need to find our own expression of the dharma, of reality. This is a simple but at the same time complex and interesting reality.

Another example of this contrast between Indian and Chinese thought is the "two truths" in Nāgārjuna's teaching versus the "three truths" in the philosophy of Tientai Zhiyi (Tendai Chigi, 538–597), the most important master in the Chinese Tientai (Tendai) school. To review, Nāgārjuna's two truths are absolute truth and conventional truth. In chapter 24 of the *Mūlamadhyamakakārikā*, "Examination of the Fourfold Noble Truth," Nāgārjuna said:

> The teaching of the Dharma by the various Buddhas is based on the two truths, namely, the relative (worldly) truth and the absolute (supreme) truth. Those who do not know the distinction between the two truths cannot understand the profound nature of the Buddha's teaching. Without relying on everyday common practice (i.e., relative truths), the absolute truth cannot be expressed. Without approaching the absolute truth, nirvana cannot be attained. We declare that whatever is relational origination is śūnyatā (emptiness). It is a provisional name (i.e., thought construction) for the mutuality (of being) and indeed, it is the middle path (24:8–10).[109]

In these passages, according to Hajime Nakamura, a Japanese Buddhist scholar, Nāgārjuna only says that relational (interdependent) origination, śūnyatā (emptiness), provisional names, and the middle path are all the same thing.

In his interpretation of Nāgārjuna's passages, Zhiyi creates three truths. The first is the conventional truth of all beings as provisional names, the second is the truth of śūnyatā (emptiness), and the third is the truth of the middle. First we need to negate the conventional truth and see emptiness. Next, we need to negate śūnyatā and enter the truth of the middle, because śūnyatā is also a provisional name. To be free from provisional names including śūnyatā is the truth of the middle. In this interpretation, provisional names and śūnyatā oppose each other and yet are the same. Freedom from and transcendence of both is the truth of the middle. To me, Zhiyi's interpretation of the three truths and Shitou's saying the root (unity) and twigs (difference) must return to the source show the same pattern of Chinese thought.

The symbol of yin and yang echoes this pattern. Yin (black) and yang (white) oppose each other, and yet yin is included in yang and vice versa. The opposite movements of each are integrated into one circle. This circle is called the "great ultimate" (Chi., *taiji*; Jap., *taikyoku*). It is the source in "Sandōkai."

"Sandōkai" as a Buddhist Text

When we read "Sandōkai" as a Buddhist text, we need to understand it from a Buddhist rather than Taoist perspective. Forms are not derived from emptiness. Unity does not give birth to difference. Five fingers are not born from one hand. Rather, one hand and five fingers are exactly the same thing.

When Shitou says, "'Noble' and 'base' are only manners of speaking," he is referring to buddhas as noble and other humans as base. We can substitute any other dichotomy—enlightenment and delusion, or universality and individuality—for noble and base. He refers here to our dualistic way of thinking and expression as "only manners of speaking." The reality before thought or explanation can only be experienced. We cannot discuss it. As soon as we try, we have already missed it. This is an important point. We can talk about our life or our zazen; but when we talk about our life, our life itself is already somewhere else. When we talk about zazen, zazen itself is somewhere else. So when we sit zazen, we should forget about what zazen is, because we are already doing it. When we think about zazen, we are not doing it; we are thinking. When we sit, we should forget what we are doing. We should forget what zazen is and just sit. That is the meaning of "just sit" or shikantaza.

How Avalokiteśvara Works with Thousands of Eyes and Hands

There is a koan that illustrates this relationship between independence and interdependence. It is a question and answer between Yunyan Tan-sheng and Daowu Yuanzhi (Dōgo Enchi, 769–835).[110] The brothers Yunyan and Daowu were disciples of Yaoshan Weiyan, who was one of Shitou's disciples. Yunyan was the younger brother and became a monk at an early age. Daowu was an official and became a monk twenty years later. Daowu attained the Way quickly, while Yunyan was never enlightened. Yunyan's main disciple was Dongshan, the founder of the Caodong (Sōtō) school in China. The relationship between two brothers, actual as well as dharma brothers, was very interesting.

Master Yunyan asked Daowu, "How does the Bodhisattva of Great Compassion use his manifold hands and eyes?" The Bodhisattva of Great Compassion is Avalokiteśvara or Kanzeon Bosatsu. He is a symbol of the Buddha's compassion. Some statues of Avalokiteśvara have a thousand hands and a thousand eyes, one on each hand. Eyes are a symbol of wisdom. So this bodhisattva has many eyes to see the differences between beings and many hands to save them. Yunyan's question is, how does Avalokiteśvara use so many hands and eyes?

Daowu replied, "It's like a man reaching behind himself in the night searching for a pillow." Sometimes in the night we lose our pillow, and have to find it in the darkness. Before electricity the night was really dark. Somehow we can find the pillow even though we cannot see it with our eyes. In a way our whole body is our eyes.

Yunyan said, "I understand."

"What do you understand?" Daowu asked.

Yunyan answered, "There are a thousand eyes all over the body."

Daowu said "That's very good, but you express only 80 or 90 percent of it." He was saying that Yunyan's understanding was not yet perfect. This is a very important point in our lineage. If you really become perfect, there is nothing more to do. Our understanding should always be 80 or 90 percent, and we need to keep inquiring.

Yunyan said, "That's my answer, how about you, elder brother?" Daowu replied, "The whole body is hands and eyes." In the chapter on the *Heart Sutra* I explained that one of the points of this koan is whether Yunyan's and Daowu's expressions are exactly the same or not. If we think they are different, we could interpret them as follows. Yunyan said there are a thousand eyes all over the body, and Daowu said the whole body is hands and eyes. In the original Chinese only two characters are different, *hen* and *tsū*, and they both mean "whole" or "entire." It might seem as though Yunyan and Daowu are saying the same thing. But *hen* means that there are hands and eyes all over the body, and in Daowu's expression, *tsū* means this whole body functions as eyes and hands. It's a subtle difference, but Daowu's statement is much more dynamic. He refers to an action or activity. Yunyan's expression is more static.

Daowu is saying that our practice, not just our zazen, but our whole life, should be lived like Avalokiteśvara. We have only two hands and eyes, and yet when we do something our whole body should become eyes. When we see something, for instance a painting in a museum, our whole body should become our eyes. We appreciate the painting with the whole body and mind, not just our eyes. When we eat, we taste not only with our tongue but with our whole body. The color and shape of food is important. The circumstances or environment of the place where we eat is also important. The taste of food depends very much on the situation. When we do something we do it with our whole body. The eye is the eye. It really is independent. Yet when we actually do something, we do it with our whole body and mind. All individual sense organs and parts of our body work together as one body and mind, as one person. This is a very practical meaning of emptiness. Everything works together to create each situation. It is our practice to awaken to this entire reality, which includes the self and all beings, creating together.

RIGHT IN LIGHT THERE IS DARKNESS

> Right in light there is darkness, but don't confront it as
>   darkness;
> Right in darkness there is light, but don't see it as light.
> Light and dark are relative to one another
> Like forward and backward steps.

Light and Darkness Interpenetrate

In the beginning of "Sandōkai," Shitou says, "The spiritual source shines clearly in the light; the branching streams flow in the darkness." This is the way he expresses the interpenetration of difference and unity, ji and ri, the absolute truth and relative truth. Here he uses light and darkness again to describe the attitude we should use to encounter and see the interpenetrating reality.

"Right in light there is darkness, but ..." This translation has "but," but I think "therefore" is better: "therefore don't confront it as darkness." Light and darkness are always together. We cannot understand our life through only one aspect. We often see darkness, unity, or nondiscrimination as enlightenment and discrimination as delusion. From this perspective, enlightenment means to give up light, differentiation, and discrimination and to live in the realm of nondiscrimination. Shitou conveys a more complex understanding. In the phrase "light and dark," light refers to samsara and dark to nirvana or nondiscrimination. But these are inseparable aspects of reality. In Mahāyāna Buddhism, our practice is not to escape samsara for nirvana. Nirvana is within samsara, which is within nirvana. We cannot make this life all nirvana or all samsara because samsara and nirvana always exist together. Right in samsara there is nirvana.

The next sentence repeats the same idea. "Right in darkness there is light, therefore don't see it as light." We cannot define this light using only one concept. Delusion and enlightenment always exist together. Delusion is a product of our mind. The fact that our brain has the power to produce delusion is reality. We cannot remove this capability from our brain. Somehow we must live with our delusions as the reality of our life. But if we forget that our delusions are created by our own minds and mistake them for reality, then we are completely caught and our life becomes a mess. We can't see where to go. We have to find a way to live with delusion without being pulled around by it.

Shitou continues, "Light and dark are relative to one another like forward and backward steps." There is no light without darkness and no darkness without light. But what do forward and backward steps mean? In walking, when the right foot is forward, the left foot is backward. When the right foot is backward, the left foot is forward. In this sense, light and darkness are like right and left feet. They are always together but sometimes we see only light and sometimes only darkness. Sometimes darkness is forward, sometimes light. But light and darkness are always together just like our feet when we are walking.

Darkness Is Negative, Light Is Positive

There are two meanings each for light and darkness. We can combine them to make three different pairs of meanings. Darkness is usually used in a negative sense, as ignorance, absence of discrimination, lack of intellection, or the inability to distinguish good from evil. Without knowledge we cannot understand what is happening. This meaning of darkness is negative because it's defined as a lack of discrimination. One meaning of light is the opposite of this first meaning of darkness; light can mean intellection. We study how to analyze, categorize, and conceptualize things. In this way we can see things outside ourselves in more detail, more clearly. This way of interacting with the things around us is called rationalism. The use of reason to understand our world is the original English meaning of enlightenment. In eighteenth-century Europe enlightenment emphasized the accumulation of knowledge.

Our suffering is caused by ignorance, so we must study more and use our reason. This is still an underlying assumption in education, not only in the West but also in the rest of the world.

Light Is Negative, Darkness Is Positive

The first meaning of light is the use of our intellect to see things not only outside of ourselves but inside as well. We call this discrimination. Abhidharma was a Buddhist form of rationalism, an attempt to understand things through reason and analysis. Abhidharma was the mainstream of Buddhist philosophy before Mahāyāna. The Abhidharma text *Abhidharmakośa bhāṣya* categorized all things into seventy-five dharmas or elements. These philosophers believed that there is no ātman or ego, no body and mind beyond a collection of elements, and that self has no substance. That's the meaning of emptiness or selflessness. They believed that the seventy-five elements really did exist and that all beings are collections of those seventy-five elements. They wrote clear definitions of each element. The five skandhas is another way to analyze a being into categories.

Mahāyāna Buddhism transcends this rationalism and conceptualization with the philosophy of emptiness. Mahāyāna Buddhism taught that the elements themselves are without substance, that they are empty. That is the meaning of the statement that the five skandhas are empty. Even the fundamental elements are empty. This means that eye, ear, nose, and tongue don't function separately, but only as a whole. They are all connected with each other. That is one meaning of emptiness. Nothing can exist as an independent entity and everything functions as part of a larger system. This perspective is called nondiscriminating mind or nondiscriminating wisdom. It is also referred to as darkness in this poem.

Going Beyond Negative and Positive

If darkness as lack of discrimination or intellection and light as rational discrimination are paired, darkness is negative and light is positive. However, we can also make a second pair with light as negative (discrimination from a limited view) and darkness as positive (a nondiscriminatory way of seeing).

In Buddhism we commonly think that nondiscrimination is the answer; that we should try to set aside discrimination and enter the realm of nondiscrimination, which is enlightenment. That's true but it's not the end of the story. There is another meaning of light called the Buddha's wisdom or "later obtained discriminating wisdom," which is also based on nondiscrimination. In our daily lives we have to discriminate to practice and to help others. In this case, nondiscrimination means nonattachment. This light is called prajñā and is described in the *Heart Sutra* as the bright mantra. It's very important that we go beyond nondiscrimination. In Zen there are some people who attain so-called enlightenment and stay in a condition of nondiscrimination. Sometimes such people cling to that condition with a kind of greed. These practitioners are called *an shō no zenji*. *An* means "darkness" and *shō* is "enlightenment." So the phrase means "enlightenment in darkness," a negative condition. Buddhism and our life itself have many dimensions. We should not stagnate in one condition. In this poem, it appears that Shitou discusses only the relationship between light and darkness, between differentiation and nondifferentiation. But the insight Shitou uses to describe the relationship between light and darkness is an example of the Buddha's wisdom, this third meaning of light. He shows us that differentiation between darkness and light is just another kind of discrimination. He discriminates between these two and then integrates them. This is a very practical wisdom, free from both discrimination and nondiscrimination. It is a more natural function of our life.

BOX AND COVER JOINING

> All things have their function—
> It is a matter of use in the appropriate situation.
> Phenomena exist like box and cover joining;
> Principle accords like arrow points meeting.

Each Thing Has Its Own Place and Function

"All things have their function." Everything and everybody has a unique function. We all have different capabilities, talents, characteristics, personalities, bodies, and languages. All things have a function appropriate to some situation. The word in Japanese for "appropriate situation" is *sho*, meaning "place." Each one of us has to find the best place to use this body and mind. This unique body and mind exists as an intersection of difference and unity. That is the place where we can create our own unique way of life. That is our practice. Our practice doesn't mean we have to make ourselves into a particular shape. We are not like cars with certain standard shapes and qualities. We have a responsibility to accept this unique body and mind and put it to use. To fulfill the potential of this body and mind, we have to find an appropriate situation and embrace it as our own life, as our own work.

Phenomena and Principle Are Like Box and Lid

Next Shitou says, "Phenomena exist like box and cover joining; principle accords like arrow points meeting." "Phenomena" is a translation for *ji*, meaning particular things or beings. "Principle" is a translation of *ri*, the unity or universality of all beings. Shitou says that phenomena exist in accord with principle, and principle exists in accord with phenomena. "Phenomena exist like box and cover joining; principle accords like arrow points meeting" is actually just one sentence. This is rhetoric used in Chinese poetry to avoid repetition of the same two subjects. Each of the two clauses is about the way phenomena and principle exist and work together. We should read, "Phenomena and principle exist like box and cover joining; principle accords with phenomena like arrow points meeting." Phenomena and principle, ji and ri, difference and unity, exist like box and cover joining. Each box is a different size with a lid that fits exactly. So there is no principle other than phenomena. Phenomena and principle are like box and cover, completely joined.

Arrow Points Meeting in the Air

"Arrow points meeting" is a reference to a classic Chinese story about two archery masters.[111] One was the teacher and the other his excellent disciple. When the student felt his skill had surpassed his teacher's, he challenged him. When they took aim at each other and shot, the arrows met in midair and fell to the ground. Both lived because they had equal skill. Shitou says that phenomena and principle, difference and unity, should meet like the arrows. Our practice is to actualize this relationship between difference and unity in each situation. For example, we cannot live by ourselves. We are part of a community, and yet no matter where I live, I am I. I cannot be another person, and yet to be a member of a community I have to transcend "I am I" and see the situation of the whole community. We have a point of view as an individual and also as a member of the sangha or community. We also have another "I" who sees the situation from both perspectives. The viewpoint of an individual person is in this case an example of difference. It's very natural that I have an opinion different from other people. We shouldn't negate our individual opinions, but as a member of a community, we have to see things as a whole. The most desirable condition is when both ways of seeing meet each other like the arrows shot by the masters. If we can perceive a situation like that, we can be really peaceful. It doesn't happen very often because it's really difficult. Our way of life is always like arrows missing each other. That's why we have pain in our social lives. There is no way another person or a god can make these arrows meet. Our practice is to find the "appropriate situation" in which this person as an individual and this person as a member of the sangha can meet like a box and cover joining, or like two arrows in midair.

DO NOT WASTE TIME

> Hearing the words, you should understand the source;
> Don't make up standards on your own.
> If you don't understand the path as it meets your eyes,
> How can you know the way as you walk?

Progress is not a matter of far or near,
But if you are confused, mountains and rivers block the way.
I humbly say to those who study the mystery,
Don't waste time.

Words and Reality

This is the final message from Shitou to us. "Hearing the words, you should understand the source." We have been reading and studying his words in this wonderful poem. He gives us the final advice that if we grasp what he has written as a theory, memorize his words, and build a system of concepts from his teaching, we will totally miss his point. All words and concepts are discriminatory. The basic function of words and concepts is to separate one thing from all other things. Even when we use the word "absolute," we have already slipped into the opposite concept, "relative." "Nondiscrimination" has meaning only in a dichotomy with "discrimination." How can we go beyond the discrimination between "absolute" and "relative," or "discrimination" and "nondiscrimination"? The only way is to see the source, the reality as it exists before being processed by our thinking mind. To do so, we need practice. Any theoretical system of concepts or thoughts is a distorted copy of reality. We can only practice it, experience it, and nod our head.

All doctrines, theories, and descriptions using words and concepts are distorted images of reality from our own point of view. When we realize this, even a distorted copy can be useful. However, if we mistake the distorted map for the true reality, we stray, making up our own standards of judgment.

Just Sitting on the Ground of Reality

Shitou asks, "If you don't understand the path as it meets your eyes, how can you know the way as you walk?" When we wake up to reality, the Way is always in front of our eyes. We are born, live, and die within this reality. We never fall out of reality. And yet, we almost always lose sight of it. By just sitting and letting go of thought, we can be within reality. Just sitting allows us to put our entire being on the ground of reality. But usually, we make up our own standards and create our distorted version of reality. Therefore, we need to constantly practice letting go. When we place ourselves on the ground of reality, we will find the path we need to walk. Otherwise, we will be lost in the map made by our minds.

Practice Is Moment by Moment

"Progress is not a matter of far or near, but if you are confused, mountains and rivers block the way." Our practice is not a race with others, a competition run from the starting point to the goal. It is not a matter of far or near. Our practice is moment by moment. When we awake, we are right in the middle of the Way. At the next moment, when we lose sight of reality, we are 100 percent off the mark. If we walk within a distorted map, no matter how long we practice, we wander far from the Way even though we are always right within the Way. We are blocked by mountains and rivers within our mind.

"I humbly say to those who study the mystery, don't waste time." No matter how hard we practice, if our practice is not based on true reality, we are wasting our time.

ENDLESS PRACTICE HERE AND NOW:
THE VERSE FOR OPENING THE SUTRA

An unsurpassed, penetrating, and perfect Dharma
is rarely met with even in a hundred thousand million kalpas.
Having it to see and listen to, to remember and accept,
I vow to taste the truth of the Tathāgata's words.[112]

THIS IS A reasonably accurate English translation of the verse
chanted before dharma talks at many American Zen centers. A
more literal translation from the original Japanese is:

An unsurpassed, most profound, subtle, and wondrous
    Dharma,
even in a hundred thousand ten thousand kalpas, it is diffi-
    cult to encounter.
I now see and listen, and I am able to accept and uphold it;
I vow (or wish) to understand the true meaning of the
    Tathāgata.

This seems to be a very simple verse. It says that since the Dharma, the
Buddha's teaching, is rarely encountered, now that I have met it, I want
to deeply understand it. I think, however, that it takes some time to
taste and really appreciate this verse.

In Japanese the first line is "Mujō jin jin mimyō no hō wa." *Mujō* means "unsurpassed." The first *jin* means "very" or "extremely," and the second means "deep" or "profound." So *mujō jin jin* means "highest and also deepest." *Mi* means "very small" or "subtle," something we cannot see with our unaided eyes. So the first line means that the Dharma or the Buddha's teaching is the highest or ultimate, and also the deepest and most subtle.

Dharma has two meanings: the Buddha's teachings, and the truth to which he awakened. So *Dharma* means both teachings about reality and the reality itself. This first line says that the Buddha's teaching is the highest, deepest, and most subtle and wondrous of teachings. It also says that the reality to which Shakyamuni Buddha awakened is the highest, deepest, and most subtle and wondrous. "Highest" implies upward movement; "deepest" implies downward. In Buddhism this pair has special meaning. To go up means to see reality with wisdom or prajñā. To go down means to use skillful means with compassion for all beings. The Buddha sees reality from the peak of wisdom and descends to help all beings awaken to and practice this reality. *Mujō jin jin* refers at the same time to the highest and deepest qualities of the Buddha's wisdom and compassion. "Subtle and wondrous" describe something we can't see with our eyes or our usual way of thinking.

The expression *jin jin mimyō no hō* is from the *Lotus Sutra*, one of the most important sources of Dōgen Zenji's teachings. For Dōgen Zenji the *Lotus Sutra* was essential because it describes the Mahāyāna Way of the bodhisattva. The expression "most profound, subtle, and wondrous dharma" is from the second chapter, titled "Expedient Devices." The first verse of the chapter in which this expression appears begins:

> The Hero of the World is incalculable.
> Among gods, worldlings,
> And all varieties of living beings,
> None can know the Buddha.
> As to the Buddha's strengths (*bala*), his sorts of
>   fearlessness (*vaiśāradya*),

His deliverances (*vimokṣa*), and his samādhis,
As well as the other dharmas of a Buddha,
None can fathom them.[113]

This passage says that none can know the Buddha; no human being can understand who the Buddha is. "Fathom" means to measure the size of something. The English unit of length is the foot, which was originally based on the length of a human foot. We measure by comparison to familiar things. To measure means to understand or grasp. Without something familiar for comparison we cannot measure anything. When we measure the size of the universe, we use a unit like the light-year. Since we can't experience a light-year, it is an abstraction, something meaningful only to scientists. To make meaningful measurements we must use our own experience as a yardstick. The Buddha and the Dharma are limitless and boundless and therefore cannot be measured. To comprehend something boundless, something infinite, we have to open our hand and become free of our yardsticks. We do this in zazen. When we stop measuring, we can understand something limitless. That is what the phrase "none can fathom them" means. This doesn't mean that 99 percent of human beings are unable but that some very superior people, sages or enlightened ones, can fathom the boundless with their special yardsticks. No one can measure something limitless because all yardsticks are limited. We can't measure without concepts based on our limited experience. When we open our hand and stop using our yardsticks, we can encounter something boundless. That's our practice. That is the quality of this Dharma.

The *Lotus Sutra* continues with the passage that is the source of the expression "profound, subtle, and wondrous Dharma."

Formerly, following numberless Buddhas,
He fully trod the various paths,
Those dharmas profound and subtle,
Hard to see and hard to understand.
Throughout countless millions of kalpas

He trod these various paths; [then]
On the platform of the Path, he was able to achieve the fruit.
This I fully know.[114]

"Kalpa" is an interesting expression. It is a unit of time, something
like a light-year, which is defined in an unusual way. Imagine that a
storehouse with a capacity of ten cubic miles is filled with poppy seeds.
Once every century someone removes a single poppy seed. A kalpa is
defined as the time it would take to empty the storehouse. The sutra
says millions of kalpas, which effectively means never. The expression
"is difficult to encounter even in a hundred thousand million kalpas"
means we can never encounter the Dharma. But then it contradicts
itself and says, "I now see and listen, and I am able to accept and uphold
or maintain it." The translation in the MZMC sutra book is "having it
to see and listen to, remember and accept." The word "having" is not
strong enough. We have to uphold, maintain, and nurture it. It's not
enough to merely have the Dharma; we also have to cultivate it.

In this translation the important word "now" is omitted. When we
merely *think* about the Dharma and try to "get it," we are unable to. As
long as we try to grasp it with our intellect, we are unsuccessful because
it's impossible. The word "now" means at this present moment, the
only reality. The past is already gone and the future has yet to come.
Neither is reality. Only this moment, *now*, is reality. And yet this *now*
is strange and wondrous. We cannot grasp it because it has no length. If
it did, we could cut it in half. Suppose I want to speak the word "now."
When I make the initial sound *na-*, the rest of the sound, *ow*, still lies
in the future; and when I do the *ow*, the *na-* is already past. So when is
the present? The present is nothing. It is empty. So the past and future
are never here, and the present is empty. It's really wondrous, and we
cannot understand it. We experience reality, actually live our lives and
do things, and yet everything is empty. When we try to grasp it there
is no substance.

Reality is empty like a phantom. This is the meaning of "form is
emptiness and emptiness is form." This is reality. This present moment,

which is zero or empty, is the only reality. It is the only time we can meet the Dharma by letting go of our limited measurement, our conventional ways of seeing and judging. To see the Dharma, the reality, we must open our hand and just accept that reality. There is no sound, and yet we have to listen for and accept this boundless Dharma. We cannot discuss the absolute. Argument doesn't work. When we discuss the nature of the Dharma, we discuss our insight, our understanding of reality. Each of us has a different life experience and different ways of seeing things. Our opinions or expressions of this reality can differ. We can discuss or argue, and yet reality itself cannot be the object of meaningful argument.

All we can do is simply accept, maintain, and uphold it. "Maintain" means to use it. "Use" doesn't mean I use the Dharma, in the sense that the Dharma is the object of my activity. Instead it means we are the Dharma itself. There is no truth or reality outside ourselves. We cannot be outside reality. We are born into and live in this reality, this Dharma. Since we are part of the Dharma, we can't observe it from outside. Everything we do in our day-to-day lives is a manifestation of this boundless Dharma. The limitless, unsurpassed, most profound Dharma should be manifested through practice with our small, limited, impermanent body and mind. Practice means more than sitting zazen in the zendō. It includes practice outside of the zendō. Our practice, our life, is the only way to manifest this infinite Dharma. The only time we can see, listen, accept, and maintain this Dharma is right now.

The *Lotus Sutra* continues:

> As to such great fruit and retribution as these,
> Such varied doctrines of nature and marks,
> I and the Buddhas of the ten directions
> Are the only ones who can know these things.
> These dharmas cannot be demonstrated;
> Words, which are only signs, are quiescent in them.
> Among the remaining kinds of living beings
> None can understand them,

Except for the multitude of bodhisattvas,
Whose power of faith is firm.

The phrase "nature and marks," which refers back to what Shakyamuni Buddha says in the prose section preceding this verse, is essential to an understanding of Mahāyāna Buddhism. The Buddha is speaking to Śāriputra, one of his ten great disciples: "Śāriputra, we need speak no more. Why is this? Concerning the prime, rare, hard-to-understand dharmas, which the Buddha has perfected, only a Buddha and a Buddha can exhaust their reality, namely, the suchness of the dharmas."[115] "Suchness of the dharmas" is a translation for *shohō jissō*. *Shohō* means "myriad dharmas" or "all beings." *Ji* means "true or real," and *ssō* is "form." So *jissō* means "reality" and "all dharmas or beings." This Dharma is the reality of all beings, not something abstract that exists outside the phenomenal world. It is the reality of all phenomenal things, including ourselves.

The sutra continues, "the suchness of their marks, the suchness of their nature, the suchness of their substance." "Marks" is translation of *sō*, which means "form." "Nature" is the characteristics of each thing. The original word translated here as "substance" is *tai*. It means "body," not substance—something impermanent or egoless. Each thing has its own body: a book, clothing, water, grass, a person—all have bodies. The list continues with "the suchness of their powers, the suchness of their functions." Each being has its own power or energy. It's not a dead thing. And anything with power or energy has function. Even though it doesn't move visibly, a mountain has functions. Dōgen Zenji says that mountains are always moving, always walking.

Finally, "the suchness of their causes, the suchness of their conditions, the suchness of their effects, the suchness of their retributions, and the absolute identity of their beginning and end."

These "ten suchnesses" were discussed in the beginning of the chapter 5. As we saw there, the first five suchnesses of all beings refer to the uniqueness of each being. And the next four imply that each and every unique being can exist only within relation with others within the network of interdependent origination throughout entire time and space.

The tenth suchness is the "absolute identity of their beginning and end." "Beginning" refers to the first suchness and "end" to the ninth, the retributions. These nine points are not independent aspects of our being but rather only one, because we cannot separate them. This last, tenth suchness is difficult to understand. Each being is unique and yet is connected with all beings, from the beginningless beginning to the endless end. When we take one being, we take all beings and all times. Nothing is substantial. Everything is empty. When we try to grasp with our intellect, using concepts, we become neurotic. When we grasp one aspect, we miss another. When we try to understand the difference between beings we differentiate and miss the connections between them. When we focus on the relationships between all beings, we miss the uniqueness of this being. These two basically contradictory aspects of the true reality of all beings are expressed in the *Heart Sutra* as "form is emptiness and emptiness is form." In "Sandōkai" the same reality is expressed as merging of difference (*ji*) and unity (*ri*).

Because it is difficult to fathom and grasp both sides of reality at once using concepts and intellect, as the *Lotus Sutra* says, we need the power of faith. Through our practice based on faith, we can experience the true reality even though we cannot see and measure it as an object.

The faith of power derives from taking refuge in the Triple Treasure. We take refuge, we take the precepts, and we take the four bodhisattva vows and continue to practice, wearing a buddha's robe and receiving offerings with gratitude from the network of interdependent origination, gifts such as air, water, food, and many more things. We keep up our effort to hear, understand, and uphold the teachings of the sutras—through texts, talks, and instructions from teachers and others—and of reality itself.

Our practice includes all activities of this body and mind—including our thoughts, which are one way to understand this wondrous Dharma. We don't need to cut off our thoughts. Thinking is, in fact, a function of the Dharma. But we should understand that thought cannot grasp reality. So we have to open our hands and work with the reality we encounter daily. When we think about each part in isolation it's really difficult to see reality as a whole and explain it. But the Buddha's teaching is really simple. It is the reality we always experience, not something mysterious or mystical beyond the phenomenal world. It's not something esoteric. Even so, it is difficult to fathom the ways all beings exist in this phenomenal world in which we live. The way we live is actually mysterious. The truth is not hidden but always here, always manifested. The goal of our practice is not to experience something different from our day-to-day lives. It is to see deep into the reality of each being, including this one. This is really wondrous and difficult to grasp. To appreciate this is to meet with the Dharma. When we really see, listen to, accept, and maintain that Dharma, we can't help but vow to understand it more deeply. That's the meaning of the last line of this verse, "I vow to understand the true meaning of the Tathāgata." We vow to deeply understand the dharmakāya into which we are born; the reality that is itself the Buddha's body, in which we live and die together with all beings.

NOTES

1. "The ancestral way come from the west I transmit east.
   Fishing the moon, cultivating clouds,
   I long for the ancient wind.
   How could red dusts from the mundane world fly up to here?
   Snowy night in the deep mountains in my grass hut."
   Dōgen, *Dōgen's Extensive Record: A Translation of Eihei Koroku*,
   trans. Leighton and Okumura (Wisdom Publications, 1995), p. 638.
2. *Buddhadharma*, Spring 2011, p. 25.
3. Dainin Katagiri, *Each Moment Is the Universe: Zen and the Way of Being Time* (Boston: Shambhala, 2007), p. 216.
4. I found this poem in the draft of *Ceaseless Effort: The Life of Dainin Katagiri*, by Andrea Martin (Minnesota Zen Meditation Center).
5. The story is based on the translation by Thomas William Rhys Davids, *Buddhist Birth-Stories: Jataka Tales* (1880) (repr., Calcutta: Srishti Publishers, 1998). Another version is found in Rafe Martin, *The Hungry Tigress: Buddhist Legends and Jataka Tales* (Berkeley: Parallax Press, 1990).
6. Martin, *Hungry Tigress*.
7. This is the translation of the verse of four bodhisattva vows in the sutra book used at Minnesota Zen Meditation Center. The translation in *Sōtō School Scriptures for Daily Services and Practice* published by Sōtōshū Shūmuchō is as follows: "Beings are numberless; I vow to free them. / Delusions are inexhaustible; I vow to end them. / Dharma gates are boundless, I vow to enter them. / The Buddha way is unsurpassable; I vow to realize it." In Japanese: "Shujō mu hen sei gan do, / Bonnō mu jin sei gan dan, / Hō mon mu ryō sei gan gaku, / Butsu dō mujō seigan gan jō."
8. This does not mean Buddhists do not pray. Originally Buddhism did not have sacred beings to pray to; but later, in Mahāyāna and Vajrayāna Buddhism, buddhas, bodhisattvas, and some guardian gods came to be considered objects of prayer.
9. Augustine Ichirō Okumura, *Awakening to Prayer*, trans. Theresa Kazue Hiraki and Albert Masaru Yamato (Washington, D.C.: ICS, 1994).

10. This is the translation of the verse from *Bosatsu-yōraku-hongōkyō* (*Bodhisattva Jewel Necklace Sutra*), Taisho, vol. 24, p. 1013.

11. This verse appears in the Mahavāgga of the Pāli Vinaya. This English translation is from Hajime Nakamura, *Gotama Buddha: A Biography Based on the Most Reliable Texts*, trans. Gaynor Sekimori (Tokyo: Kosei, 2000), p. 228.

12. This poem was published in the MZMC newsletter, Spring 1991, on the occasion of the first anniversary of Katagiri Roshi's death.

13. D. T. Suzuki, *Living by Zen: A Synthesis of the Historical and Practical Aspects of Zen Buddhism* (London: Samuel Weiser, 1972).

14. D. T. Suzuki, *Zen ni yoru Seikatu*, trans. Kobori Sōhaku, Suzuki Daisetsu Zen senshu, vol. 3 (Tokyo: Shunjūsha, 1975), p. 173.

15. D. T. Suzuki, *Outlines of Mahayana Buddhism* (New York: Schocken Books, 1963), p. 307.

16. Kōshō Uchiyama, *Opening the Hand of Thought* (Boston: Wisdom, 2004), p. 157.

17. Shohaku Okumura, *Shikantaza: An Introduction to Zazen* (Kyoto: Kyoto Sōtō Zen Center, 1985), p. 63.

18. Shohaku Okumura and Taigen Dan Leighton, trans., *The Wholehearted Way: A Translation of Eihei Dōgen's Bendōwa with Commentary by Kōshō Uchiyama Roshi* (Boston: Tuttle, 1997), p. 23.

19. This saying appears in the third chapter of the *Lotus Sutra*, "Simile and Parable." Burton Watson, trans., *The Lotus Sutra* (New York: Columbia University Press, 1993), p. 69.

20. Taigen Dan Leighton and Shohaku Okumura, trans., *Dōgen's Pure Standards for the Zen Community: A Translation of Eihei Shingi* (Albany: State University of New York Press, 1996), pp. 47–49.

21. Ibid.

22. Ibid. p. 48.

23. Ibid. p. 37.

24. Ibid. p. 48.

25. Ibid. pp. 48–49.

26. Guishan Lingyou (Isan Reiyū) lived from 771 to 853 CE during the golden age of Chinese Zen. He founded the Guiyang (Igyō) school, one of the five schools of Zen in China. Guishan was a dharma successor of Baizhang Huihai (Hyakujō Ekai). Baizhang is known for his *Baizhang Qingguei* (*Hyakujō Shingi*), a compilation of the regulations for a Zen monastery. With Baizhang's regulations, Zen monastic practice was formally established.

27. This is my translation. Another can be found in Gudo Nishijima and Chodo Cross, trans., *Master Dōgen's Shōbōgenzō, bk. 2* (BookSurge, 2006), p. 170. Zen Master Dayuan is the honorific title given by the emperor to Guishan.

28. This lecture at the Sōtōshu Kyōka Kenshūsho (Sōtō School Propagation and Research Institute) was translated by Rev. Rosan Yoshida and appeared in the MZMC newsletter in three parts: Fall 1990, Spring 1991, and Summer 1991.

29. Hōkyōji is a country practice center in Southeastern Minnesota established in 1978. In 2007 it became independent from the MZMC and is currently named Hōkyōji Zen Practice Community.

30. This is a part of a conversation between Hongzhi and his teacher Donxia Zichun (Tanka Shijun, 1074–1117), which appeared in Hongzhi's biography in *The Record of Hongzhi* (Chi., Hongzhi-lu; Jap., Wanshi-roku). Originally this saying was by Baima

Xingai (Hakuba Gyōai) and appeared in *The Record of the Transmission of the Dharma Lamp* (Chi., *Jingde chuandeng lu*; Jap., *Keitoku Dentōroku*), vol. 23.

31. This expression by Dōgen Zenji appears in Dharma discourse no. 2 in *Eihei Kōroku*. See Taigen Dan Leighton and Shohaku Okumura, trans., *Dōgen's Extensive Record: A Translation of the Eihei Kōroku* (Boston: Wisdom, 2004), p. 76.

32. The translation in the *Sōtō School Scriptures for Daily Services and Practice* is "All my past and harmful karma, / born from beginningless greed, hate, and delusion, / through body, speech, and mind, / I now fully avow."

33. This is based on the theory of the origin of Mahāyāna Buddhism held by Japanese scholars such as Akira Hirakawa. When I lectured on these matters in 1993 I did not know about Western scholars' criticism of the hypothesis that Mahāyāna Buddhism was originally a lay Buddhist movement. Today few scholars support this hypothesis.

34. Here "ego" is used as a translation of the Sanskrit *ātman*, which is usually translated as "self" or "soul." "Egolessness" is a translation of *anātman*, "no-self." According to *The Shambhala Dictionary of Buddhism and Zen* (Boston: Shambhala, 1991), *ātman* means "the real immortal self of human beings, known in the West as the soul." In Mahāyāna Buddhism, not only the "soul" of human beings, but also the substance of material things is negated.

35. This is my translation from *Busso-shōden Zenkaishō (Essence of Buddha Ancestors' Authentically Transmitted Zen Precepts)*, Taisho, vol. 82, no. 2601.

36. This is my translation from Sōtan Oka, *Kaitei Busso-shōden Zenkaishō Kōwa (Lecture on the revised Busso-shōden Zenkaishō)* (Tokyo: Kōmeisha, 1931), pp. 44–48.

37. The translation in *Sōtō School Scriptures for Daily Services and Practice* is "I take refuge in buddha. / May all beings / embody the great way, / resolving to awaken. / I take refuge in dharma. / May all living beings / deeply enter the sutras, wisdom like an ocean. / I take refuge in sangha. / May all beings / support harmony in the community, / free from hindrance." This verse was originally a part of the longer verse in chapter 11 of the *Avataṃsaka Sutra*, titled "Purifying Practice." The English translation is as follows. "Taking refuge in the Buddha, / They should wish that all beings / Continue the lineage of Buddhas, / Conceiving the unexcelled aspiration. / Taking refuge in the Teaching, / They should wish that all beings / Enter deeply into the scriptures / And their wisdom be deep as the sea. / Taking refuge in the Community, / They should wish that all beings / Order the masses, / All becoming free from obstruction." Thomas Cleary, trans., *The Flower Ornament Scripture: A Translation of The Avatamsaka Sutra* (Boston: Shambhala, 1993), pp. 315–16.

38. This is my translation. Another translation is in Nishijima and Cross, *Master Dōgen's Shōbōgenzō*, bk. 4, p. 178.

39. Thanissaro Bhikkhu, trans., *Dhammapada: A Translation* (Barre, Mass.: Dhamma Dana, 1998), v. 160, p. 46.

40. H. Saddhatissa, trans., *The Sutta-Nipata* (London: Curzon, 1994), p. 88.

41. *Dasheng-yi-zhang (Jap., Daijō-gi-shō, The meanings of Mahāyāna Teaching)*, written by Huiyuan (Eon) in the Sui dynasty (589–618), Taisho, vol. 44, no. 1851, p. 654.

42. This is the translation in the MZMC sutra book, p. 1. The translation in *Sōtō School Scriptures for Daily Services and Practice* is "How great, the robe of liberation, / a formless field of merit. / Wrapping ourselves in Buddha's teaching, / We free all living beings." This verse also appears in *Chanyuan Qinggui (Rules of Purity for the Chan Monastery)*, vol. 8, in the section describing the precepts-receiving ceremony for novices (*shami*).

There is one character different from the version we chant. The third line reads, "Wearing the Tathāgata's precepts."

43. This is my translation. Another translation appears in Nishijima and Cross, *Master Dōgen's Shōbōgenzō*, bk. 1, p. 146.

44. This story appears in Vinaya texts. See, for example, I. B. Horner, trans., *The Book of the Discipline (Vinaya-piṭaka)*, vol. IV (London: Luzac, 1951), p. 407.

45. This is my translation. See also Nishijima and Cross, *Master Dōgen's Shōbōgenzō*, bk. 1, p. 127.

46. As far as I know, an English translation of *Kyōjukaimon* has not yet been published. In *Shōbōgenzō Kie-sanbō (Taking Refuge in the Three Treasures)*, Dōgen introduces four kinds of Three Treasures, including the three mentioned here. See Nishijima and Cross, *Master Dōgen's Shōbōgenzō*, bk. 4, p. 177.

47. This is a free translation from Japanese. The English translation from Pāli is in H. Saddhatissa, *The Sutta-Nipata*, p. 8.

48. Leighton and Okumura, *Dōgen's Pure Standards*, p. 36.

49. Ibid., pp. 83–84.

50. Robert A. F. Thurman, trans., *The Holy Teaching of Vimalakīrti: A Mahāyāna Scripture* (College Park: Pennsylvania State University Press, 1988), p. 27.

51. Leon Hurvitz, trans., *Scripture of the Lotus Blossom of the Fine Dharma* (New York: Columbia University Press, 1976), p. 22.

52. Ibid., p. 23.

53. The texts of meal chants in chapter 5 are from *Sōtō School Scriptures for Daily Services and Practice*, p. 75, not from the sutra book of the Minnesota Zen Meditation Center.

54. Maurice Walshe, trans., *The Long Discourses of the Buddha: A Translation of the Dīgha Nikāya* (Boston: Wisdom, 1987), p. 263.

55. Red Pine, trans., *The Diamond Sutra: The Perfection of Wisdom: Text and Commentaries translated from Sanskrit and Chinese* (Washington, D.C.: Counterpoint, 2001), p. 3.

56. Thomas Cleary, trans. *The Blue Cliff Record* (Boulder, Colo.: Shambhala, 1977), case 1, p. 3.

57. *Fahuawengou*, Taisho, vol. 34, #1718, p. 0128a16.

58. Translation by the Buddhist Text Translation Society with a few minor changes by Okumura. http://www.purifymind.com/BrahmaNetSutra.htm.

59. My translation. See also Nishijima and Cross, *Master Dōgen's Shōbōgenzō*, bk. 4, p. 178.

60. Menzan Zuihō (1683–1769), one of the greatest Sōtō Zen monk-scholars of the Tokugawa period, wrote a commentary on this "Verse of Five Contemplations" titled *Jujikigokan-kunmo* (Instruction on the Five Contemplations for Receiving Food) in 1720. He said that these five contemplations were first mentioned in a Vinaya text by Nanshan Daoxuan (Nanzan Dōsen), the founder of the Chinese Ritsu (Vinaya) School. Later the verse was rewritten by one of the famous Chinese literati of the Song dynasty who was also a Zen practitioner, Huang Tingjian (Kō Teiken, 1045–1105). It also appears in *Chanyuan Qinggui (Zen'en Shingi, Rules of Purity for the Chan Monastery)* by Changlu Zongze (Chōro Sōsaku, ?–1107). Dōgen Zenji took the verse from the Chinese Standards. However, modern scholars doubt Huang's authorship because the same verse is found in a text that precedes his birth.

61. These are parts of my unpublished translation of *Shōbōgenzō* "Hachidainingaku" (Eight Points of Awakening of Great Beings). Another translation is found in Nishijima and Cross, *Master Dōgen's Shōbōgenzō*, bk. 4, pp. 233–34.

62. Rewata Dhamma, *The First Discourse of The Buddha* (Boston: Wisdom, 1997), p. 17.
63. Gene Reeves, trans. *The Lotus Sutra: A Contemporary Translation of a Buddhist Classic* (Boston, Wisdom Publications, 2008), pp. 93–94.
64. Nishijima and Cross, *Master Dōgen's Shōbōgenzō*, bk. 4, p. 173.
65. Leighton and Okumura, *Dōgen's Pure Standards*, p. 98.
66. This is my translation. Another is in Kazuaki Tanahashi, ed., *Enlightenment Unfolds: The Essential Teachings of Zen Master Dōgen* (Boston: Shambhala, 1999), p. 23.
67. Bhikkhu Bodhi, trans., *The Connected Discourses of the Buddha*, vol. 1 (Boston: Wisdom, 2000), p. 233.
68. Ibid., p. 950.
69. Three vehicles are the Mahāyāna categorization of Buddhism. *Śrāvaka* means "hearer" and refers to the disciples of the Buddha. *Pratyekabuddha* means "solitary awakened one" and refers to the practitioners who attain awakening without a teacher and do not teach others. From the Mahāyāna point of view, both were *Hīnayāna*, "lesser vehicles."
70. When I gave this talk in 1993, heart transplants were not yet legal in Japan. In 1997 the procedure was legalized, but it is still very rarely performed.
71. I live in America as a foreigner and need a great deal of patience. Katagiri Roshi's name Dainin means Great Patience. I think it was a very suitable name for him as a teacher in the United States, where the spiritual and cultural backgrounds are very different from Japan. American Buddhist practitioners who practice with teachers from Japan or other Asian Buddhist countries must need the same sort of patience. Actually, any two people who live or work together will sometimes have conflicts and need to practice patience.
72. Edward Conze, trans., *Perfect Wisdom: The Short Prajñāpāramitā Texts* (Devon: Buddhist Publishing Group, 1973), p. 140.
73. Katagiri Roshi's translation appeared in *Zen no Kaze* (Wind of Zen), a magazine published by Sōtōshū Shūmuchō. The translation of this sentence in *Sōtō School Scriptures for Daily Services and Practice* is "Avalokiteśvara Bodhisattva, when deeply practicing prajñā pāramitā, clearly saw that all five aggregates are empty and thus relieved all suffering."
74. *Shōbōgenzō* "Kannon" is included in Nishijima and Cross, *Master Dōgen's Shōbōgenzō*, bk. 2, p. 211.
75. Yunyan was the teacher of Dongshan (Tōzan), the founder of Chinese Caodon (Sōtō) Zen. He is mentioned below.
76. If you are interested in the discussion of this koan, study case 54 in the *Book of Serenity* and case 89 in the *Blue Cliff Record*. Thomas Cleary, trans., *Book of Serenity: One Hundred Zen Dialogues* (New York: Lindisfarne Press, 1990), p. 229. Cleary, *Blue Cliff Record*, p. 489.
77. Shohaku Okumura, trans., *Realizing Genjōkōan: The Key to Dōgen's Shōbōgenzō* (Boston: Wisdom, 2010), app. 2, p. 207.
78. Conze, *Perfect Wisdom*, p. 140.
79. Kenneth K. Inada, trans., *Nāgārjuna: A Translation of His Mūlamadhyamakakārikā with an Introductory Essay* (Tokyo: Hokuseidō Press, 1970), p. 146. (Chapter and verse numbers are cited in the text.)
80. This is my translation. Another translation is in Nishijima and Cross, *Master Dōgen's Shōbōgenzō*, bk. 4, p. 221.
81. Inada, *Nāgārjuna*, p. 39.
82. Ibid., p. 59.

83. This is my translation from the Chinese, which Kumārajīva translated with Pingala's commentary, Taisho, vol. 30, no. 1564, p. 8a07.

84. Okumura, *Realizing Genjōkōan*, p. 1.

85. Ibid., p. 3.

86. Ibid.

87. Francis Cook, trans., *The Record of Transmitting the Light: Zen Master Keizan's Denkōroku* (Boston: Wisdom, 1996), pp. 193–94.

88. Conze, *Perfect Wisdom*, p. 140.

89. Okumura, *Realizing Genjōkōan*, p. 209.

90. Nakamura, *Gotama Buddha*, p. 319.

91. My translation. Another is found in Nishijima and Cross, *Master Dōgen's Shōbōgenzō*, bk. 3, p. 55.

92. Shohaku Okumura, trans., *Shōbōgenzō-zuimonki: Sayings of Eihei Dōgen Zenji* (Tokyo: Sōtōshū Shūmucho, 1987), p. 124.

93. Inada, *Nāgārjuna*, p. 103.

94. When I gave this talk in 1994 my son was three years old and I was forty-five. That was the first time I felt I was aging.

95. One of the oldest temples in Japan, Shitennōji was built by Prince Shōtoku in the sixth century at the very beginning of Japanese Buddhism. At that time Osaka and Nara were the two main cities. Nara was the capital, and Osaka was a port for travel to Korea and China. The prince also built a temple in Nara called Hōryūji. Hōryūji has the world's oldest wooden structure, almost fifteen hundred years old.

96. This translation, in the MZMC sutra book, p. 8, is by Thomas Cleary and is included in Cleary, *Timeless Spring: A Sōtō Zen Anthology* (Tokyo and New York: Weatherhill, 1980), p. 36. In the sutra book the word "patriarch" in the original translation was changed to "ancestor."

97. The word *Sandōkai* derives from the title of a Daoist text on the *Yijing* (Book of Changes) written during the Han dynasty (206 BCE–220 CE).

98. John McRae, *Seeing Through Zen: Encounter, Transformation, and Genealogy in Chinese Chan Buddhism* (Berkeley: University of California Press, 2003), p. 61.

99. Ibid., p. 62.

100. Yoshito S. Hakeda, trans., *The Awakening of Faith* (New York: Columbia University Press, 1967), p. 31. This is one of the most important texts on the theory of *tathāgata-garbha*, or buddha-nature, which is an essential part of Zen teachings.

101. Hakeda says, "Since it has been made clear that the essence of all things is empty, i.e., devoid of illusion, the true Mind is eternal, permanent, immutable, pure, and self-sufficient; therefore, it is called 'nonempty'" (ibid., p. 35).

102. Zongmi's discussion about the differences among the four schools appears in "Chart of the Master-Disciple Succession of the Chan Gate That Transmits the Mind Ground in China." See Jeffrey Lyle Broughton, trans., *Zongmi on Chan* (New York: Columbia University Press, 2009), pp. 69–100.

103. Okumura, *Realizing Genjōkōan*, p. 2.

104. Inada, *Nāgārjuna*, p. 146.

105. Hakeda, *Awakening of Faith*, p. 31.

106. Sheng-yen, *The Infinite Mirror: Commentaries on Two Chan Classics* (Boston: Shambhala, 1990), p. 25. Sheng-yen translates *Sandōkai* as "inquiry into matching halves." "Inquiry" is *san*, "matching" is *dō*, "halves" is *kai*. This is very different from the Japanese interpretation.

107. Translation by Shohaku Okumura and Hozan Alan Senauke, in *The Bodhisattva's Embrace: Dispatches from Engaged Buddhism's Front Lines*, by Alan Senauke (Berkeley: Clear View Press, 2010), p. 215.

108. Stephen Mitchell, trans., *Tao Te Ching* (New York: HarperCollins, 1988), pp. 40–42.

109. Inada, *Nāgārjuna*, pp. 146–48.

110. This kōan is called Yunyan's "Great Compassion" in *Congronglu* (Shōyōroku), case 54. Cleary, *Book of Serenity*, p. 229.

111. This story appears in the Chinese Daoist classic *Liezi*, vol. 5.

112. This verse in the *Sōtō School Scriptures for Daily Services and Practice* is: "The unsurpassed, profound, and wondrous dharma / is rarely met with, even in a hundred, thousand, million kalpas. / Now we can see and hear it, accept and maintain it. / May we unfold the meaning of the Tathāgata's truth."

113. Hurvitz, *Scripture of the Lotus Blossom*, p. 23.

114. Ibid.

115. Ibid., p. 22.

GLOSSARY OF NAMES

Note: Sources for this glossary include *Bukkyōgo Daijiten* (Nakamura Hajime, Tokyo Shoseki), *Zengaku Daijiten* (Taishūkan Shoten), *Bukkyō Daijiten* (Shōgakkan), and *The Shambhala Dictionary of Buddhism and Zen* (Shambhala).

Ānanda: One of the ten great disciples of the Buddha. He was the personal attendant of the Buddha for twenty years and memorized all the teachings of the Buddha. His exposition of the Buddha's discourses formed the basis for the sutras at the first council.

Aśvaghoṣa: Indian monk-poet who lived in the first to second centuries CE. He wrote *Buddha-carita: Life of the Buddha*. Another work, *Awakening of Faith in Mahāyāna*, was attributed to Aśvaghoṣa, but some scholars today think the text was written in China.

Avalokiteśvara: One of the most important bodhisattvas of Mahāyāna Buddhism, considered to be the symbol of the Buddha's compassion.

Baizhang Huihai (Hyakujō Ekai, 749–814): An important Zen master of the Tang dynasty in China. He was a dharma successor of Mazu Daoyi and master of Guishan Lingyou and Huangbo Xiyun.

Traditionally he was considered to be the author of the first rules of purity (*Qinggui, Shingi*).

Baotang Wuzhu (Hotō Mujū, 714–774): The founder of the Baotang school of Zen in the Tang dynasty.

Bodhidharma (Bodaidaruma): The twenty-eighth ancestor after Shakyamuni Buddha in the Indian lineage, who came from India to China and became the first ancestor of the Zen tradition.

Butsuju Myōzen (1184–1225): A disciple of Myōan Eisai who transmitted Rinzai Zen tradition to Japan and was Dōgen's first Zen teacher in Japan. Myōzen and Dōgen went to China together, but Myōzen died while practicing at Tiantong monastery.

Changlu Qingliao (Chōro Seiryō): A Chinese Caodong (Sōtō) Zen master, a dharma heir of Danxia Zichun (Tanka Shijun), and the elder dharma brother of Hongzhi Zhengjue.

Changlu Zongze (Chōro Sōsaku, ?–1107): The Chinese Zen master who compiled *Chanyuan Qinggui* (*Zen'en Shingi*, Rules of Purity for the Chan Monastery).

Dai Daoxin (Daii Dōshin, 580–651): The fourth ancestor of Chinese Zen and the master of Doman Hongren. Dai and Doman's assemblies were later called East Mountain Dharma Gates.

Dainin Katagiri Roshi (1928–1990): The founder of Minnesota Zen Meditation Center. He came to the United States in 1963 and assisted Shunryū Suzuki Roshi at the San Francisco Zen Center until Suzuki Roshi's death in 1971. He moved to Minneapolis to establish the MZMC in 1972.

Dajan Huineng (Daikan Enō, 638–713): The sixth ancestor of Chinese Zen and dharma heir of the fifth ancestor, Daman Hongren. He is considered the founder of the Southern school of Chinese Zen.

Daman Hongren (Daiman Kōnin, 602–675): The fifth ancestor in the Chinese Zen tradition, from whom the Northern and Southern schools were derived.

Daowu Yuanzhi (Dōgo Enchi, 769–835): A dharma heir of Yaoshan Weiyan and dharma brother of Yunyan Tansheng.

Dongshan Liangjie (Tōzan Ryokai, 802–869): The dharma heir of Yunyan Tansheng. Dongshan was the founder of the Chinese Caodong school.

Edward Conze (1904–1979): A British Buddhist scholar who taught in England and the United Sates. The author of many books on the *Prajñāpāramitā Sutras*.

Eihei Dōgen (1200–1253): A dharma heir of Tiantong Rujing, Dōgen is the founder of Japanese Sōtō Zen Buddhism.

Emperor Wu (464–549): The first emperor of the Rian dynasty. He supported Buddhism and himself lectured on Buddhist sutras such as the *Parinirvana Sutra*. In the Zen tradition it is said that he met with Bodhidharma.

Feixiu (Haikyū, 797–870): A government official of the Tang dynasty. He studied Fayen (Kegon) Buddhism with Guifeng Zongmi and Zen with Huangbo Xiyun.

Guifeng Zongmi (Keihō Shūmitsu, 780–841): A scholar-monk of the Fayen school and also a Zen master in the Tang dynasty. He wrote *The Chart of the Master-Disciple Succession of the Chan Gate That Transmits the Mind Ground in China, Prolegomenon to the Collection of Expressions of the Chan Source*, and many other texts.

Guishan Lingyou (Isan Reiyū, 771–853): A dharma heir of Baizhang Huihai. Together with his disciple Yangshan Huiji, he is considered the founder of one of the five schools of Chinese Zen, the Guiyang school.

Hārītī (Kishimojin): The daughter of a demonic being (*yaksa*) in Rājagriha. She had five hundred (or one thousand or ten thousand) children to whom she fed the babies of others. When she heard the Dharma from the Buddha, she repented her misdeeds and vowed to protect Buddhism. In Japan she is invoked for an easy delivery and the health of children.

Heze Shenhui (Kataku Jinne, 668–760): A disciple of the sixth ancestor, Huineng. He attacked the Northern school and insisted that Huineng was the legitimate successor of the fifth ancestor. He is considered to be the founder of Heze school.

Hongzhi Zhengjue (Wanshi Shōkaku, 1091–1157): A famous Chinese Caodong (Sōtō) Zen master who served as abbot of Tiangtong monastery. Hongzhi was well known for the excellence of his poetry, and he composed verses to supplement a hundred koans. Wansong Xingxie later wrote commentaries on these verses and created the *Congronglu* (Shōyōroku).

Huang Tingjian (Kō Teiken, 1045–1105): A famous poet and calligrapher of the Song dynasty in China. He was a lay disciple of the Linji Zen master Huanglong Zuxin.

Ichirō Okumura (1923–): Father Ichiro Okumura entered the Catholic Church in 1948 and was ordained to the priesthood within the Order of Discalced Carmelites in 1957.

Jingzhong Wuxiang (Jōshu Musō, 684–762): A Tang dynasty Zen master from Korea and the teacher of Baotang Wuzhu.

Kōdō Sawaki (1880–1965): A modern Sōtō Zen master, and Kōshō Uchiyama's teacher. He was a professor at Komazawa University but never had his own temple or monastery. He was called "homeless Kōdō" because he traveled throughout Japan to teach.

Kōshō Uchiyama (1912–1998): Kōdō Sawaki's dharma heir who succeeded Sawaki at Antaiji. He wrote many books, several of which have been translated into English and other languages.

Kumārajīva (344–413): One of the most important translators of Buddhist texts from Sanskrit to Chinese. He translated many Mahāyāna texts including the *Lotus Sutra, Vimalakīrtinirdeśa Sutra, Mūlamadhyamakakārikā,* and *Mahāprajñāpāramita-Śāstra.*

Longtan Chongxin (Ryūtan Sōshin): A Tang dynasty Zen master in Shitou Xiqian's lineage. Shitou's disciple Tianhuang Daowu was his teacher and Deshan Xuanjian his disciple.

Mahākāśyapa: One of the ten major disciples of Shakyamuni Buddha. He was famous for his strict discipline living in the forest even after the Buddha founded monasteries. After the Buddha's death he became the leader of the sangha and took the leadership for the first council of five hundred arahats. In the Zen tradition he is considered the first ancestor in the Indian lineage, since he received dharma transmission from the Buddha.

Maitreya Buddha: The next buddha. Maitreya is in Tuṣita heaven now as a bodhisattva and is expected to come to this world in the future.

Mañjushrī: The bodhisattva of wisdom. In Zen, Mañjushrī is enshrined in the center of the monks' hall.

Mazu Daoyi (Baso Dōitsu, 709–788): One of the most important Tang dynasty Zen masters. Mazu was a disciple of Nanyue Huairang. He had many disciples, including Baizhang Huihai and Nanyuan Puyuan.

Menzan Zuihō (1683–1769): One of the important Sōtō Zen monk-scholars in the Tokugawa period. Dharma heir of Sonnō Shūeki, he studied Dōgen extensively and wrote many commentaries on *Shōbōgenzō* and other writings of Dōgen.

Myōan Eisai (1141–1215): The first Japanese master, who transmitted the Rinzai Zen tradition to Japan. He established several Zen monasteries including Kenninji Kyoto, where Dōgen practiced Zen with Eisai's disciple Myōzen.

Nāgārjuna: One of the most important philosophers of Buddhism and the founder of Mādhyamika school of Mahāyāna Buddhism. His most important work is *Mūlamadhyamakakārikā*. In the Zen tradition he is considered to be the fourteenth ancestor.

Nanshan Daoxuan (Nanzan Dōsen, 596–667): A Buddhist master in Tang dynasty China. He was the founder of the Nanshan (Nanzan) Ritsu-shū (Vinaya school).

Nanyue Huairang (Nangaku Ejō, 677–744): A Tang dynasty Zen master. He was dharma heir of the sixth ancestor, Huineng, and the master of Mazu Daoyi.

Niutou Farong (Gozu Hōyū, 594–657): A Tang dynasty Zen master. He was considered the disciple of the fourth ancestor, Daoxin, and the founder of the Niutou (Ox Head) school of Zen.

Qingyuan Xingsi (Seigen Gyōshi, 660?–740): A Tang dynasty Zen master. One of the dharma heirs of the sixth ancestor, Huineng, he was the master of Shitou Xiqian.

Samantabhadra: One of the most important bodhisattvas in Mahāyāna Buddhism, who is venerated as the protector of all those who teach the Dharma.

Shakyamuni Buddha: The founder of Buddhism. Shakyamuni means "sage from the Shākya clan."

Śāriputra: One of the ten great disciples of Shakyamuni Buddha. He is considered to be the person with the deepest wisdom in the Buddha's assembly.

Shitou Xiqian (Sekitō Kisen, 700–790): A Tang dynasty Zen master. The dharma heir of Quingyuan Xingsi and the master of Yaoshan Weiyan, he is famous for his poems "Merging of Difference and Unity" (Sandōkai), and "Song of the Grass Hut."

Shōtoku Taishi (574–622): Prince of Emperor Yōmei. He served as prince regent for his aunt, Empress Suiko. He played a key role in establishing Buddhism in Japan. He founded Hōryūji in Nara and Shitennōji in Osaka.

Sōen Nakagawa (1907–1984): A modern Japanese Rinzai Zen master. He was the abbot of Ryūtakuji temple.

Subhūti: One of the ten great disciples of Shakyamuni Buddha, considered to have the deepest understanding of emptiness.

Śuddhodana: King of the Shākya clan and Shakyamuni Buddha's father.

Tianhuang Daowu (Ten'nō Dōgo, 748–807): A Tang dynasty Zen master, one of Shitou Xiqian's disciples.

Tientai Zhiyi (Tendai Chigi, 538–597): One of the most important Chinese Buddhist masters. The Chinese Tientai (Tendai) school is based on his teachings.

Tiantong Rujing (Tendō Nyojō, 1163–1227): A Song dynasty Zen master who was the abbot of Tiantong monastery when Dōgen practiced in China. Dōgen received dharma transmission from Rujing.

Vairocana Buddha: The main Buddha of the *Avataṃsaka Sutra* is the sambhogakāya buddha. Maha Vairocana (Dainichi Nyorai) is the dharmakāya buddha and the main Buddha in Vajrayāna Buddhism.

Vimalakīrti: The principal character of *Vimalakīrtinirdeśa Sutra*. He was a rich lay student of the Buddha who had better understanding of emptiness than the Buddha's disciples.

Vipaśyin Buddha: The first of the seven buddhas in the past. The seventh is Shakyamuni.

Xuanzang (Genjō, 600–664): One of the most important translators in the history of Chinese Buddhism. He traveled to India by himself and stayed there for seventeen years and transmitted the teaching of the Yogācāra school and established the Faxiang (Hossō) school.

Yangshan Huiji (Gyōsan Ejaku, 807–883): A Tang dynasty Zen master, dharma heir of Guishan Lingyou, and considered as the co-founder of the Guiyang (Igyō) school of Zen.

Yunyan Tansheng (Ungan Donjō, 780–841): A Tang dynasty Zen master, dharma heir of Yaoshan Weiyan, and the teacher of Dong-shan Liangjie.

Yuquan Shenxiu (Gyokusen Jinshū, 606–706): A Tang dynasty Zen master, a disciple of the fifth ancestor, Daman Hongren, and the founder of the Northern school of Zen.

Glossary of Terms and Texts

Abhidharma: The earliest compilation of Buddhist philosophy and psychology. It took form in the period between the third century BCE and the third century CE. Its interpretations and explanations of concepts in the sutras reflect the views of individual Buddhist schools.

Absolute Three Treasures (*ittai sanbō*): One of the three categories of the Three Treasures mentioned in Dōgen's comments on the sixteen precepts. See *ittai sanbō*.

Āgama Sutra: The name used in China for collections of early Buddhist sutras, comparable to the Pāli Nikāya.

aggregate (Skt., *skandha*): A bundle, pile, or collection.

ambrosia: An English translation for the Sanskrit word *amṛta*, in Japanese *kanro*. This is a drink for heavenly beings. When one drinks it one attains immortality. It symbolizes nirvana and the Buddha's teachings.

anātman: Nonself, nonessentiality; one of the three marks of everything that exists. The anātman doctrine is one of the central teachings of Buddhism; it says that no self exists in the sense of a permanent, eternal, integral, and independent entity within an individual. Thus, in Buddhism, the ego (self) is no more than a transitory, fluid process that is a result of the interaction of the five aggregates. In early Buddhism this analysis is limited to the personality. In Mahāyāna it is applied to all conditionally arising beings. This freedom from self-nature is called emptiness.

ancient buddha (*kobutsu*): Dōgen used this expression as a title of the Zen masters who truly attained the Dharma, such as Zhaozhou, Hongzhi, and his teacher Tiantong Rujing.

Antaiji: A Sōtō Zen temple located in Kyoto, Japan, where Kōdō Sawaki Roshi and Kōshō Uchiyama Roshi taught. It moved to Hyōgo Prefecture in 1976.

asura: One of the six realms of samsara. English translations are "fighting spirit," "demon," "evil spirit," and "titan."

ātman: According to Brahmanism, the real immortal self of human beings, corresponding to what is known in the West as the soul. It is the nonparticipating witness of the *jīva* (unchanging essence) beyond body and thought, and, as absolute consciousness, is identical with *brāhman*, the underpinning of all reality. By virtue of its identity with *brāhman*, its characteristic marks (*ātmakara*) are identical: eternal absolute being, absolute consciousness, and absolute bliss. In Buddhism the existence of an *ātman* is denied: neither within nor outside of physical and mental manifestations is there anything that can be designated as an independent, imperishable essence.

Avataṃsaka Sutra (Flower Ornament Sutra): A Mahāyāna sutra that is the basis of the teachings of the Chinese Huayen (Kegon) school, which emphasize "mutual interpenetration."

Awakening of Faith in Mahāyāna (Daijōkishinron): One of the most important Mahāyāna Buddhist texts, which advocates tathāgata-garbha theory (see *buddha-nature*). This text greatly influenced many Chinese and Japanese Buddhist teachings.

Bhagavat: One of the ten epithets of the Buddha, World-Honored One.

Bodhgayā: One of the four sacred places of Buddhism, where Shakyamuni Buddha attained complete enlightenment.

bodhi tree: The fig tree under which Shakyamuni Buddha attained complete enlightenment.

bodhi-mind (Skt., *bodhi-citta*): awakened mind, the mind of enlightenment; Way-seeking mind.

bodhisattva: In early Buddhism, Bodhisattva refers to Shakyamuni Buddha before he attained buddhahood. In Mahāyāna Buddhism, a bodhisattva is a person who has aroused bodhi-mind, taken the bodhisattva vows, and walks the bodhisattva path.

bonnō: A Japanese word for the Sanskrit *kleśa*. Although usually translated as delusion, illusion, or passion, this word has much wider connotations, including worldly care, sensual desire, suffering, and pain.

Brahma Net Sutra (Brahmajāla Sūtra; Jap., *Bonmōkyō*): A Mahāyāna Buddhist sutra that contains the ten major precepts and forty-eight minor precepts of bodhisattvas.

Brahma: Brahma was originally one of the gods in Indian mythology. In Buddhism, Brahma is considered to be one of the guardian gods of Dharma.

buddha-nature (Skt., *buddhata*): The same concept as *tathāgatagarbha*; tathāgata's embryo or womb. The true, immutable, and eternal nature of all beings.

Caodong school: Caodong (Jap., Sōtō) is one of the five schools of the Chinese Chan (Zen) tradition founded by Dongshan Liangjie and his disciple Caoshan Benji. This lineage was transmitted from China to Japan by Eihei Dōgen and continues today.

causality: The principle of cause and result. The Buddha said that without cause, nothing exists. It can be expressed as "If this exists, that exists; if this comes into being, that comes into being; if this is not, that is not; if this ceases to be, that ceases to be."

Chanyuan Qinggui (*Zen'en Shingi*, Rules of Purity for the Chan Monastery): The earliest Chan (Zen) monastic code, compiled by Changlu Zongze in 1103.

"Chiji Shingi" (Pure Standards for the Temple Administrators): One part of Dōgen's *Eihei Shingi*. *Chiji* refers to the six monastic administrators: director (*tsūsu*), assistant director (*kansu*), treasurer (*fūsu*), supervisor of the monks' conduct (*inō*), chief cook (*tenzo*), and work leader (*shissui*).

consciousness (Skt., *vijñāna*): The fifth of the five aggregates (*skandhas*). When the six sense organs encounter their objects, six consciousnesses arise: eye consciousness, ear consciousness, nose consciousness, tongue consciousness, body consciousness, and mind consciousness. In Yogācāra teaching, two deeper consciousnesses are added: *manas vijñāna* (ego-consciousness) and *ālaya vijñāna* (storehouse consciousness).

dāna-pāramitā: One of the six *pāramitās*, it is the practice of giving or generosity. There are two kinds of *dāna*: offering Dharma and offering material things.

Deer Park (Mṛgadāva): One of the four sacred places in Indian Buddhism. After attaining enlightenment Shakyamuni Buddha went to the Deer Park in Sārnāth, on the outskirts of Vārāṇasī, and taught the five monks. This is called the first turning the dharma wheel.

dependent origination: see *interdependent origination*.

Dhammapada: One of the oldest and most well-known Buddhist scriptures, included in the Khuddaka Nikāya.

Dharma gate (Skt., *dharma mukha*): The teachings of the truth; the gate to the truth.

Dharma/dharmas: A term with various meanings. *Dharma*, with a capital *D*, refers to the truth or reality to which the Buddha awoke and the teachings of the Buddha as expressions or explanations of this truth. With a lowercase *d*, and in the plural, *dharma* refers to phenomenal beings, norms of behavior and ethical rules, objects of thought, ideas, and reflections of things in the mind.

dharma-nature (Skt., *dharmatā*; Jap., *hosshō*): The true nature of all beings; thusness or emptiness.

dharmadhātu (dharma-realm): In Mahāyāna Buddhism, the notion of a true nature that permeates and encompasses all phenomena. As a space or realm, the realm of dharmas is the uncaused and immutable totality in which all phenomena arise, dwell, and perish.

dharmakāya: One of the three bodies of a buddha in Mahāyāna Buddhism. Dharmakāya is the true nature of the Buddha, which is identical with ultimate reality, the essence of the universe. The dharmakāya is the unity of the Buddha with all beings in the universe. At the same time it represents the dharma, the teaching expounded by the Buddha. The other two bodies are sambhogakāya (reward body) and nirmāṇakāya (transformation body).

Diamond Sutra (Skt., *Vajracchedikā-prajñāpāramitā Sūtra*). Sutra of the Diamond-Cutter of Supreme Wisdom. One of the sutras in the group of *Prajñāpāramitā Sutras*. It shows that all the forms of phenomenal beings are not ultimate reality but rather illusions, projections of one's own mind.

duḥkha: Sanskrit word usually translated as "suffering." It is the first of the four noble truths. Duḥkha not only signifies suffering in the sense of unpleasant sensations, it also refers to everything, both material and mental, that is conditioned, subject to arising and perishing, comprised of the five aggregates, and not in a state of liberation. Thus everything that is temporarily pleasant is suffering, since it is subject to change and must end. Duḥkha arises because of delusive desire and craving and can be transformed by the elimination of desire through practicing the eightfold noble path.

eightfold noble path (Skt., *aṣṭāṅgika-mārga*): The fourth of the four noble truths; the path leading to cessation of suffering, comprising right view, right thinking, right speech, right action, right livelihood, right effort, right mindfulness, and right concentration.

Eihei Kōroku: *Dōgen's Extensive Record*, a collection of Eihei Dōgen's dharma hall discourses at Kōshōji, Daibutsuji, and Eiheiji, including dharma words and Chinese poems compiled by his disciples Ejō, Senne, and Gien.

Eihei Shingi: The collection of Dōgen's writings regarding monastic regulations: "Instructions for the Cook" (Tenzokyōkun), "The Model for Engaging the Way" (Bendōhō), "The Dharma for Taking Meals" (Fushukuhanpō), "Regulations for the Study Hall" (Shuryō Shingi), "The Dharma when Meeting Senior Instructors of Five Summer Practice Periods" (Taitaiko Gogejarihō), and "Pure Standards for the Temple Administrators" (Chiji Shingi).

ejiki (Skt., *durvarṇī-karaṇa*): Muted color of the *okesa*, or square robe. In ancient India Buddhist monks picked up discarded pieces of cloth, washed and dyed them an ochre color, and sewed them into a robe.

emptiness (Skt., *śūnyatā*): An expression used in Mahāyāna Buddhism, such as in the *Prajñāpāramitā Sutra*, for the nonexistence of the permanent self (*anātman*) and interdependent origination.

Enmei-jukku-kannon-gyō: A very short sutra with only forty-two Chinese characters on Kanzeon Bosatsu (Avalokiteśvara Bodhisattva) originating in China.

fearlessness (Skt., *abhayadāna*; Jap., *muise*): Freedom from anxiety. One of the three kinds of offering (*dāna*). The other two are offering of material and offering of the Dharma.

feeling or sensation (Skt., *vedanā*): The second of the five aggregates. When each of the six sense organs contacts its objects, we receive pleasant, unpleasant, or neutral sensations.

form (Skt., *rūpa*): The first of the five aggregates: material elements. In the case of human beings, the body is *rūpa*, whereas the other four aggregates are functions of mind.

formations (Skt., *saṃskāra*; Jap., *gyō*): The fourth of the five aggregates. Formations include all volitional impulses or intentions that precede an action.

four benefactors (Jap., *shion*): There are different sets of the four benefactors in various texts. The most common set is (1) father and mother, (2) all living beings, (3) king of the country, and (4) the Three Treasures.

four gross elements: The constituents of all living beings and things: the earth element, occurring in solid things such as bones; the water element, such as blood and other body liquids; the fire element, as in body heat; and the wind element, or movement.

four noble truths (Skt., *ārya-satya*): The most basic teaching of Buddhism. The noble truths are suffering (*duḥkha*), the origin of suffering, the cessation of suffering, and the path that leads to the cessation of suffering.

fukuden (Skt., *puṇya-kṣetra*): The field (rice paddy) which brings about the harvest of happiness or merit (*puṇya*). *Puṇya* refers to the karmic merit gained through good actions such as generosity and reciting sutras. Offerings to the Three Treasures, especially to the Buddha and monks, bring merit. Therefore the sangha of monks was considered to be a field of happiness.

"Fushukuhanpō" (The Dharma for Taking Meals): A section of *Eihei Shingi*, written by Eihei Dōgen. It describes the procedure of formal morning and noon meals at the monks' hall.

genzen sanbō: One of the three alternative ways to define the Three Treasures, in terms of the historical origins of Buddhism: Shakyamuni Buddha is the Buddha Treasure; the Buddha's teachings are the Dharma Treasure; and the Buddha's disciples and lay students are the Sangha Treasure. The other two definitions are the Absolute Three Treasures (*ittai sanbō*) and the Maintaining Three Treasures (*jūji sanbō*). See also *Three Treasures*.

great ultimate (Chi., *taiji*; Jap., *taikyoku*): A Chinese cosmological term for the supreme, ultimate state of undifferentiated absolute and infinite potentiality, contrasted with the *wuji* (without ultimate). The great ultimate is the source of the two opposing powers, yin and yang, that produce all things.

hachidainingaku (eight points of awakening of great beings): The eight points to watch in practice appear in the *Sutra of the Last Discourse of the Buddha* (*Butsu-yuikyōgyō*). This is also the title of the final chapter of Dōgen's *Shōbōgenzō*, written in the year he died.

head monk (*shuso*): The head monk of a practice period, who, as an exemplary monk, shares teaching responsibilities with the abbot and leads and encourages other monks' practice. He is one of the six heads of the different monastic departments.

hikkyo-kisho: The place to which we ultimately return. Dōgen says that we should take refuge in the Three Treasures because they are the place to which we finally return.

Hongzhou school: Hongzhou (Jap., Kōshū) is the school of Chinese Zen founded by Mazu Daoyi. Hongzhou is the name of the province where many of his disciples lived.

hṛdaya: A Sanskrit word translated into Chinese as *xin* (mind/heart). The original meaning is the heart as a part of the body. It also means "essence," as in the title of the *Prajñāpāramitā-hṛdaya Sutra*.

impermanence (Skt., *anitya*): One of the three marks of all beings. The other two are suffering (*duḥkha*) and no-self (*anātman*).

Indra's net: A metaphor used to illustrate the concepts of emptiness, interdependent origination, and interpenetration, found in the *Avataṃsaka Sutra*. The metaphor shows that all phenomenal beings are intimately connected. Indra's net has a multifaceted jewel at each vertex, and each jewel is reflected in all of the other jewels.

interdependent origination (Skt., *pratītya-samutpāda*; Jap., *engi*): A cardinal Buddhist teaching about causality. Other translations are "dependent origination" and "dependent arising."

ittai sanbō: One of the three categorizations of the Three Treasures, the Absolute Three Treasures. *Ittai* literally means "one body." The Buddha Treasure is the dharmakāya Buddha; the Dharma Treasure is the way all beings are; and the Sangha Treasure is the interconnection of all beings within the Indra's net of the universe. See also *Three Treasures*.

Jātaka: Part of the Khuddaka Nikāya, a collection of the stories regarding the Buddha's previous lives. In these stories the Buddha is called a bodhisattva.

ji: phenomenal, concrete things, as opposed to principles; the relative, as opposed to and the absolute. See also *ri*.

jijuyū zammai: Self-receiving and self-employing samādhi. This term, used by Dōgen as a foundation for his teachings on zazen, points to the dropping off of conceptual boundaries such as "self," "other," "myriad beings," and "practice" in zazen or any wholehearted practice.

joyful mind: One of the three minds discussed in Dōgen's "Tenzo-kyōkun." The other two are the magnanimous mind and the nurturing mind.

jūji sanbō: The Maintaining Three Treasures, one of the three categorizations of the Three Treasures. The Buddha symbolized by Buddha images is the Buddha Treasure; the printed Buddhist texts are the Dharma Treasure, and the sangha members in each Buddhist sangha is the Sangha Treasure. These have maintained Buddhist tradition since Shakyamuni Buddha's death. See also *Three Treasures*.

jukai ceremony: We become a Buddhist through this ceremony in which we receive the Buddhist precepts as the guideline of our lives.

kalpa: An exceedingly long period of time. To express the length of a kalpa two similes are used. In the first, a kalpa is how long it would take to empty a ten-cubic-mile container of poppy seeds by removing a single seed once every one hundred years. In the second, if once every one hundred years a heavenly woman brushes a solid one-cubic-mile rock with her silk sleeve, a kalpa is the time it would take for the rock to wear away.

Kapilavastu: The name of the city where Shakyamuni Buddha's father Śuddhodana was king. The Buddha was born in the Lumbinī Park near the city. One of the four sacred places of Indian Buddhism.

karma: A deed that is produced by the action of the mind, body, or speech, and which will produce an effect in the future.

kaṣāya (Jap., *kesa*): The square robe for Buddhist monks. This word refers to the color of the robe, usually muted black, blue, or red. Monks were allowed to own three kinds of *kaṣāya*: *saṃghāti*, *uttarāsaṃgha*, and *antarvāsa*.

kesa (okesa): Traditional monk's robe sewn by hand and originally pieced together with discarded fabric. Okesa is a polite form of kesa.

kitō: Praying to buddhas, bodhisattvas, or other guardian gods of Buddhism for some specific purpose. This was originally a practice in esoteric Buddhism, but later it was practiced in other Buddhist schools including Zen.

Kuśinagara: Place where Shakyamuni Buddha entered nirvana. One of the four sacred places in Indian Buddhism.

kuyō: A Japanese word for making an offering to the Buddha, the Dharma, and the Sangha, or to deceased persons through actions of body, speech, and mind.

Kyōjukaimon: Eihei Dōgen's comments on the sixteen precepts recorded by his dharma heir, Koun Ejō. This short text is the basis of the teaching on morality in Sōtō Zen tradition.

kyōzō (Skt., Sūtra Piṭaka): One of the three divisions of the Buddhist scriptures, a collection of the Buddha's discourses. The other two are the Abhidharma Piṭaka (psychological compilations of his teachings) and the Vinaya Piṭaka, the collection of the Buddha's admonitions regarding monk's misdeeds. Later in China and Japan *kyōzō* came to refer to the building in which Buddhist scriptures are stored.

lotus posture: Cross-legged posture used in sitting meditation. Originally in esoteric Buddhism this term referred to the Hindu yoga posture known as *padmāsana*. In Zen Buddhism the terms *kekkafuza* (full lotus) and *hankafuza* (half lotus) have been used.

Lotus Sutra (Skt., *Saddharmapuṇḍarīka Sūtra*; Jap., *Myōhō-renge-kyō*): One of the most important sutras in Mahāyāna Buddhism, especially popular in China and Japan. The Tientai (Tendai) and Nichiren schools are based on its teachings. Since Dōgen was originally ordained and trained in the Tendai tradition before starting to practice Zen, he valued the *Lotus Sutra* as the king of all sutras.

Lumbinī Park: One of the four sacred places in Indian Buddhism. Shakyamuni Buddha was born in this park near Kapilavastu, the capital of the Shākya clan.

Magadha: North Indian kingdom at the time of Shakyamuni Buddha. Rājagriha was the capital of the kingdom where the first Buddhist monastery, Veluvana (Bamboo Grove) Vihāra, was founded. The king of Magadha, Bimbisāra, and his son Ajātasatru supported Shakyamuni and his sangha.

magnanimous mind: One of the three mental attitudes all Zen practitioners need to maintain, mentioned in Dōgen's "Instructions to the Cook" (Tenzokyōkun). The other two attitudes are nurturing mind and joyful mind. A magnanimous mind is like a mountain or ocean, immovable and without discrimination.

mahāsattva: Literally, "great being"; a term for bodhisattvas.

Mahāyāna Buddhism: Literally means "great vehicle." Mahāyāna is one of the two main branches of Buddhism that originated in India, the other being Theravāda. In the Mahāyāna tradition one aims to attain buddhahood together with all living beings.

mantra: A syllable or series of syllables that is believed to have special power and to manifest cosmic forces and aspects of the buddhas. Sometimes a mantra is the name of a buddha. Continuous repetition of mantras, also called dhāranīs, is a meditation practice in many Buddhist schools, particularly in esoteric Buddhism. In the Zen tradition the use of mantras shows the influence of esoteric Chinese Buddhism.

mārga: The Buddhist path, specifically the fourth of the four noble truths: the eightfold noble path that leads to the cessation of suffering.

"Merging of Difference and Unity": A translation of the title of the poem "Sandōkai," composed by Shitou Xiqian.

Middle Way (Skt., *madhyama-pratipad*): A term for the practice of the eightfold noble path taught by Shakyamuni Buddha, who said that the two extremes, self-indulgence and self-mortification, should be avoided. Later in the Mahāyāna, Nāgārjuna described the Middle Way as refraining from choosing between opposing positions in relation to the existence or nonexistence of all things. Therefore his school was called Mādhyamika.

mind-ground: A translation of the Japanese word *shinchi*, synonymous with expressions such as mind-nature and mind-source. *Mind* here refers to a mind of absolute suchness. This mind is like a ground from which all different plants, grasses, grains, trees, and so forth arise and grow.

Mount Hiei: The mountain east of Kyoto and the site of the main monastery of the Japanese Tendai school, Enryakuji. Eihei Dōgen became a monk at this monastery.

mui (Skt., *asaṃskṛta*): "Unconditioned" or "unproduced." Things that are beyond conditioned existence, beyond arising, dwelling, changing, and perishing. In the original teaching, only nirvana was regarded as unconditioned. The Sarvāstivāda school had three kinds of unconditioned space and two kinds of dissolution (*nirodha*).

mujūsho-nehan: One of the three kinds of nirvana, the nirvana of nonabiding. This is the nirvana of bodhisattvas who, because of their wisdom, do not stay on the shore of samsara and because of their compassion do not dwell on the far shore of nirvana.

mumyō (Skt., *avidyā*): Ignorance, one of the three poisonous minds. Ignorance of the four noble truths and the reality of all beings is the primary cause of suffering within samsara.

mushotoku: Without gaining. Freedom from the desires to gain any desirable result form Buddhist practice. This expression appears in the *Prajñāpāramitā Sutras*, such as the *Diamond Sutra* and the *Heart Sutra*. Eihei Dōgen put emphasis on practice without gaining mind in "Gakudōyōjinshū" (Points to Watch in Practicing the Way).

nirvana (Jap., *nehan*): Literally *nirvana* means "extinction" or "blowing out" of the fires of greed, anger/hatred, and ignorance; it is the state of perfect peace of mind. In early Buddhism it meant departure from the cycle of rebirth in samsara and entry into an entirely different mode of existence. Nirvana is unconditioned, beyond arising, abiding, changing, and perishing. In Mahāyāna, nirvana is not different from samsara or from the ultimate nature of the dharmakāya. The duality of samsara and nirvana exists only from a conventional viewpoint.

Niutou school: Niutou (Oxhead; Jap., Gozu) is one of the schools of Chinese Zen founded by Niutou Farong, a disciple of the fourth ancestor, Daoxin.

Northern school: One of the schools of Chinese Zen. The Northern and Southern schools separated after the time of the fifth ancestor, Daman Hongren. The founder of the Northern school was Yuquan Shenxiu, a senior dharma brother of Huineng.

nurturing mind (Jap., *rōshin*): One of the three minds mentioned in Dōgen's "Tenzokyōkun." Another possible translation is "parental mind": the mind that takes care of others the way parents nurture their children.

okesa: see *kesa.*

One Mind (Jap., *isshin*): This expression can refer both to the mind in the aspect of phenomena (*jishin*) and to the mind in the aspect of the absolute (*rishin*). The former is the discriminating mind, the latter the mind beyond discrimination.

ōryōki (Skt., *pātra*): A set of eating bowls that Zen monks receive at their ordination. In a narrower sense *ōryōki* refers to the largest of these bowls. In India, Buddhist monks used only one bowl for begging and eating, a bowl much larger than the ōryōki of the Zen tradition today.

pāramitā: Literally means "perfection" of certain virtues. In Mahāyāna Buddhism the six pāramitās—giving, morality, patience, diligence, concentration, and wisdom—are considered to be the bodhisattva practice.

perception (Skt., *saṃjñā*): The third of the five aggregates. Perception denotes not only the construction of mental images and the formation of concepts but also the concepts themselves.

phenomenal beings (Skt., *saṃskṛta*; Jap., *ui-hō*): Conditioned beings. All interdependent and conditioned phenomenal beings which arise, abide, change, and perish. Everything conditioned is empty, impermanent, without substance.

prajñā (Jap., *hannya*): Wisdom, a central concept of Mahāyāna Buddhism and one of the six pāramitās of bodhisattva practice. This wisdom sees emptiness, the true reality of all things.

precept (Skt., *śīla*): One of the six pāramitās of bodhisattva practice: perfection of morality, ethics, virtue, proper conduct. Guidelines for conduct may be further specified as explicit precepts for the various types of practioners.

prophecy (Skt., *vyākaraṇa*; Jap., *juki*): Prophecy given by a buddha regarding someone's attainment of buddhahood in a future life.

repentance (Skt., *kṣamā*; Jap., *sange*): An important part of Buddhism from its beginning. Twice a month each sangha gathered for a ceremony known as *uposatha* (Jap., *fusatsu*). During the gathering, the leader of the sangha recited the Vinaya precepts and monks who violated the precepts made repentance.

ri: principles, as opposed to phenomenal, concrete things; the absolute, as opposed to the relative. See also *ji*.

Rig Veda: The oldest collection of the verses of wisdom called Vedas
in Indian thought.

saba: Small pieces of food offered by practitioners to unseen beings
such as hungry ghosts during ōryōki meals at Zen monasteries.

samādhi (Jap., *zammai*): Concentration of the mind, one of the three
foundations of the study of Buddhism, the other two being morality (*śīla*) and wisdom (*prajñā*). Dōgen called his practice of zazen
jijuyū-zammai.

samsara: Literally *samsara* means "continuous flow," that is, the cycle
of birth, life, death, and rebirth within the six realms. This cycle
ends in the attainment of liberation and entrance into nirvana.

sangha: The Buddhist community. In a narrow sense the sangha consists of monks, nuns, and novices. In a wider sense the sangha also
includes lay followers.

sanshin: Three minds or mental attitudes for practitioners in a Zen
monastery, mentioned in Dōgen's "Tenzokyōkun": joyful mind,
nurturing mind, and magnanimous mind.

sentient beings: The mass of living beings subject to illusion, suffering,
and transmigration within samsara.

sesshin: Literally, "touching or embracing the mind/heart." This refers
to the intensive practice periods in Zen monasteries during which
monks focus on sitting meditation practice.

shikantaza: "Just sitting." Originally this expression was used by Tiantong Rujing, Eihei Dōgen's teacher. Dōgen also taught a practice of
wholehearted sitting without any special meditation technique.

Shingon school: Japanese esoteric Buddhist school founded by Kūkai
(774–835).

Shitennōji: One of the oldest Buddhist temples, founded by prince Shōtoku in Osaka in the seventh century.

Shōbōgenzō: True Dharma Eye Treasury. The title of the collection of Eihei Dōgen's essays. The *Shōbōgenzō* is considered the most profound work in Zen literature and the most outstanding work of Buddhist literature of Japan.

śramaṇa (Jap., *shamon*): Wandering ascetic monk. Another name for a Buddhist monk.

skillful means (Skt., *upāya*; Jap., *hōben*): A skillful method or expedient device used by buddhas and bodhisattvas to guide beings. This is also the title of the second chapter of the *Lotus Sutra*.

sōdō (monks' hall): One of the seven basic buildings of Zen monasteries in which monks sleep, practice meditation, and eat meals.

Sōtō Zen tradition: Sōtō or Caodong is one of the five schools of Chinese Zen, founded by Dongshan Liangjie and his disciple Caoshan Benji. This tradition was transmitted from China to Japan by Eihei Dōgen and continues today.

Southern school: One of the schools of Chinese Zen founded by the sixth ancestor, Huineng. The central teaching of this school is sudden enlightenment.

stūpa: Originally stūpas were memorial monuments for Shakyamuni Buddha built at various sacred places such as Lumbinī Park, where the Buddha was born; Bodhgayā, where the Buddha attained enlightenment; Sārnāth, where the Buddha gave his first discourse to five monks; and Kuśinagara, where the Buddha entered nirvana.

suchness: "Suchness," "thusness," and "as-it-is-ness" are translations for the Sanskrit word *tathātā* and the Japanese word *shinnyo*, which refer to the reality of all beings as it is. Suchness is a synonym for *dharmatā*.

suffering: see *duḥkha*.

śūnyatā: see *emptiness*.

Suttanipāta: A collection of short sutras. One of the oldest scriptures of Buddhism, included in the Khuddaka Nikāya.

takuhatsu (Skt., *piṇḍapāta*): Traditional religious begging practiced by Buddhist monks from the Buddha's time in India. This is still practiced in the Theravāda tradition and by Zen monks in Japan. In Japan today the monks receive mainly monetary donations instead of food.

Tathāgata: One of the ten epithets for the Buddha, literally the "thus-come one" or "thus-gone one."

tathātā: "Suchness," "thusness," "as-it-is-ness." One of the central concepts of Mahāyāna Buddhism, which refers to the true reality of all beings.

"Tenzokyōkun" (Instructions for the Cook): The first section of *Eihei Shingi*. Eihei Dōgen wrote this text to teach the importance of communal work as a practice, using the example of cooking.

thought construction (Skt., *prapañca*; Jap., *keron*): One of the important expressions in Nāgārjuna's teachings on emptiness. It refers to the deluded conceptualization of the world through the use of ever-expanding language and concepts, all rooted in the delusion of self. Other translations are conceptual proliferation or self-reflexive thinking.

three poisonous minds: The three destructive, deeply rooted human tendencies—greed, hatred, and delusion—that are the source of all suffering. All result from ignorance of our true nature.

Three Treasures: Same as the Three Jewels, or the Triple Gem: three things in which a Buddhist takes refuge and looks to for guidance—the Buddha, the Dharma, and the Sangha. Can be defined in three complementary ways. See also *ittai sanbō, genzen sanbō,* and *jūji sanbō.*

transmigration: Transmigration, or reincarnation, is believed to occur after death when the soul or spirit comes back to life in a newborn body. This doctrine is a central tenet within the majority of Indian religious traditions, such as Hinduism, Jainism, and Sikhism. The Buddhist concept of rebirth is also often referred to as reincarnation.

Tripiṭaka: The three baskets (of Buddhist scriptures): the Sutra Piṭaka, Abhidharma Piṭaka, and Vinaya Piṭaka.

Tuṣita heaven: The heaven where Shakyamuni Buddha stayed before he was born. It is believed that Maitreya is residing there and will be born in this world several billions of years from now.

twelve links of dependent origination: see *interdependent origination.*

Two Truths: conventional truth and ultimate truth. Nāgārjuna is the first Buddhist master who clearly mentioned the two truths, in his *Mūlamadhyamakakārikā.*

unsurpassable mind: A translation of the Japanese word *mujōshin,* a synonym for *bodaishin* (Skt., *bodhi-citta*). *Bodhi-citta* is considered to be a shortened form of *anuttarā-samyaksambodhi-citta.* "Unsurpassable" is a translation of *anuttarā.*

Vajrayāna: A school of Buddhism that emerged in sixth- or seventh-century India. This school is also called esoteric Buddhism or Tantric Buddhism. It developed out of Mahāyāna Buddhist teachings strongly influenced by Hinduism. It reached into China, Japan, and Tibet. The Shingon school founded by Kūkai is a Japanese form of Vajrayāna Buddhism.

Vinaya: One of the three *piṭaka* (baskets) of Buddhist scriptures. Vinaya is a collection of the rules and regulations for the communal life of monks and nuns.

Vishnu: The Supreme God in the Vaishnava tradition of Hinduism.

Vow (Skt., *pranidhāna*): In Mahāyāna Buddhism, bodhisattvas take a vow stating that they will strive to liberate all sentient beings from samsara and lead them to enlightenment. Bodhisattvas do not seek to awaken solely for themselves, but rather endeavor to free all beings and help them reach nirvana.

Vulture Peak (Skt., Gṛdhrakūṭa): A mountain near the city of Rāja-gṛha. Shakyamuni Buddha often gave discourses on this mountain. It is said that the *Lotus Sutra* was expounded on this mountain. In Zen the transmission from the Buddha to Mahākāśyapa took place there when the Buddha held up a flower and smiled.

wheel-turning king (Skt., *cakravarti-rāja*): In the Indian tradition, an ideal king who rules the world by rolling the wheel he receives from heaven at his enthronement. The wheel of his chariot rolls everywhere without obstruction.

Yogācāra school: One of the two Mahāyāna schools in India, founded by Maitreyanātha, Asaṅga, and Vasubandhu.

zendō: An abbreviation of *zazendō*, a hall for zazen practice; meditation hall in Zen tradition.

INDEX

ABOUT THE AUTHOR

 SHOHAKU OKUMURA was born in Osaka, Japan in 1948. He is an ordained priest and Dharma successor of Kōshō Uchiyama Roshi in the lineage of Kōdō Sawaki Roshi. He is a graduate of Komazawa University and has practiced at Antaiji with Kōshō Uchiyama Roshi, Zuioji with Narasaki Ikkō Roshi in Japan, and Pioneer Valley Zendo in Massachusetts. He taught at Kyoto Sōtō Zen Center in Japan and Minnesota Zen Meditation Center in Minneapolis. He was the director of the Soto Zen Buddhism International Center (previously called Soto Zen Education Center) in San Francisco from 1997 to 2010.

His previously published books of translation include *Dōgen's Extensive Record: A Translation of the Eihei Kōroku*; *Shikantaza: An Introduction to Zazen*; *Shōbōgenzō Zuimonki: Sayings of Eihei Dōgen Zenji*; *Heart of Zen: Practice without Gaining-mind* (previously titled *Dōgen Zen*); *Zen Teachings of "Homeless" Kōdō*; *Opening the Hand of Thought*; *The Whole Hearted Way: A Translation of Eihei Dōgen's Bendōwa with Commentary by Kōshō Uchiyama Roshi*; and *Dōgen's Pure Standards for the Zen Community: A Translation of Eihei Shingi*. Okumura is also the editor of *Dōgen Zen and Its Relevance for Our Time*; *Soto Zen: An Introduction to Zazen*; and *Nothing is Hidden: Essays on Zen Master Dōgen's*

Instructions for the Cook. He is the author of *Realizing Genjōkōan: The Key to Dōgen's Shōbōgenzō.*

He is the founding teacher of the Sanshin Zen Commuinity, based in Bloomington, Indiana, where he lives with his family.

REALIZING GENJOKOAN
The Key to Dōgen's Shobogenzo
Shohaku Okumura
Foreword byTaigen Dan Leighton

THE ZEN TEACHING OF HOMELESS KODO
Shohaku Okumura and Kosho Uchiyama

DŌGEN'S EXTENSIVE RECORD
A Translation of the Eihei Kōroku
Eihei Dōgen
Taigen Dan Leighton, Shohaku Okumura, John Daido Loori, and
Steven Heine
Foreword byTenshin Reb Anderson

OPENING THE HAND OF THOUGHT
Foundations of Zen Buddhist Practice
Kosho Uchiyama, Tom Wright, Jisho Warner, and Shohaku Okumura

About Wisdom Publications

Wisdom Publications is the leading publisher of classic and contemporary Buddhist books and practical works on mindfulness. To learn more about us or to explore our other books, please visit our website at wisdomexperience.org or contact us at the address below.

Wisdom Publications
199 Elm Street
Somerville, MA 02144 USA

We are a 501(c)(3) organization, and donations in support of our mission are tax deductible.

Wisdom Publications is affiliated with the Foundation for the Preservation of the Mahayana Tradition (FPMT).